New Heart, New Spirit

BIBLICAL HUMANISM FOR MODERN ISRAEL

by ARIE LOVA ELIAV

Translated by Sharon Neeman

Foreword by Herman Wouk

Introduction by Amos Oz

THE JEWISH PUBLICATION SOCIETY
Philadelphia • New York • Jerusalem
5748–1988

*To dear Sallie Lewin
and Sam Lewin
very good friends
and of mine
with best Shalom of Israel
wishes
Lova Eliav
Jerusalem
4/3/89*

The English renderings of passages from the Hebrew Bible conform generally to *Tanakh: The Holy Scriptures* (JPS, 1985). In some cases, however, an alternative translation has been used by the author.

Copyright © 1988 by Arie Lova Eliav
First edition   All rights reserved
Manufactured in the United States of America
Library of Congress Cataloging in Publication Data

Eliav, Arie L., 1921–
  [Lev ḥadash ve-ruaḥ ḥadashah.   English]
  New heart, new spirit : biblical humanism for modern Israel / by
Arie Lova Eliav; translated by Sharon Neeman.—1st ed.
    p.   cm.

  Translation of: Lev ḥadash ve-ruaḥ ḥadashah.
  ISBN 0-8276-0317-7
  1. Ethics in the Bible.   2. Zionism—Philosophy.   3. Nationalism—
Israel.   4. Israel—Politics and government.   I. Title.
BS1199.E8E4513 1988
296.3'877'095694—dc19
                                                        88-12953
                                                           CIP

Introduction copyright © 1986 by Amos Oz, to appear as "A New Heart and a New Spirit" in his forthcoming *The Slopes of Lebanon* (Harcourt Brace Jovanovich, Inc.). Originally published in Hebrew in *Davar*, October 17, 1986.

Designed by Jonathan Kremer

CONTENTS

Foreword

ARIE LOVA ELIAV AND I HAVE EXACTLY THE SAME POINT OF departure on the subject of this book, stated simply and beautifully in an early passage:

> Without the Bible, Zionism would lose not only its right to Zion and to the land of Israel but its very soul. . . . Although the Bible existed long before Zionism and can go on existing without Zionism, Zionism cannot survive without the Bible. At best it can be a soulless, empty shell.

So far, so good. Thereafter we go our separate Biblical ways; Lova as a humanist, I as the writer of *This Is My God*. The author of *New Heart, New Spirit* is a man I profoundly admire, sometimes disagree with, and always hold in affection. In this attitude toward Lova I am far from alone. I would venture that in Israel, where he is universally known, that may be the general feeling about him.

A few months ago Lova received his country's highest civilian honor, the Israel Prize. I flew to Jerusalem to be present at the ceremony. Next day he was off to Nitzana, his current settlement project in the Negev desert. Happily I managed to see him again, because the president of Israel, Chaim Herzog, decided to visit Nitzana and was kind enough to take me along in the plane he piloted.

We saw there the kind of thing Lova has been doing for forty years and more. Lova Eliav has received the Israel Prize for his extraordinary batting average in making discouraging projects work and impossible dreams come true. Lova believes that Ben Gurion was right in the first place, to see Israel's future in the Negev. For Lova, to believe is to act, and so he is building Nitzana in sandy wilds on the Egyptian border. That is perhaps his chief distinction. He puts his life where his thoughts are. Those thoughts have led him through a political career of sharp ups and downs; but in his recent return to the fold of the Labor Party, he has leaped to a leadership position, after long years as a voice crying in the wilderness.

Crying for what? For new ideas. For authentic democracy. For the courage to have visions and to make them realities. Above all, for peace! Whatever else Arie Lova Eliav is, he is without question Israel's preeminent peacenik. When some ultrasensitive negotiation with the Arabs must go forward, any Israeli government is likely to call on Lova. Even Israel's foes admire and have affection for this Jew. So I recommend to the reader *New Heart, New Spirit* as a revealing glimpse into the mind and spirit of a remarkable Israeli.

The passage I have quoted is the key to Lova's newest book, its reason for being. He states his case for the relevance of the Bible not only to Zionism in general, but to the lives and thoughts of Israel's freethinkers, its "humanists." Lova wants to reclaim the Hebrew Bible from the exclusive possession of the ultra-Orthodox and the Orthodox; to show that Scripture speaks in humanist accents as well as ritualist absolutes, and belongs as much to his brand of Jewish awareness as to the viewpoint dramatized in black garments, black hats, and strict observance. He knows his Scripture. Being a polemicist, sometimes a fierce one, he quotes the fiery rebukes of the Prophets with zest; but being a dreamer, he is at home with their Messianic visions, too. Lova is an intense and interesting writer, saturated in current Jewish themes. When he wants to, he can raise his voice so that you must hear, whether you agree or not.

He closes his book with a fervent plea for the political solutions he has long advocated. He is abrasive in his denunciation of trends in Israel that he considers misguided, dangerous, or corrupt. In this he may be supplying ammunition to malicious foes, but Arie Lova Eliav has always called things as he sees them. Not being an Israeli, not sharing their burdens and their joys, I tend to reserve my opinions on these matters. For what it is worth, I agree with Lova here no more than I do on religious issues. But again, he makes his case, and one cannot choose but hear.

Amos Oz, a humanist like Lova, is one of Israel's premier novelists. His appreciation of *New Heart, New Spirit,* included in this volume, sheds the clear light of a gifted writer's eloquence on the passions and commitments of Israel's humanists, exemplified in Eliav and in himself.

It may well be that Arie Lova Eliav here succeeds in reclaiming our eternal Hebrew Bible for the humanists. That would be in itself a praiseworthy and significant service to Zionism and to Jewry. My own modest notion is that one of these years the Bible will reclaim the humanists. Meantime, wherever you stand on this long-lived dilemma, my friend's book is eminently worth your while. He is a Jew, a mentsch, and an *ohev Yisrael*, with an outstanding record as both a warrior and a peace-lover; and I wish some of my Orthodox acquaintances knew and loved the Bible as this "humanist" does.

AMOS OZ

Introduction

THROUGH MOST GENERATIONS, THE JEWS TENDED TO LIVE WITH an emotional, spiritual relationship to the distant and glorious past and to some distant messianic future. The present and immediate future were almost always perceived as a "valley of tears," whose hardships it is permitted to lament but against which there is nothing to be done and about which there is no point in expending too much emotional energy. The Messiah will come, realizing the lofty future, and in doing so will revitalize the wondrous past. The sorrows of the present will disappear.

The word "before" in Hebrew means "forward" (in space) but "backward" (in time). This reflects a contradiction between the perception of time and the perception of space that runs through the Hebrew language. It helps us to understand how it is that the Jews, in most generations, stand with "their faces to the past."

The years of my childhood and adolescence, years of Zionist enthusiasm, were almost entirely centered on the present and immediate future. Zionist society was a future-oriented society. "Yesterday is left behind us, but long is the path to the future," we sang.

And now we have regressed to being a past-oriented society. "Tomorrow is left behind us" and yesterday reigns over all. People are involved, almost obsessively, with the past: with the very distant past, with the recent historical past, and with questions about who said what in which argument, and who was right. The Bible, which was, during the good years of the Zionist revolution, a source of inspiration for renewers and world reformers, is becoming the authorization for opposition to any innovation, for refraining from the present and for an emotional stance "with our face to the past."

In this respect, there is something refreshing in the title that Lova Eliav has chosen to give his book: *New Heart, New Spirit.* Lova is one of those people whose face is turned toward the future and who, even when they dive into the past—whether to write a memoir or whether, as in the book before us, to study the Bible—do not attempt to recreate the past, to commune with the dead, to invoke ghosts, but rather to illuminate something from the past (personal or national) that will serve the present and the future.

The truth is that there has always been in Zionism a dialectical tension between deep longing for the distant beauty of days of yore and fierce aspirations to turn over an entirely new leaf. In important issues and in petty ones, the tension between the "recreation impulse" and the "innovation impulse" was found: The names given by early Zionists to their children, to their villages, and to their books bear witness to the covert battle between "renew" and "our days as of yore." And indeed in the partial phrase "renew our days as of yore"—words that became a common Zionist slogan—one can see the essence of this dialectic: The precondition for recreation of the past is renewal. Without renewal there is no past, and vice-versa—and that is almost all of Zionism in a nutshell.

But Zionism was fundamentally a movement of rebellion and the shattering of conventions, although there is a tendency today to blur this, to smooth the edges, to "Judaize" the Zionist revolution and erase the sharp contradiction between Zionism and the Judaism of orthodox ritualism. Zionism was a rebellion against the fossilization that was increasingly strong in Judaism—against the negation of all innovation and change.

For thousands of years the Jews lived outside of history and in opposition to it, as if saying: The "game" of history is the business of Gentiles, and the Jews must not dirty themselves in it. We Jews must wait with humility and accept our agonies with love until the coming of the Messiah, like a group of victims of a catastrophe who stand or lie down on a mountain slope waiting for the tornado to pass. History will pass and come to an end, and afterward the Messiah will come and carry us off in a magical chariot to the glorious past, to the days of the Temple and the monarchy and even before, to the days of the Garden of Eden. All we have to do is purify ourselves, distance ourselves from sin, to hunker down and wait. As long as we find ourselves, disastrously, within history we can have only one goal: to survive, to get out of history safely. Not to try to change it, to attempt to shape it; not, God forbid, to pressure the heavens; and not "to take it into our own hands." History, said the Jews for thousands of years, must be endured like a prolonged illness from which we emerge directly into the days of the Messiah, who will come. The Messiah will cancel out history, restoring us to our land and redeeming us in the fullness of redemption.

Zionism came to overthrow this passive approach. It was not a simple rebellion. A relative handful of "heretics," "upstarts," and "overthrowers of the Yoke of Torah" decided to take history and Jewish destiny into their own hands, to cease waiting for the Messiah, to shape the future actively within the bounds of history and politics.

Opposing them were adversaries from various directions, among them adversaries who waved the Bible and other sacred texts at them, shouting: "The Bible forbids innovation." They insisted that this generation of Jews was forbidden to do anything that had not been done by its forebearers. In other words: It must sit and wait with patience, humility, and meekness of spirit for the coming of the Messiah. And until that time, it must only purify itself, suffer, and pray. It is forbidden to renew, forbidden to change the customs of our dead ancestors. Only to them, not to future generations, are we accountable. We are obligated to think, to say, and to do only what our dead ancestors thought, said, and did. We must dress like they did in every place, in every age, and in every climate. We are forbidden to move.

The battle between the Zionist revolutionaries and the guardians of Orthodoxy was a unique one, with both sides drawing their arguments and proofs from the Bible and sacred texts. Zionism did not treat its Orthodox opponents the way most revolutions treated their adversaries. It did not say to the Orthodox, "take your sacred writings and go to hell." It did not say, "we shall destroy the Old World to its foundations." It sought and succeeded in the creation of legitimacy for itself from its enemies' perspective. In other words, it based itself on "their" texts, on "their" sources, on "their" predecessors. It claimed not to boycott the heritage but to give it a new interpretation, within the framework of the familiar, recognized, and legitimate game of interpretation, by which Judaism has sustained itself in each generation. Zionism did not usually say that Jewish heritage is "of no concern to us"; rather "we are the inheritors with the right not only to interpret but to place new emphasis and to downplay the centrality of previous emphasis, just as our forebears have done in every generation."

Lova Eliav, in dealing with the Bible in the manner he has chosen in *New Heart, New Spirit*, is thus engaged in a classic Zionist act: He interprets by his own rights and emphasis in accordance with his vision—without making claim to exclusivity, without banishing other interpretations beyond the pale, without ostracism and excommunication of other positions. The crux of the argument between the Zionists and their Orthodox adversaries is not that the rebels cast the Bible to the wind, ignore the heritage of the people of Israel, and seek to create a new nation, but rather that they, the Zionist rebels, see themselves as the inheritors of a large library, the library of their parents and grandparents and a hundred generations. They claim that in their parents' time there were books that stood on the night table next to the bed, and there were books that stood on a high shelf, reachable only by ladder. In their grandparents' time certain books were in the cellar and others were "close at hand." Even their grandparents' grandparents set priorities, and this generation thus has the right to reorganize the library: to put certain books on the upper shelves and to take others down to be close at hand. This is Lova's starting point. Like a person walking through a field pointing out certain plants as edible or therapeutic and others as poisonous, he does not seek to destroy the poisonous plants nor to ignore them; he seeks to know them, to classify them, to analyze them, but not to be nourished by them.

To my regret, this intellectual position is not common among today's secularists in Israel. As a result of accumulated fatigue, quarrels, and religious coercion and politicking, many secularists now tend to say impatiently, "Okay, enough already. To hell with all of it! The Bible and the Talmud, the poetry

and the legends and the prayers, let the Orthodox take it all
and leave us alone." In the eyes of such secularists, the Bible
has acquired the scent of medieval, Hasidic clothing, of Yid-
dish, of West Bank settlements, of shooting and oppression.
Thus the tendency to thrust all of Jewish heritage into the
hands of the Orthodox: Take it and good riddance—we'll
make do with the best-seller list. Or with other imported
goods, among products of real quality.

Alongside this extraordinary concession you also find its
opposite: self-deprecation before the Orthodox. Hasidic rabbis and Sephardic holy men are the most Jewish Jews. World-
class. After them come the messianic-nationalist settlers on
the West Bank. National league. Beneath them are those who
observe tradition—Kashrut, fast at least on the Day of Atonement, travel on the Sabbath, but not to non-Kosher restau-
rants. Beneath them are "plain folks." And the least Jewish
are the leftists, the Arab lovers, the ones who preach and
scream "justice, justice" like old-time Christians when they
think someone is doing some one wrong.

It is to this position that Lova throws out his challenge.
The Bible is not the inheritance of Hasidic rabbis, nor is
Jewish heritage the property of messianic nationalists. Seekers
of peace and condemners of injustice are, at least in their own
eyes, not less but more "Jewish" than bus-stop burners, murderers of Arab pupils, or vandalizers of the graves of Jewish
converts. Lova Eliav's perception of Judaism requires no self-
justification or self-effacement. Perhaps the opposite. It has
no cause for shame or meekness before the Orthodox. This
is not to say that the Judaism of socially progressive Zionists
is immune to argument or that we are forbidden to dissent
or reconsider it. The Orthodox may come and point out
instances of spiritual poverty or moral defilement among secularists and say, "Look where your approach to Judaism
leads." Certainly Eliav's kind of Judaism has to be ready to
defend itself, and more importantly—to test itself. His Judaism is better disposed to this than the Judaism of the Orthodox, which never tests itself—except to make sure it is
an automatic copy of its parents and grandparents.

True, revolutionary Zionist Judaism had grandiose hopes

that were not fully realized. Far from it. But who said that the effort to build a creative, just, self-sustaining society, even if it succeeded in only 5 or 10 percent of its dreams, is less "Jewish" than shaving the heads of kosher Jewish wives? Who has declared that the attempt to create a model of social justice, without exploitation or oppression, is less "Jewish" than strictures of a *mezuzah* on every doorframe?

Lova Eliav reads the Bible as a legitimate heir. And he does exactly what has been done by teachers and interpreters in previous generations: puts aside and brings together. He draws a thick blue line under some passages, emphasizes others with a red line of warning. It is possible, says Eliav, to find in the Bible "The wolf shall dwell with the lamb" (Isa. 11:6); "Nation shall not take up sword against nation" (Isa. 2:4); and "You shall not let a soul remain alive" (Deut. 20:16). We also can find "To me, O Israelites, you are just like the Ethiopians" (Amos 9:7); as well as "Fair Babylon, you predator . . . a blessing on him who seizes your babies and dashes them against the rocks" (Psalms 137:8−9); "visiting the guilt of the parents upon the children, upon the third and upon the fourth generations" (Exod. 20:5); and "A person shall be put to death only for his own crime" (2 Kings 14:6). These contradictions have been intepreted and rationalized and softened by teachers in past generations, but contemporary Jews have no less right to interpret the contrasts and to choose among them. The concept of "chosen people," for example, has been open to various interpretations, some of them monstrous, and with support from the Bible: "Moab would be my washbasin; on Edom I would cast my shoe" (Psalms 60:10); or "They shall pounce on the back of Philistia to the west, and together plunder the peoples of the east" (Isa. 11:14). But one can and should interpret it as a contract obligating the "chosen" to responsibilities without granting any privileges. We can break the correlation, so fashionable today, between the concept of "choosing" and the contemptible and despicable concept of a "master race." It is a matter of interpretation. If we leave the field of interpretation in primitive hands, we should not be surprised if primitive interpretations abound.

Eliav states in the introduction to his book, "The basis of the book is found in the study of seven moral values of the Bible that are perceived by the author as central: the sanctity of life, justice, freedom, equality, fraternity, compassion, and peace."

I believe this to be an important sentence, not because of the magic number "seven," nor because of the beautiful list of values, nor because of the unfortunately slightly worn phrase "moral values." I believe this sentence is important because of the words "perceived by the author as central." Eliav does not claim that these, then, are the central values in the Bible. Nor does he say that these are the values that our ancestors saw as central. Nor that these values must be central. No. They "are perceived by the author as central." This is an intellectual position, which is touched by humility—someone else is permitted to emphasize other values—as well as intellectual independence. Eliav asks no one's permission before deciding what he believes should be considered central. In this matter he accepts authority from previous generations but not from the prejudices of the religious establishment.

One could certainly find no inconsiderable Biblical confirmation for the opposites of the values that Eliav has chosen to emphasize: confirmation for the denigration of life, injustice, oppression, discrimination, hatred, brutality, and aggression. Eliav does not ignore them. On the contrary, he presents famous examples and discusses their terrible implications. But his starting point is that every generation and every reader is entitled to decide what to underline with a blue pencil of admiration and what to underline with a red pencil of warning and what not to underline at all now. In contrast to the wars of Joshua, which are so fashionable now and serve as support for brutality and savagery, we have the example of King Solomon, who granted twenty cities to Hiram, King of Tyre. We did not hear of fire descending from the sky to devour him and his household as a result of his act nor have the militant religious nationalists called King Solomon a traitor and troublemaker to Israel. Imagine what would happen to a "King of Israel" today were he to grant twenty cities to a neighboring state—with what Biblical quotes he would be attacked, not to mention sticks and stones and bullets.

Lova Eliav's insistence on his right to choose his values is, I believe, a classic Zionist act and is moreover the indubitable stance of a free Jew. Because the battles among us are not left to the "Bible guardians" and those who would forfeit the Bible, not between the good Jews and the Hellenists. Rather, they are battles between differing visions of Judaism: some of them humanist, some of them primitive, and some of them in between the two. They are all, regretfully, legitimate visions with a basis for support.

Lova Eliav wrote *New Heart, New Spirit* in an attempt to rescue the Bible from the hands of those who would use it as a club, an attempt to project the humanistic light that shines in some portions of the Bible. In the words of its author, "this book is therefore an attempt to wave, once again, the banner of human values—both Jewish and universal—sanctified in the Book of Books. And it is a call to rally around this banner." His face is turned to the future. He turns to the past, to the Bible, because he hopes to influence what will come after these evil days.

Preface

NEW HEART, NEW SPIRIT CONFRONTS THE ETHICAL AND MORAL values of the Bible in the context of the critical situation that Israel and Zionism are currently facing. It has sprung from the profound concerns of an Israeli Jew who fears for the fate of Zionism and Israel. The bonds of personal and national ethics that linked Zionism with the best of biblical values are now weakening—in some circles, to the point of cutting off the People of Israel from its sources of life. Zionism is becoming defiled. A considerable number of Zionists have abandoned the pure wells of the Prophets in favor of the muddy precipitates at the bottom of our glorious tradition. Instead of continuing as a movement of life and peace, justice and freedom, equality, brotherhood, and mercy, Zionism is in danger of turning into a movement that glorifies war while allowing internal social injustice, love of power, and hatred of aliens to flourish unchecked. Most frightening of all, extremist forces are attempting to justify—and even to glorify—these negative values by extracting and distorting fragments of Biblical verses. For example, those who choose dominion over a "Greater Israel" rather than territorial compromise leading to peace with Israel's Arab neighbors constantly invoke "Holy Words" to justify their position.

It now seems that the Bible—along with the entire Jewish tradition founded upon it—has been imprisoned by extremist factions in Judaism, Zionism, and Israel. These factions each claim to be the sole authorized interpreter of the Bible and of Judaism and seek, by virtue of their "exclusive" nature, to convert members of Israeli society to their cause.

The Bible is not only the cornerstone of Judaism. It is a universal asset, an integral part of the history of civilization. Without it there can be neither Judaism nor Jews. Without it, for that matter, neither Christianity nor Islam could have been founded. This means that most of human culture and history would have been vastly different and severely impoverished had the Bible not been written.

The Bible is a work of exalted religious and moral revelation. But it is also a compendium of rules and laws, a continuous history of the People of Israel, and a chronicle recording the creation of the world and the roots of humanity. In it are books of prophecy and poetry, wisdom and philosophy; its lines are set with symbols, legends, mysteries. Yet, above all, it is a book of ethics, an appeal to peace and social justice among the nations and all humankind.

Ever since the completion of the Bible more than two millennia ago, the Sages of Israel have used it as a firm foundation on which to build layer upon layer of spiritual and moral superstructure. In the following centuries, generations of great scholars compiled the Mishnah and the Gemarah, or Talmud. Since then, and to this very day, further levels of knowledge and wisdom have been added to the legacy termed by Jews the Oral Law or Oral Tradition. The Oral Law, no mere commentary on the Bible, transformed the Torah into a living, breathing work on which the People of Israel chose to base their lives throughout the prolonged agonies of exile. In every generation the Sages of Israel considered it their prime duty to find ways to implement the central principles of Torah. One illustration of this is a succinctly written passage from the *Book of Principles* by Rabbi Yosef Albo, one of the most important figures in medieval Jewish thought:

> The Torah of God, Blessed be His Name, cannot possibly be complete in such a way as to suffice for all time, as the details of human existence are constantly changing . . . they are too great to be included in one book. Therefore, certain general things briefly hinted at in the Torah were conveyed orally to Moses on Mount Sinai, so that the sages would be able to extract from them the changing details of every generation. (BOOK OF PRINCIPLES, ART. III, CHAP. 23)

In this way, throughout the generations of exile, the Jews created and maintained a continuous spiritual independence linked to the Bible, which sustained them in their times of trouble.

When Zionism arose in the nineteenth century as the national renaissance movement of the Jewish People, it too drew its strength and values from the Bible. The Zionist movement sought to fulfill the comforting visions of the Prophets by bringing about the long-awaited redemption of Israel. Toward that end, the Great Book has served the Zionists as both "bill of rights" and marching orders, from the immigration of the pioneers from Russia and Yemen more than a hundred years ago, to the creation of the state more than four decades ago.

Zionism began as an idea taken from the Biblical storehouse of hidden light, and, through the exertion of immense mental and spiritual energies, it was transformed into a shining vision. That vision in turn flourished into a living reality whose zenith is the State of Israel.

The basic idea and vision of Zionism stemmed from the doctrines of the Prophets, who spoke of a return to Zion and the rebuilding of the foundations of truth, justice, righteousness, and peace. Admittedly, contemporary Zionism has also drawn from other universal ideologies—such as liberalism and socialism—to forge tools appropriate to the era in which it functions. Nevertheless, its most basic source is the Bible. Without the Bible, Zionism would lose not only its right to Zion and to the Land of Israel but its very soul. Thus we see that although the Bible existed long before Zionism and can go on existing without Zionism, Zionism cannot survive without the Bible. At best, it can only be a soulless, empty shell.

World recognition was vital to the success of Zionism. The Balfour Declaration of 1917, designating a "Jewish home" in Palestine, and the United Nations resolution of 1947 proposing the establishment of a Jewish state, were crucial milestones in its path to realization. But even they fade to insignificance when compared to the book that determined the basic, historical, and inalienable right of the People of Israel to its homeland.

But the doctrine of the Bible does not limit itself to this basic right; it places just as strong an emphasis on the image of the People of Israel following its return to its homeland. It is up to that people to choose between goodness and pure faith in the One God, Creator of heaven and earth, and relinquish its evil instincts to iniquity and self-aggrandizement. Unfortunately, in Israel today fanatics raise baser interpretations of the Bible as banners in their march toward intolerance and racism.

Discussions of the Bible, its historic tales, and its social and ethical values accompanied the resurgent Jewish national movement as it grew, keeping pace with the increasing fulfillment of Zionism in the Land of Israel. And small wonder: The Bible contains the essential history of the People of Israel and most of the geography of the Land of Israel—that land whose resettlement had been dreamed of by Jews throughout the ages, Jews who longed to restore its former glory as "a land flowing with milk and honey."

Following the establishment of the State of Israel and the renewed contact with the physical and geographical Land of Israel, the Bible has become even more relevant. Now, more than ever before, discussion of the Great Book and its values is of supreme and unparalleled importance in determining the future of Zionism and of Israel. Our affinity with the Bible, despite the 2,000 years that have elapsed since its completion, stems from the fact that from many standpoints it has remained a "modern" work—that is, it corresponds to the basic national circumstances of our life much more than many subsequent layers of moral and political philosophy.

In this connection, it should be remembered that the Mishnah, the Talmud, and all of the great rabbinical literature that followed them were written by and about a *nonsovereign* Jewish society. True, some of the Oral Law was composed in the Land of Israel; however, at the time of its writing, the country was ruled by the Roman Empire. Moreover, most of the Oral Law arose in the Diaspora, within a Jewish society dwelling in exile on alien soil.

The Bible, on the other hand, deals with the issues of a *complete*—that is to say, a *sovereign*—society living in its own homeland, and with the ethical and moral standards required by such a society. The Torah, despite the fact that the People of Israel received it during their wanderings in the wilderness, covers the most minute details of individual and collective life in the framework of a nation in its own country. This is at least as true of the books of the Prophets and the Writings, most of which were written in the Land of Israel.

It was a land admittedly engaged in a continual struggle for existence but nevertheless an independent, sovereign country, with the People of Israel comprising the vast majority of its population. It may therefore be said that the Bible treats the problems of society and state in a direct, contemporary manner, whereas many of the subsequent legal texts seem relatively abstract and divorced from the reality of nationhood.

Furthermore, the Bible remains close to our hearts because, in addition to matters concerned with interpersonal relationships, or with those between human beings and their Creator, it also delves into problems that transcend time and space: problems of ethical and moral attitudes to social and political phenomena that continue to perplex us to this day. The Bible discusses various forms of state government: from the concept of kingship, through power struggles between tribal elders, judges, priests, and kings, to the quasi-presidential rule envisioned by several of the Prophets. The Bible analyzes the elements of justice and righteousness, and attitudes toward the weak and minorities that should prevail in the state established by the People of Israel. The Bible expounds on universal equality before the law, and on the problems of social justice: specifically, on preventing the exploitation of individuals and classes by individuals or groups seeking wealth and power.

Of no less importance, the Bible ceaselessly explores problems of war and peace, borders, territories, and alliances. Such subjects as relations between neighboring nations or between the superpowers and ordinary countries of the period fill page after page. In this regard the Prophets were not only great visionaries of peace—both regional peace and much-longed-for world peace—but also supporters of explicit political opinions on the various states of war and peace in their time.

During the 1,878 years that elapsed between the destruction of the Second Temple in the year 70 and the declaration of Israel's independence on May 15, 1948, the Jewish nation had no sovereignty. Whether under occupation on their own soil or—as was generally the case—dispersed among a multitude of alien nations, the Jews could neither declare war nor conclude peace, neither crown their own king nor elect their own legislative, executive, and judiciary institutions according to their own national guidelines, without the benevolent permission of foreign rulers.

But once the Jews had restored their sovereignty in the Land of the Bible and had again assumed responsibility for their own destiny, Biblical values resumed their former role as guidelines for the State of Israel. Indeed, the country's Declaration of Independence is imbued with these values.

New Heart, New Spirit focuses on seven universal ethical values expressed in the Bible and considered by this author as cardinal: the sanctity of life, justice, freedom, equality, brotherhood, mercy, and peace. These values closely resemble the seven attributes of goodness defined in Jewish tradition and prayer: peace, goodness, blessing, life, grace, lovingkindness, and mercy.

Yet even the Bible has another side—one of negative values or "anti-values"; even the Bible contains evidence of evil and cruelty, slavery and oppression, hatred and war. The Bible may be compared to a great forge in which the moral spirit of the Torah and the Prophets blazes with amazing force. Nevertheless, that spirit did not operate in a vacuum. Not only were the People of Israel "a stiff-necked people"—within them, as within all of humankind, the divine image struggled against the instincts of evil and destruction. Nor should it be forgotten that the People of Israel were constantly influenced by their idolatrous environment, with its rites, witchcraft, and human sacrifices.

In this millennial forge, the ethical values of the Bible underwent an age-long process of purification and distillation, shining out in all their glory and illuminating the path traveled by Judaism and by much of humanity. Yet, though the light of those values still glows steadily, the bottom of the forge has naturally remained coated with the dross of tribal behavior, punitive laws, and the cruel customs of war.

The composers of the Oral Law and subsequent Sages of Israel sought to lessen some of the severity of these impurities while leaving the foundations of the Bible undamaged. For example, they interpreted "an eye for an eye" as "an eye for the cash value of an eye"—that is, retribution via monetary fines rather than via physical affliction. They shunned the indiscriminate use of the death penalty, to the extent that a Sanhedrin (Jewish High Court) that prescribed execution, even infrequently, was called a "bloody" Sanhedrin. Polygamy, which had led to the oppression and subservience of women, was formally banned by Rabbenu Gershom, one of the greatest Jewish lawgivers of the Middle Ages.

The Sages of Israel realized that the Torah was handed down at a time and in an environment scarcely conducive to the subtleties of moral values. Rabbenu Bahye Ibn Paquda, a medieval sage from Spain, wrote:

> Those persons to whom the Torah was given were in a situation in which their animal lusts conquered them. (THE DUTIES OF THE HEARTS, SEC. 3, CHAP. 3)

The Rambam—Rabbi Moses ben Maimon (Maimonides), "great eagle" of wisdom—understood that the Torah deals with sacrifices as a function of ancient customs, including those of the People of Israel:

> It would be unnatural to expect humankind to abandon everything to which they have become accustomed at once. . . . And the famous custom in the everyday world at the time, the ordinary way of worship in which we were brought up, was that of the sacrifice of various animals. . . . And therefore, these types of worship were assumed to be exalted, and were continued. (GUIDE OF THE PERPLEXED, PT. 3, CHAP. 32)

This process of adopting the principles of good detailed in the Bible, while rejecting its impurities, guided the direction of Judaism for two thousand years and ultimately engendered Zionism. Now, however, it has come to a halt. Worse, it appears that we are now witnessing an inverse process: Judaism, Zionism, and Israel are being poisoned by polluted streams that have sprung from our darkest recesses to distort their basic moral essence.

Individuals and movements within our midst have begun to take up—and even to venerate—the dregs of ritual in the Bible, with a wild, fanatic worship foreign to the true spirit of Judaism. Before our very eyes, these fundamentalists are attempting to adopt as a political slogan "a people that shall

dwell alone, and shall not be reckoned among the nations."
Thus—supposedly in the name of the Bible—modern-day
Jewish extremists are flying the xenophobic flag of "holy
wars" focused on power, land, and blood.

This book is an outcry and a challenge against this dangerous process. Its author's intention is to represent the ranks
of Israeli humanists who are attempting to rescue the Bible
from its captors and to set it and its values free again in Israel.
It is an attempt to raise anew the banner of human values—
Jewish and universal—sanctified in the Great Book, as well
as an appeal to rally round that banner.

—A.L.E.

CHAPTER ONE

The Sanctity of Life

LET US BEGIN AT THE BEGINNING, WITH GENESIS. THAT BOOK, in its first eleven chapters, creates and formulates the philosophy of life that characterizes the entire Bible. It lays the foundation not only for the Biblical theory of life but also for the doctrine of monotheism—belief in one God, "Creator of heaven and earth." In those few short chapters we face the problems of existence that prevail in our world and our lives to this very day, and with which we must cope on a daily basis: birth and death, good and evil, reward and punishment. There, wonderfully narrated and depicted, are portrayals of space and eternity, light and darkness. There we are presented with eternal questions: Where do we come from? What aim, what purpose, is there to our lives?

The rest of the Bible, from Genesis 12 to its last verse, is essentially a Jewish document. Nearly all of its stories, laws, and prophecies are concentrated in the history and fate of the People of Israel. Nevertheless, its first eleven chapters deal with *human beings*—not with races, tribes, or nations, but with individuals, their motive forces and their achievements. What is true of Adam or Eve, Cain or Abel, is true of each and every one of us. These eleven chapters do not even hint at the racial traits of the first human beings. Were they white or black, yellow or red? Did Adam have blue eyes or brown; was Eve's hair straight or kinky? What was the shape of Abel's skull; how thick were Cain's lips?

No wonder, then, that these tales of Genesis were later adopted by myriad peoples throughout the world—from the Eskimos and Lapps of the frozen North, to the Bushmen and Zulus of Africa. Each and all of these could and did identify with the first characters of Genesis and with their tales of age-old, universal drives and instincts, transcending all ethnic and geographical frameworks, equally applicable to every human being.

The greatest—indeed, one may say, most terrible—question that we encounter is: What sort of creature is this Man, whom God created on the sixth day? Humankind, supposedly, is the jewel in the crown of Creation, the summation of divine activity. It seems that God's motive in taking the trouble to fashion the universe—the celestial bodies, the sea and land, and all that lives and grows therein—was for the sake of humankind. Moreover, God seems to have delegated some of His essence to His handiwork, as He announces, in glorious festivity:

> Let us make man in our image, after our likeness. (GENESIS 1:26)

This marvelous intention is, indeed, realized:

> And God created man in His image, in the image of God He created him; male and female He created them. (1:27)

So, then, all is good. . . Or is it? It seems, for an instant (meaning, of course, one of the eternal instants of Creation), that all is not just "good" but "very good":

> And God saw all that He had made, and found it very good. And there was evening and there was morning, the sixth day. (1:31)

But what happens next? If the creation of humankind was indeed a "very good" thing; if Man was indeed made in the divine image, as the Psalmist sings:

> You have made him little less than divine. (PSALMS 8:6)

If all of this is true, what happened to cause God to declare definitively, such a short time later:

> . . . how great was man's wickedness on earth, and how every plan devised by his mind was nothing but evil all the time. (GENESIS 6:5)

And only two chapters later, God repeats this conviction with even greater emphasis:

> The devisings of man's mind are evil from his youth. (8:21)

May we, then, assume from this that humankind is born corrupt, that evil reigns within our hearts from the very beginning of our lives? Many prophets and philosophers have concentrated on this theme throughout the generations. Jeremiah asks whether Man's evil nature is at all capable of change:

> Can the Ethiopian change his skin, or the leopard his spots? Just as much can you do good, who are practiced in doing evil! (13:23)

And Ecclesiastes cries out:

> Men's hearts are full of sadness, and their minds of madness. (9:3)

If this is indeed the case, it seems but natural that God should have regretted creating human beings—should even have gone so far as to wish, for a moment, to destroy humankind and all living things:

> The Lord said: "I will blot out from the earth the men whom I created—men together with beasts, creeping things, and birds of the sky; for I regret that I made them." (GENESIS 6:7)

The questions arising from these passages probe the very quintessence of divinity and humanity. Their solution, or lack of solution, has preoccupied every feeling heart and thinking mind since the dawn of knowledge. The initial great question is twofold. First, how could a good, loving, and omniscient God have made something evil and flawed, only to regret that creation later? Second, how could humans—formed in God's own image, the supposed embodiment of perfection—be inherently evil?

The first part of the question is answered by Isaiah:

> I form the light and create darkness, I make weal and create woe—I the Lord do all these things. (45:7)

In other words, the fact that the Supreme Being Himself created these drastic contrasts in His world only shows Him to be far above them. Indeed, according to Genesis *(1:2)*, the existence of darkness preceded even that of light. The light came later, springing forth out of the darkness in response to the divine command:

> Let there be light. (1:3)

According to this view, ever since its creation, the world has included elements of darkness and light, of evil and good, of war and peace. These elements intermingle, producing an eternal struggle between the Kingdom of Day and the Kingdom of Night, the angels and the demons. This struggle, in turn, fills our universe with interminable tension. And caught up in the very midst of this tension is humankind—which, ever since the expulsion from Eden, has been dominated by evil instincts, even (some say) to the point of becoming evil in nature. Nonetheless, even in humans lies hidden, deep and dormant, the element of good—the image of God.

The central theme of the Bible, in essence, is the struggle *against the evil element in human nature*. To this end, God has been enlisted in all His might and power. "To do good in the eyes of God," to achieve the human potential for good, to expose the hidden light of our innermost souls—this is the substance of the Prophets' ethical doctrine. The campaign against humanity's evil nature must be waged in God's name; the series of precepts included in "doing good" must be definitively sanctioned by God. Our doing good and being good must be achieved as if against our will.

The doctrine of Moses and the Prophets, then, would seem to consist of a constant and incessant swimming upstream. Since the human inclination to evil is persistent, the precepts of doing good must be forced upon humanity unceasingly and without respite. Useful in this endless process of coercion are such tools as divine commands, precepts of "You shall" and "You shall not," and study of the Bible and its teachings. Without all these, the human race will no doubt revert to ways of sin.

This struggle—first for the souls of individuals, and later for the collective souls of families, tribes, societies, peoples, and the whole of humanity—is a predominant theme throughout the entire Bible. Through the Bible and its successors—the Mishnah and the Talmud—the struggle has been brought to the hearts of the People of Israel. Through Christianity and Islam, built on the foundations of the Bible, it has penetrated the consciousness of untold millions. The struggle goes on everywhere, each day, each hour, within each one of us. According to the Prophets it will not cease until the messianic "end of days," when good will vanquish evil totally and eternally.

ON MURDER

In the very first pages of Genesis, which describe the young Early Man's first steps on his native earth, he is overcome by his evil instincts. He (or, more correctly, his son) then commits the most heinous of crimes: He slays a human being.

Of the four humans then living on this planet—Adam, Eve, Cain, and Abel—one becomes the first victim of bloodshed, another the first murderer:

Cain set upon his brother Abel and killed him. (GENESIS 4:8)

Intentionally and dramatically, the first mention of crime in the Bible deals with the most serious crime of all: murder. It was neither theft, nor robbery, nor even rape, but the killing of one human being by another. Murder, then, has accompanied humankind since the dawn of Creation.

Indeed, it seems that the human animal was created as a beast of prey. God apparently had no intention of making us vegetarians; like any other carnivore, humankind kills other animals for food. Even before we began to herd sheep and tend the soil, we were hunters of flesh, ever sharpening our senses and our instinct to kill—our beastly instincts, aptly described by Ecclesiastes:

Man has no superiority over beast. (3:19)

So animal-like is mankind that many primitive civilizations are known to have fed on human flesh. The Bible cites no facts on cannibalism; however, in more than one passage prophesying periods of great famine and distress, it paints bloody pictures of human beings liable to be forced by starvation into this gruesome last resort:

You shall eat the flesh of your sons and the flesh of your daughters. (LEVITICUS 26:29)

And also:

> You shall eat your own issue, the flesh of your sons and daughters that the Lord your God has assigned to you, because of the desperate straits to which your enemy shall reduce you. (DEU-TERONOMY 28:53)

Admittedly, by Biblical times, most Middle Eastern cultures had adopted the taboo against cannibalism. Yet we humans of the twentieth century can hardly pronounce ourselves "above that sort of thing," knowing that some human tribes in remote areas still consume human flesh, especially that of their enemies; and that conditions of war and extreme famine still occasionally drive even civilized persons to eat the flesh of their fellows.

Nevertheless, the ancient taboo proscribing the eating of human flesh does not apply to any other form of murder—and murders are still committed for myriad reasons: to gain possession of others' food (or of the means whereby others produce their food—land, water, money); out of hatred and revenge; "to preserve one's honor"; sexual murder; ritual murder; political murder. All these, and many more, are motives for murder of individuals by individuals. Group murder, or war, will be discussed later.

The authors of the Bible knew that murder—any murder—could be prevented by nothing less forceful than a divine prohibition. This, in fact, is clearly, concisely, and impressively handed down in the story of the first murder, when God Himself cries out to the murderer, Cain:

> What have you done? Hark, your brother's blood cries out to Me from the ground! (GENESIS 4:10)

Immediately following this accusation, God pronounces a fearful doom:

> Therefore, you shall be more cursed than the ground, which opened its mouth to receive your brother's blood from your hand. If you till the soil, it shall no longer yield its strength to you. You shall become a ceaseless wanderer on earth. (4:11–12)

Cain, the first murderer, does not protest his innocence, nor declare his doom unjust. He merely appeals against its severity:

> My punishment is too great to bear! (4:13)

This passage is the first Biblical illustration of the relationship between murder, blood, and the spirit of life:

> For the blood is the life (DEUTERONOMY 12:23)

—and the life of a human being is a living soul, given by God:

> The Lord God formed man from the dust of the earth. He blew into his nostrils the breath of life, and man became a living being. (GENESIS 2:7)

Thus, anyone who spills the blood of any human being sins against God, as only God has the right to return a human soul to its Creator—to whom all human souls belong. The shedding of human blood is prohibited by divine edict:

> Whoever sheds the blood of man, by man shall his blood be shed; for in His image did God make man. (GENESIS 9:6)

Moses, foremost of the Prophets, proclaims God's law concerning murder to the People of Israel in simple, straightforward words:

> You shall not murder. (EXODUS 20:13)

This is a clear-cut, definitive, and irrevocable command, meaning "You shall not murder any human being"—man or woman, child or adult, Jew or Gentile, anyone at all. There are no qualifications, no loopholes, no ways around the edict. Murder is forbidden by the word of God.

Once that divine command was set down, its enforcement became the responsibility of the police, the judiciary, and the elders of the people. Nevertheless, the concept of "blood vengeance" by the families of murder victims was still hard to eradicate from the nomad society of the ancient Hebrews. (In fact, as we twentieth-century dwellers know all too well, the concept persists to this day.) This is the reason behind the Biblical concept of "cities of refuge," places where involuntary slayers of human beings would be safe from undeserved revenge:

> You shall provide yourselves with places to serve you as cities
> of refuge to which a manslayer who has killed a person unin-
> tentionally may flee. The cities shall serve you as a refuge from
> the avenger, so that the manslayer may not die unless he has
> stood trial before the assembly. (NUMBERS 35:11–12)

The extent to which an entire people could respond in
avenging the death of one innocent person is amply illustrated
in the Book of Judges, in the story of the concubine in Gibeah.
The terrible testimony given by the murdered woman's hus-
band, the Levite, sets forth her multiple rape and brutal murder by the men of Gibeah in Benjamin:

> They meant to kill me, and they ravished my concubine until
> she died. (20:5)

The response of the assembled people, according to the
Bible, was to rise up "as one man," demanding that the Benjamites deliver up "the base fellows that are in Gibeah" for
punishment, with a view toward driving such evil out of
Israel. The Benjamites' refusal to extradite the rapist-mur-
derers resulted in a bloody civil war that nearly wiped out
the entire tribe of Benjamin.

Yet even more impressive and dramatic examples of blood
vengeance appear in the books of the Prophets, those brave
souls who carried the banner of justice and righteousness
throughout the Bible. The first of these courageous chal-
lengers was Nathan, prophet to King David. The Bible, initially preserving a seemingly neutral, unprejudiced attitude,
tells us how King David forcibly lay with Bath-sheba, wife
of Uriah the Hittite; how he killed Uriah—not by his own
hand but certainly by his own order; and how he then took
Bath-sheba, pregnant with his child, to wife.

Up to this point, the story is no more than a historical
episode, similar to many others: A heroic, much-admired king
observes a beautiful nude woman and desires her. When he
finds out that she is married to an officer in his army, he
sends the loyal officer to die in battle. All of this is ostensibly
known only to a chosen few within the royal court and could
conceivably have gone unnoticed, or at least uncommented.

The crucial, astonishing turning point lies in the appearance
of the prophet, a figure of justice and truth, who—like the
God he serves—sees and knows all:

> And the Lord sent Nathan to David. He came to him and said,
> "There were two men in the same city, one rich and one poor.
> The rich man had very large flocks and herds, but the poor man
> had only one little ewe lamb that he had bought. He tended it
> and it grew up together with him and his children: it used to
> share his morsel of bread, drink from his cup, and nestle in his
> bosom; it was like a daughter to him. One day, a traveller came
> to the rich man, but he was loath to take anything from his own
> flocks or herds to prepare a meal for the guest who had come
> to him; so he took the poor man's lamb and prepared it for the
> man who had come to him." (2 SAMUEL 12:1–4)

The Bible relates nothing of Nathan's origins. Was he a
noble of the court, or a simple plebeian? The reader is not
advised as to how Nathan dared approach King David, nor
why a king much burdened with the work of ruling would
receive this man and hear his tale of lambs. It is, however,
immediately clear that, in Israel in those days, all anyone
needed to open doors in the highest places—whether out of
respect or out of awe—was a reputation as a prophet.

On hearing the account of the rich man's behavior, the
king becomes incensed at the injustice:

> David flew into a rage against the man, and said to Nathan, "As
> the Lord lives, the man who did this deserves to die! He shall
> pay for the lamb four times over, because he did such a thing
> and showed no pity." (12:5–6)

This, then, was David's verdict and sentence, passed down
upon the as yet unidentified oppressor. How great his shock
and fear must have been to hear the prophet's answer—a
bold accusation of murder:

> That man is you! (12:7)

Speaking in the name of God, Nathan rebukes the king:

> Why then have you flouted the command of the Lord and done
> what displeases Him? You have put Uriah the Hittite to the

sword; you took his wife and made her your wife and had him killed by the sword of the Ammonites. (12:9)

He then delivers the sentence:

> Therefore the sword shall never depart from your House. . . . I will make a calamity against you from within your own house; I will take your wives and give them to another man before your very eyes and he shall sleep with your wives under this very sun. You acted in secret, but I will make this happen in the sight of all Israel and in broad daylight. (12:10–12)

David, humbled by the prophet's words, admits his crime and accepts the punishment, saying:

> I stand guilty before the Lord. (12:13)

Only a few generations later, following the split in what had been David's kingdom of Israel and Judah, Ahab, son of Omri, became king in Israel. His spouse and partner in evil was Jezebel, daughter of Ethbaal, king of the Zidonians.

Ahab, who covets the vineyard of Naboth the Jezreelite, desires to purchase it for his own. When Naboth refuses to sell the land that had been his fathers' for generations, wicked Queen Jezebel launches a campaign of rumors against him. With the aid of base, lying witnesses, she brings about his accusation as a traitor. He is condemned and stoned to death by the people.

Once more we read of an iniquitous king, faced by a prophet of doom. This time, the prophet is Elijah, who does not even bother with parables:

> Then the word of the Lord came to Elijah the Tishbite: "Go down and confront King Ahab of Israel who [resides] in Samaria. He is now in Naboth's vineyard; he has gone down there to take possession of it. Say to him, 'Thus said the Lord: Would you murder and take possession? Thus said the Lord: In the very place where the dogs lapped up Naboth's blood, the dogs will lap up your blood too.' " (1 KINGS 21:17–19)

Ahab, long familiar with Elijah, and with the prophet's hatred of and anger against the king and his ways, realizes that he has been caught with his hands dripping with innocent blood. Elijah pronounces Ahab's fearsome punishment:

I will bring disaster upon you. I will make a clean sweep of you, I will cut off from Israel every male belonging to Ahab, bond and free. . . . And the Lord has also spoken concerning Jezebel: "The dogs shall devour Jezebel in the field of Jezreel. . . ." (21:21–23)

The king accepts his fate with subdued humility: He tears his clothes, dons sackcloth, fasts, and submits completely.

It would appear, then, that where "You shall not murder" is concerned, there is an authority above that of the general law-enforcement system—an immeasurably higher authority: God Himself. The Lord personally seals the doom of those who break this commandment—no matter how high and mighty the transgressors—using the Prophets as His voice on earth. The appearance of prophets as direct messengers of God, is unique to the People of Israel. The power and the burden of speaking the truth and chastising the people—each one of the people, from the humblest child to the king himself—were borne by the Prophets of Israel, in bravery and agony, throughout their days.

ON SACRIFICES

The first time we read about sacrifice in the Bible is in the story of Cain and Abel. Linked with animal blood at the beginning, the story ends horribly with the spilling of human blood—the first murder. It is interesting to note that the Hebrew word for sacrifice (*ḥurban*) is identical to the word for "victim."

The first rites of sacrifice were conducted ages ago, in the dawn of prehistory. Ritual instruments used in idol worship, along with the bones of sacrifices offered to those idols, have been unearthed in archeological excavations in and around human dwellings from ancient periods. Many of those idols were related to the primeval elements of nature: earth, fire, and water; sun, moon, and stars; wind, lightning, and thunder.

The Bible abounds in descriptions of such idols, made of wood and stone. Again and again, the Prophets mock and scorn them and their fashioners. But is it all that ridiculous for primitive persons, in the earliest stages of life as a human species, to have been awed and frightened by the fearsome forces that these idols represented? It was, after all, just such forces that could preserve their very lives—or, just as arbitrarily, condemn them to death. What could have been more natural than to pray to them and to shower their earthly representations with gifts and offerings in hopes that they, in turn, would show favor to the givers?

This, then, was the origin of the sacrificial rite. The two most common types of sacrifices were, in fact, those cited in the story of Cain and Abel: fruit on one hand, and beasts on the other. This, too, is understandable, as the idols were thought to own the earth and all its creatures, meaning that the first fruits of the animal and vegetable kingdoms were theirs by right.

Over the course of long generations, many different sacrificial rituals developed: ceremonies and supplications, dances and songs. A special class of people—the priests—came to be responsible for performing the actual offering; the priests enjoyed a privileged and protected status, as well as sharing in the foodstuffs sacrificed. Days and occasions for sacrifice soon became fixed in the calendar as holidays.

It may thus be seen that the world of the Biblical lawgivers was one surrounded by sacrifices. These, however, were not limited to offerings of crops and animals. Several neighboring cultures, predating that of the Hebrew nomads, had long included in their worship a cruel and terrible rite: the sacrifice of human beings to the gods. Human sacrifices—especially those of children, and frequently firstborn sons or daughters—were prevalent throughout the ancient Near East.

What was the Hebrew forefathers' attitude to sacrifices following their discovery of the One God, Maker of Heaven and Earth, and of monotheism, the faith in that One God? Abraham, the first known monotheist, built altars and offered sacrifices throughout his journeys with his flocks, all over the Land of Canaan. This custom, at first glance, appears no different from that of prior and contemporary tribal chiefs.

One fundamental difference, however, did exist: The sacrifice of human flesh was utterly prohibited.

The attempted sacrifice of Isaac draws the reader's attention to this fact, in a remarkable manner. God apparently wished to test Abraham, in order to determine the extent of his loyalty and faith. He therefore instructed him to offer his only, beloved son, Isaac, as a sacrifice. Abraham, in whose world such a demand was neither incomprehensible nor unusual, took his young son, bound him to the altar, and even raised the ritual knife to slay his child. And then, in one of the Bible's most dramatic moments, he hears the divine command:

Do not raise your hand against the boy. . . . (GENESIS 22:12)

Strictly speaking, the command was given to Abraham. However, it may also be interpreted as God's comment to Himself: I, the One God, will never test My true believers in this way again. Thus, that awesome scene became the occasion of an edict unmistakably clear to all those who followed the Hebrew God: No more human sacrifices! (The sacrifice of beasts, however, was still permitted—and, in fact, one such sacrifice was implemented later in the tale of Abraham and Isaac. A ram, caught by his horns in a nearby bush, was offered by a grateful Abraham to God as a substitute for his beloved child.)

From that time and throughout the Bible, the spiritual leaders of the People of Israel—mainly, of course, the Prophets—fought a fierce, grueling, and protracted campaign against the sacrifice of human beings by Hebrews. Not just the common folk of Judah and Israel, but even nobles and kings continued to transgress against this prohibition for many generations, offering their children to the fire of Moloch as well as to additional idols of Canaan and other nations whose sheltering of Hebrew wanderers exposed them to foreign faiths.

In only a single, exceptional instance is a human sacrifice mentioned in the Bible without condemnation. This is the case of the judge Jephthah the Gileadite, who sacrificed his only daughter on the altar of the One God to keep the vow that he had made to God following his victory over the Ammonites—a sort of primitive relapse into the ancient, bloody ritual ceremony.

By contrast to the sacrifice of human beings, the offering of animals was adopted and favored by the Bible. Indeed, considerable portions of the Pentateuch are devoted to detailed instructions in the laws of sacrifice. Yet even there, these sacrifices were accompanied by offerings of fruits and vegetables—gifts that did not require bloodshed of any kind.

Praiseworthy are the skill and foresight with which the lawgivers of the Bible created a connection between the great events that befell the then nomadic People of Israel—such as the Exodus from slavery in Egypt and the gift of Torah on Mount Sinai—and the holidays of nature in their annual cycle, the feasts of a people celebrating the land on which it dwells and by whose bounty it is fostered. Passover commemorates the departure from Egypt; but it also marks the Omer—the first day of the grain harvest. Shavuot, the Feast of Weeks, celebrates the gift of Torah; yet it also denotes the Feast of First Fruits and the end of the grain harvest. Sukkot, the Feast of Tabernacles, also recalls the Exodus, when the People of Israel dwelled in flimsy booths in the desert; but it signifies the ingathering of field crops as well.

How beautiful are the ceremonies of these feasts: the sheaf of grain, held high aloft on the first intermediate day of Passover; the basket of first fruits on Shavuot; the prayers over the seven varieties of produce on Sukkot. How simple and clean they are, compared to the slaughter and sacrifice of cattle, sheep, and doves!

With the conquest of the Land of Israel, the Hebrew tribes began to build more permanent altars. Shiloh, Beth-el, and many other places became centers of religious ritual and sites of animal sacrifice, and the priesthood became an established class of special status. The zenith of this process, of course, was the naming of Jerusalem as capital of Judah and Israel during the reign of King David, and the building of the Temple by his son, King Solomon.

Yet, concurrently with this institutionalization of religious ritual and sacrificial ceremonies, the People of Israel began to witness another, quite different process: the struggle of the Prophets, those wonderful champions of truth and justice, whose sharp eyes and sensitive hearts told them that animal sacrifice had become much more wrong than rite. The Prophets perceived that the sacrificial ceremonies were fast becoming a religion of rote—and worse, that the bringers of sacrifices believed that the bird or beast offered to God would win them an effortless free pardon in exchange, thinking that any crime, whether against one's fellow human beings or against God Himself, could be forgiven and forgotten merely by killing a calf or a young goat.

Samuel, angered by King Saul's disregard of the divine command, asks:

> Does the Lord delight in burnt-offerings and sacrifices as much as in obedience to the Lord's command? (1 SAMUEL 15:22)

By this Samuel means that it is far better, far more important, to listen to the word of God than to spill the blood of animals.

This, however, is but the beginning of the Prophets' struggle for drastic and comprehensive changes in the individual and collective scale of values adopted by the People of Israel. The struggle was to last hundreds of years, throughout the entire Prophetic period, from Amos to Malachi. The importance of that struggle to the formation and the future of the Jewish People, and indeed to that of all humanity, has proven to be immeasurable.

The principal change called for by the Prophets was that of granting precedence to a moral code of justice and mercy, rather than to an elaborate system of ritual and ceremony in general, and animal sacrifice in particular. The struggle was constant and far-ranging. One prophet after another took up the case, each with a voice unique unto himself. First was Amos, the dresser of sycamore trees from Judah, who arrived in Samaria, exalted capital of the Kingdom of Israel, in the days of Jeroboam II—Jeroboam, the son of Joash, a great conqueror who annexed vast territories to his kingdom. These conquests were accompanied by huge feasts and profuse sacrifices, phenomena quite common in the wake of military

victories, and generally followed by corruption and conspicuous consumption. Amos, observing this licentious living,
storms:

> I loathe, I spurn your festivals, I am not pleased by your solemn
> assemblies. If you offer Me burnt-offerings—or your meal-
> offerings—I will not accept them; I pay no heed to your gifts
> of fatlings. Spare Me the sound of your hymns, and let Me not
> hear the music of your lutes. But let justice well up like water,
> righteousness like an unfailing stream. (5:21–24)

Hosea, who prophesied in the Kingdom of Israel a short
time after Amos, was also a witness to the country's moral
degradation. Although Hosea's heart brimmed with compassion and love for his people, he could not accept sacrifice as
a means of remedying the disastrous social situation prevailing in Israel:

> For I desire goodness, not sacrifice; obedience to God, rather
> than burnt-offerings. (6:6)

The superiority of prayer—the speech of lips and heart—
over animal sacrifice in the eyes of God is portrayed in the
Book of Hosea for the first, but by no means the last, time
in the prophecies:

> Instead of bulls we will pay [the offering of] our lips. (14:3)

Not many years later, a true giant among prophets arose
in Judah: Isaiah, son of Amoz. His very first prophecy—
addressed to the residents of Jerusalem and to his people,
whom he referred to as a "brood of evil-doers, depraved
children" —is marked by an incisive condemnation of animal
sacrifice and ceremonial rites by those no less vile, in his eyes,
than the sinners of ancient Sodom and Gomorrah. Moved by
righteous anger, he extorted the rulers and people of Judah:

> Hear the word of the Lord, you chieftains of Sodom; give ear
> to our God's instruction, you folk of Gomorrah! "What need
> have I of all your sacrifices?" says the Lord. "I am sated with
> burnt-offerings of rams, and suet of fatlings, and blood of bulls;
> and I have no delight in lambs and he-goats. That you come to
> appear before Me—who asked that of you? Trample My courts

no more. Bringing oblations is futile, incense is offensive to Me. New moon and sabbath, proclaiming of solemnities, assemblies with iniquity I cannot abide. Your new moons and fixed seasons fill Me with loathing; they are a burden to Me, I cannot endure them. And when you lift up your hands, I will turn My eyes away from you; though you pray at length, I will not listen. Your hands are stained with crime—Wash yourselves clean; put your evil doings away from My sight. Cease to do evil; learn to do good. Devote yourselves to justice; aid the wronged. Uphold the rights of the orphan; defend the cause of the widow." (1:10–17)

Note how Isaiah—like Amos before him—describes God's attitude toward sacrifices in harsh and bitter terms: burden, iniquity, hatred, abomination. His reference to the blood of oxen, spilt by sacrifice-bringers whose hands drip with human blood, evokes powerful and gory associations in the minds and hearts of his readers. Disgust and revulsion at the ritual slaughtering cry out from every line—indeed, from nearly every word. In vivid contrast to this practice, Isaiah calls for purity and goodness, law and justice, mercy and knowledge of God.

Micah, a younger contemporary of Isaiah, deals with this same theme via a series of questions and answers, an argument between God and his corrupt people. The people are represented as asking:

With what shall I approach the Lord, do homage to God on high? Shall I approach him with burnt-offerings, with calves of a year old? Would the Lord be pleased with thousands of rams, with myriads of streams of oil? Shall I give my first-born for my transgression, the fruit of my body for my sins? (6:6–7)

The prophet's reply to these questions is an unequivocal "No." The Lord, according to Micah, has no use for any of these. Rather, God requires of man:

Only to do justice and to love goodness, and to walk modestly with your God. (6:8)

Another few generations after Micah, the Kingdom of Israel was razed by Assyria, and its people sent into exile. Still the people of Judah neither mended their ways nor even realized the extent of their wickedness. Jeremiah, most tragic of prophets, raised his voice in protest against rulers and common folk alike, demanding social reform and an utter reversal of official policies.

Jeremiah, too, mentioned sacrifices. Not content with accusing his people of being "greedy for gain" and "deal[ing] falsely," he reproached them in God's name:

> What need have I of frankincense that comes from Sheba, or fragrant cane, from a distant land? Your burnt-offerings are not acceptable and your sacrifices are not pleasing to Me. (6:20)

What God desires of Israel, as expressed by Isaiah, is not sacrifices but, rather, a cessation of sin. Nor does Isaiah differentiate between an evildoer who sacrifices to the God of Israel and an idolater:

> As for those who slaughter oxen and slay humans, who sacrifice sheep and immolate dogs, who present as oblation the blood of swine, who offer incense and worship false gods—Just as they have chosen their ways and take pleasure in their abominations. . . . (66:3)

The anti-sacrificial theme continues to be repeated by prophet after prophet down to the last of them, Malachi. They ceaselessly proclaim the futility and hypocrisy of sacrifice and implore the people of Israel to turn to the ways of righteousness and justice.

ON FASTING

In early religions, fasting—in addition to sacrifices—was one of the more common ways of warding off evil or asking forgiveness and atonement from God. Fasts were accompanied by various ceremonies: special prayers, rending one's garments, wearing sackcloth, scattering ashes on one's head, and the like.

Fasting is given ample room in both the Bible and Jewish

religious ritual. Nevertheless, at one stage, the People of Israel began to treat fasting lightly, as they had sacrifices. It became a cheap, routine way to atone for serious crimes and iniquities.

The Prophets, principally Isaiah, campaigned against fasting and its attendant, hypocritical "pretended torture" and "mock starvation." Fasting—which of itself is neither a positive nor a negative act—is boldly, clearly, and beautifully contrasted by Isaiah with the essential virtue of doing good. This marvelous prophecy opens with a rhetorical question from the fasting "penitents" to God:

> Why, when we fasted, did You not see? When we starved our bodies, did You pay no heed? (58:3)

And God's answer, through the prophet:

> Is such the fast I desire, a day for men to starve their bodies? Is it bowing the head like a bulrush and lying in sackcloth and ashes? Do you call that a fast, a day when the Lord is favorable? No, this is the fast I desire: To unlock fetters of wickedness, and untie the cords of the yoke To let the oppressed go free; To break off every yoke. It is to share your bread with the hungry, and to take the wretched poor into your home; when you see the naked, to clothe him, and not to ignore your own kin. Then shall your light burst through like the dawn and your healing spring up quickly. . . . (58:5-8)

Zechariah, prophet during the rebuilding of the Second Temple, also appealed in God's name to the entire community, with their incessant fasting and lamentation for the ruined First Temple. He too asked whether their fast was really directed at God, and whether God could enjoy a mere abstinence from food, with no sign of regret for the sins of the past.

ON DOING GOOD

In a process drawn out over hundreds of years, the Prophets slowly taught the people of Israel that doing "good"—a concept that they very carefully defined—is more important than sacrificial rites and ceremonial fasting. Who, if not the Prophets, knew the strength of evil impulses, both among individuals and in human society in general? Who, if not they, knew just how apt God's words to Cain in Genesis had been:

> Sin couches at the door; its urge is toward you, yet you can be its master. (4:7)

The Prophets were well aware of the dark drives common to all humanity. They also knew that the process of introducing good to the people would be long, wearying, and bitterly resented; that they would be widely scorned and mocked, and more than occasionally flogged and imprisoned.

We must remember that the small People of Israel was surrounded by a riotous profusion of idols and idolaters and that these idols—or rather, their bloodthirsty priests—customarily demanded the immoral slaughter of animals and even humans. Nor should we forget that the Kohanic priesthood kept a zealous grip on sacrificial ritual among the People of Israel, and on its accompanying laws and ceremonies. As such, the priests cast baleful eyes on the Prophets and their teachings. Many kings, rulers, and aristocrats were also enthusiastic supporters of the sacrificial rites. As for the common people, they were by far more capable of understanding sacrifice than of comprehending the Prophets' abstract theories.

Undaunted by the opposition, the Prophets continued to spread their faith with constant, unflagging perseverance. One step at a time, they laid the ground for the great revolution that was to take place at the end of the Second Temple period. This revolution came too late for the Prophets to witness; but its fruits nourish the Jewish People and all of humanity to this very day. The underlying principle of this revolution was, quite simply, the placing of supreme emphasis on fulfillment of religious precepts—primarily on those concerned with doing "good": truth, justice, mercy, and peace. These maxims, by their very nature, are in no way related to altars and ritual bloodshed; they do not require priestly mediators. The most fundamental of all:

Love your fellow as yourself. (LEVITICUS 19:18)

—which Hillel the sage defined as the essence of Torah—calls for neither rite nor ceremony. It is a "one-on-one" precept, a mandate of "I and Thou."

Another facet of the revolution inspired by the Prophets concerned prayer: pure, simple prayer. Such worship need not be conducted in mass convocations—although the Prophets, in fact, had nothing against such convocations; indeed, Isaiah, in a vision of the distant future, spoke of the Temple:

My house shall be called a house of prayer for all peoples. (56:7)

Whether individual or congregational, the Prophets taught that the most valid sort of prayer is that which stems directly from the springs of the heart. Such prayer is described in the story of Hannah, wife of Elkanah, who prayed in Shiloh:

Hannah was praying in her heart; only her lips moved, but her voice could not be heard. So Eli thought she was drunk. Eli said to her, "How long will you make a drunken spectacle of yourself? Sober up!" And Hannah replied, "Oh no, my Lord! I am a very unhappy woman. I have drunk no wine or other strong drink, but I have been pouring out my heart to the Lord." (1 SAMUEL 1:13–15)

The Prophets considered precisely this sort of pure prayer to be the essential contact between man and God. In the words of the Psalmist:

May the words of my mouth and the prayer of my heart be acceptable to you, O Lord, my rock and my redeemer. (19:15)

This is the source of the Prophets' demand, or entreaty, that the People of Israel be granted an open heart, a good heart, a sensitive and understanding heart; and of their conviction that, even though the people had not yet been given such a heart, it was not yet too late for them to turn their own heart to good. Ezekiel, for example, exhorted the People of Israel to do just that:

> Cast away all the transgressions by which you have offended, and get yourselves a new heart and a new spirit, that you may not die, O house of Israel. For it is not My desire that anyone shall die—declares the Lord God. Repent, therefore, and live. (18:31–32)

And again, in a later passage:

> And I will give you a new heart and put a new spirit into you. I will remove the heart of stone from your body, and give you a heart of flesh. (36:26)

The Prophets' ultimate goal, then, was the extirpation of evil from the individual and collective hearts of humankind.

The teachings of the Prophets gave shelter and comfort to the People of Israel when the destruction of the Second Temple put an end to sacrifices in Judaism. This, in essence, shows the uniqueness of the Jewish People: Even after the destruction of its capital, the exile of many of its children, the razing of its Temple—till then the focal point of its religious ritual—and the loss of political independence, the people preserved its spiritual teachings, both those in writing and those carried within the heart. The heritage of the Prophets helped the Jewish People to establish new spiritual homes in any village, town, or city in which Jews could live. The house of prayer became the synagogue, where the faithful could pray, purify their hearts, and hope for better days, when:

> The Lord rebuilds Jerusalem; He gathers in the exiles of Israel. (PSALMS 147:2)

Till that day comes, remote though it may be, Jews can gather in any synagogue, even the most humble; even there, Jews can and do pray, study, and learn how to do good.

The post-Biblical teachings of the Sages provide an expansion, an interpretation, and an application of the doctrine of the Prophets. According to those worthy sources, human conduct is based on the solid foundations laid by the Prophets of Israel. Or, in the words of Simeon the Just, one of the great Sages of the first century:

> By three things is the world sustained—by the Law, by . . . service, and by deeds of loving-kindness. (MISHNAH AVOT 1:2)

Rabbi Johanan ben Zakkai, first and foremost among the rehabilitators of the Jewish People after the destruction of the Second Temple, tells his students:

> Go forth and see which is the good way to which a man should cleave. R. Eliezer said, A good eye. R. Joshua said, A good companion. R. Yose said, A good neighbor. R. Simeon said, One that sees what will be. R. Eleazar said, A good heart. He said to them: I approve the words of Eleazar ben Arak more than your words, for in his words your words are included. (2:9)

Is this not a wonderful sequel to the words of the Prophet Ezekiel on "a new heart and a new spirit?"

The supreme importance of doing good is stressed by Rabbi Simeon:

> There are three crowns—the crown of the Law, the crown of the priesthood, and the crown of kingship; but the crown of a good name excels them all. (4:13)

The foundations provided by the Prophets of the Bible, with their love of life and goodness, supported the mighty building of the Talmud. Together, the Written Torah and the Oral Torah continue to support, to this day, an edifice of Jewish ethics based on the sanctity of life.

The doctrine of the Prophets had, and continues to have, an immense effect on the majority of humankind. Their principles of truth and justice; their critical attitude toward religious ritual as an entity stripped of all good works; their condemnations of the trappings of the priesthood as devoid of righteousness—all these were passed on to the world at large by Christianity and Islam.

Thus, ever since the Prophets of Israel first required their People to be:

Children-of-the-Living-God (HOSEA 2:1)

and not the children of a God worshiped by sacrifice of living beings—the children of a God who holds life, not ritual, sacred—ever since then, the doctrine of the Prophets has become a Book of Life and a guiding light to vast portions of humanity.

The fact that the Prophets of Israel were not always listened to in their lifetime, and that the majority of the human race did not often choose to follow their teachings, by no means diminishes the intrinsic value of their doctrine of life.

Justice in the Gate

T HE FIVE BOOKS OF MOSES—THE BASIC LEGAL CODE OF THE People of Israel—deal with the problems of good and evil, and, naturally, with justice. We have already seen, in our discussion of the sanctity of life, that the basic premise on which the Book of Genesis believes the human character to be founded is a pessimistic one:

The devisings of man's mind are evil from his youth. (8:21)

And:

How great was man's wickedness on earth, and how every plan devised by his mind was nothing but evil all the time. (6:5)

In the very first chapters of Genesis, we encounter this evil in all its power: murder, hatred, jealousy, falsehood, and violence. Violence, indeed, is the collective name for all the evil accumulated in humanity—as it is written:

The earth became corrupt before God; the earth was filled with lawlessness. (6:11)

Opposite all this evil, opposite the instinctive violence with which the heart of humankind is so deeply imbued, stand goodness and justice. Opposite Cain, the first murderer, the embodiment of evildoing, stands Noah:

Noah was a righteous man; he was blameless in his age; Noah walked with God. (6:9)

God, indeed, has very definite attitudes toward perpetrators of evil and doers of good, the wicked and the righteous. To Cain, his brother's murderer, God says:

You shall be more cursed . . . (4:11)

Noah, the good-hearted and just, who walked in innocence before God, resembled the divine image that God had sought to recreate in humankind. But, as the story of Noah attests, the righteous are in the minority—in fact, they may well be the smallest of minorities. Most human beings are corrupt by nature, impelled to violence by their evil character and instinct. As such, they must be coerced into ways of goodness and justice by divine commands. If the burden of these precepts is not imposed upon them, they will persist in their evil ways.

The laws of justice laid down in the Pentateuch, then, are intended to restrain the evil of the human heart. If we admit that human beings—all human beings—have the potential of committing murder, adultery, and theft, of bearing false witness and coveting their neighbor's belongings, we will realize that the Torah's great, thundering "You shall not," brought down from the mountain as the Word of God by Moses, greatest of lawgivers, was intended to fetter the demon who dwells within each one of us.

The Pentateuch is not merely a book of laws, but a work founded on divine law. It is the great legal code of the People of Israel. Therefore, due to their basic nature as laws, the commands of the Five Books of Moses are short, decisive, and utterly unambiguous. In the laws of "You shall" and "You shall not," there is no room for bargaining between God and the recipient, the People of Israel. There is no "may" or "might" about these laws. They are absolute precepts to which the People of Israel have no choice but to answer, "We will do and obey." The Five Books of Moses contain no abstract arguments on good and evil, justice and violence. They contain only a framework of unassailable definitions.

This is by no means the case with the Books of the Prophets, created more than a thousand years after the Pentateuch. These books are filled with developments, ramifications, and philosophical debates on justice, good, and evil. They ring with exhortations for the achievement of justice and social reform, which was to come about not in some undefined latter day, but in what was, for each Prophet, present reality. They offer meditations, challenges, and searching questions. Why do the righteous fail while the wicked succeed? Why should children die for the iniquity of their parents? Why does the

People of Israel deserve such a cruel fate? Why are there such vast differences between extravagant wealth and degrading poverty?

One of the first things we must remember when discussing the Five Books of Moses is the fact that they were handed down to a people surrounded by idolatrous cultures—Babylonian, Egyptian, and Canaanite. The influence of the environment and the times on some of the Biblical laws is unmistakable. What is truly amazing is how, in a world of such stark cruelty, the lawmakers of the Pentateuch rose above their surroundings and succeeded in formulating laws of justice that were not only valid for their time but have remained relevant for thousands of years.

We must also keep in mind that the Israelites of those days were a nomadic people. As such, their lives—compared to those of a society of peasants, tied to the land—were free and relatively egalitarian. Of course, a strict hierarchy did exist among the People of Israel; but the social pyramid was much less complicated, with fewer strata and much less room for extremes than that of village society, or the even more complex urban society.

The laws of justice as expressed in the Pentateuch are so vast that, for the sake of good order, they must be divided into several subtopics. Yet the difficulty inherent in such a division is obvious: The Pentateuch, after all, is no mere dry compilation of laws. It is a work of history, the chronicles of a people; a work of poetry and prophecy; and, perhaps most of all, a great religious epic, depicting unparalleled mystic and dramatic occurrences involving believers and their God. Moreover, the laws appearing in the Five Books are not arranged in alphabetical order, or even by any kind of legal logic. The Mosaic laws have their own internal logic, which—though not always comprehensible to their readers—has provided a basis for innumerable commentaries by Jewish sages throughout the millennia.

Here, laws governing justice will be discussed in four categories: protection of the weak; matters between one individual and another; the relationship between the individual and society; and procedure for a fair, just trial.

PROTECTION OF THE WEAK

The nomadic herding society of the Hebrews in Moses' day was, relatively speaking, simple in structure. There were, admittedly, rich shepherds and tribal chiefs—such as Abraham—while other shepherds within the same tribe were relatively poor. However, the tribe as a social unit possessed various means of regulating and narrowing inordinate discrepancies in property.

Nevertheless, even in this society—and how much more so in societies whose property is measured in land—there were weak, vulnerable human beings. Such are the poor and destitute: persons who, for whatever reason, have suffered at the hands of fate and have been left with no property whatsoever—not even the "one little ewe lamb" of the poor man in Nathan's parable, not even one small plot of earth. Such unfortunates have been part of human society since the dawn of creation. Even the Bible admits the truth of this fact:

> For there will never cease to be needy ones in your land. (DEU-
> TERONOMY 15:11)

Other weak individuals recognized by the Pentateuch are widows and orphans. Ancient societies—including that of the Hebrews—were characterized by a difficult struggle for survival in the face of natural disasters and beasts of prey, especially in the face of the incessant hostilities between neighboring tribes and nations. Vast numbers of fighting men died before their time, leaving their wives widowed and their children fatherless.

Mosaic law recognizes an additional category of weak persons—some of them congenitally so: the sick and handicapped. Indeed, in what society has this vulnerable group not existed?

And there was yet another group in need of protection in the ancient Hebrew society—a group which, though not exactly weak and unfortunate, was certainly different from the majority: the Levites. The tribe of Levi owned no land in Israel; its members filled the role of "public servants" in spiritual, religious, and ritual fields. Yet officially they were without property, dependent for their living on tithes doled out by the public.

Another group, the non-Jewish residents, will be discussed in the chapter on equality.

These five groups—the poor, the orphans, the widows, the sick, and the Levites—are protected in the Pentateuch by a series of impressive "shalls" and "shall nots":

> You shall not ill-treat any widow or orphan. If you do mistreat them, I will heed their outcry as soon as they cry out to Me. . . . If you lend money to My people, to the poor among you, do not act toward them as a creditor: exact no interest from them. (EXODUS 22:21–22, 24)

And, concerning the sick and handicapped:

> You shall not insult the deaf, or place a stumbling block before the blind. You shall fear your God: I am the Lord. (LEVITICUS 19:14)

And, regarding the Levites:

> And to the Levites, I hereby give all the tithes in Israel as their share in return for the services that they perform, the services of the Tent of Meeting. (NUMBERS 18:21)

The Pentateuch repeats its demand for justice and assistance toward the weak, emphasizing that this is the will of God Himself Who:

> . . . upholds the cause of the fatherless and the widow, and befriends the stranger, providing him with food and clothing. (DEUTERONOMY 10:18)

In Deuteronomy, the laws covering protection of the weak are quite detailed. And the lawgivers repeatedly stress that those of limited property must not be deprived of their basic clothing or tools of livelihood, that pains must be taken to ensure that their wages are paid on time:

> A handmill or an upper millstone shall not be taken in pawn, for that would be taking someone's life in pawn. . . . You shall not subvert the rights of the stranger or the fatherless; you shall not take the widow's garment in pawn. Remember that you were a slave in Egypt and that the Lord your God redeemed you from

there; therefore do I enjoin you to observe this commandment. (24:6, 17-18)

On the dramatic occasion when the Levites publicly adjure the people to keep the main "You shall not" precepts of the Pentateuch, the Book of Deuteronomy lists among the transgressions some relevant to the protection of the weak:

Cursed be he who removes his fellow countryman's landmark. ... Cursed be he who misdirects a blind person on his way. Cursed be he who subverts the rights of the stranger, the fatherless, and the widow. (27:17-19)

The Book of Ruth enlightens its readers on many aspects of life in the Biblical Land of Israel, and how the laws of protection applied to Naomi and Ruth: Naomi, the poor widow; Ruth, the poor stranger. When Naomi returns to the city of Bethlehem with her Moabite daughter-in-law who could not bear to leave her, she sends Ruth to glean in the field after the reapers. The owner of the field, Boaz, deems her actions to be fitting and proper, based on Biblical precept—even before Ruth and Boaz fall in love.

LAWS BETWEEN INDIVIDUALS

Most Biblical laws of this type deal with criminal offenses. Besides murder, the most heinous of crimes, the other offenses detailed in the Bible are sins and transgressions commonly practiced to this day: theft, robbery, false witness, trespassing, bribery, nonpayment of wages, and so forth.

These offenses are countered in the Pentateuch by myriad proscriptions such as:

Keep far from a false charge; do not bring death on those who are innocent and in the right, for I will not acquit the wrongdoer. Do not take bribes, for bribes blind the clear-sighted, and upset the pleas of those who are in the right. (EXODUS 23:7-8)

And:

You shall not steal; you shall not deal deceitfully or falsely with one another. You shall not swear falsely by My name, profaning the name of your God: I am the Lord. You shall not defraud your fellow. You shall not commit robbery. The wages of a hired laborer shall not remain with you until morning. (LEVITICUS 19:11–13)

And:

When you enter another man's vineyard, you may eat as many grapes as you want until you are full, but you must not put any in your vessel. When you enter another man's field of standing grain, you may pluck ears with your hand; but you must not put a sickle to your neighbor's grain. (DEUTERONOMY 23:25–26)

These examples show how the Bible became the paradigm for Western common law.

LAWS DETERMINING PROCEDURE FOR A JUST TRIAL

The Pentateuch repeatedly emphasizes a number of foundations of laws such as justice without favor, rules of evidence and witnesses, and deterrent verdicts and sentences. These Biblical rules, which also comprise the legal system of the Judges of Israel, are expressed as divine commands.

The commandment of behaving righteously and justly is handed down by God as early as Abraham's time. In God's words to Abraham:

He may instruct his children and his posterity to keep the way of the Lord by doing what is just and right, in order that the Lord may bring about for Abraham what He has promised him. (GENESIS 18:19)

God's promise to make Abraham into "a great nation" is, then, defined from the beginning as contingent upon Abraham's doing righteousness and justice. In later years, when the prophets in Judah and Samaria cried out for justice and righteousness, one of their central arguments was that the doers of evil and violence among the people—including the corrupt kings and rulers—had broken the covenant between God and the People of Israel, and that their transgressions had brought wars, disasters, and destruction upon their people.

The most concise definition of justice is given in Deuteronomy:

When there is a dispute between men and they go to law . . . a decision is rendered declaring the one in the right and the other in the wrong. (DEUTERONOMY 25:1)

The Biblical rules of justice start with the Ninth Commandment:

You shall not bear false witness against your neighbor. (EXODUS 20:13)

The books of Leviticus and Deuteronomy spell out in detail all the procedures that are meant to ensure equality and justice before the law. Of equal significance to the lawgivers of the Pentateuch is the central problem of justice. For example, should punishment for crime and iniquity constitute part of one's inheritance? Should children suffer for the misdeeds of their parents? Can a man be liable for a sin that he himself did not commit?

No clear-cut answer is provided in the Pentateuch to this difficult situation, as described by Jeremiah:

Parents have eaten sour grapes and children's teeth are blunted. (JEREMIAH 31:29)

In fact, we find two types of answers—one could almost say, two schools of thought—on the issue. On the one hand:

I the Lord your God am an impassioned God, visiting the guilt of the parents upon the children, upon the third and upon the fourth generations of those who reject Me. (EXODUS 20:5)

Yet, on the other hand:

Parents shall not be put to death for children, nor children be put to death for parents: a person shall be put to death only for his own crime. (DEUTERONOMY 24:16)

This moral-philosophic problem is discussed, time and time again, by the Prophets; and the manner of its discussion casts light on the reality in which they lived. For example: Should Zedekiah, king of Judah and a descendant of King Manasseh, be punished because his ancestor did that which was evil in the sight of God?

The first biblical discussion of the laws of monarchy may also be found in the Five Books of Moses. The People of Israel, at the time they received the Torah, did not yet have a king; they were a nomadic society, with no capital and no palaces. Their leaders were spiritual giants—Moses, of course, chief among them—but had not yet received the crown and scepter. Nevertheless, the lawmakers of the Pentateuch foresaw that the people might well desire a king in the future. In preparation for that day, they drew up a list of conditions of and limitations to the institution of monarchy:

> If, after you have entered the land that the Lord your God has assigned to you, and taken possession of it and settled in it, you decide, "I will set a king over me, as do all the nations about me," you shall be free to set a king over yourself, one chosen by the Lord your God. Be sure to set as king over yourself one of your own people; you must not set a foreigner over you, one who is not your kinsman. Moreover, he shall not keep many horses . . . [nor] wives . . . [nor] gold. (DEUTERONOMY 17:14–17)

The Pentateuch also recognizes the relationship between righteousness and justice, a subject which, at first, appears extraneous to law and legality *per se*: love of one's fellow human beings—and, first of all, nonhatred:

> You shall not hate your kinsfolk in your heart. Reprove your kinsman but incur no guilt because of him. You shall not take vengeance or bear a grudge against your countrymen. Love your neighbor as yourself: I am the Lord. (LEVITICUS 19:17–18)

These lines constitute commandments of the heart, which cannot be measured or enforced. There is no way to look into a human heart and determine whether, and to what extent, its owner hates his brother; no way to measure love of one's neighbors, nor to compare it with love of oneself. Yet precisely these commandments illustrate the greatness of the Torah. For it is the fostering, promotion, and development of these supreme, altruistic emotions that distinguish true humanity—the divine image—from the bestial creature that lurks within our hearts.

Not by chance did the Pentateuch weave these verses into a tractate of rigid, unambiguous laws. It may be safely assumed that this was done with the deliberate intent of ensuring that these ethical and emotional precepts would be honored as definitive commands. And it was certainly no coincidence that impelled Hillel the Sage to define "You shall love your neighbor as yourself" as the essence of the entire Torah; certainly no coincidence that led Rabbi Akiva to state that this command was "a great rule of the Torah."

Obviously, those who entirely fulfill the precept "You shall love your neighbor as yourself" have brought their good instincts to a true and final victory over their evil instincts. Just as obviously, this blessed state is reached by very few—perhaps by a mere handful. As the legend has it, there may be only thirty-six such righteous persons throughout the entire world. Still, the attempt to achieve such love remains the supreme goal that humankind can set for itself.

Following the era of the Pentateuch came the generations of Joshua and the Judges. This was a period of conquest and colonization, studded with cruel wars against the indigenous peoples—a period without much room for righteousness and justice. Much of that time, in fact, may be characterized by the short Biblical phrase:

> In those days there was no king in Israel; every man did as he pleased. (JUDGES 17:6)

It is certainly true that nations fighting for their lives seldom take time to consider such values as justice or righteousness. In fact—and this can scarcely be insignificant—the books of Joshua and Judges hardly even mention those concepts. In the entire Book of Judges, for example, the word "righteous" appears only once. The word "judgment" (in Hebrew *mishpat*, the same word used for "justice") also appears in only one verse. Both of these terms are used in connection with Deborah the Prophetess:

> The Israelites would come to her for judgment. (4:5)

And, in Deborah's song of victory:

> Let them chant the righteous acts of the Lord, His gracious deliverance of Israel. (5:11)

The stories of the remaining judges do not center on descriptions of their judging but, rather, on their heroic deeds, their courage, and their cunning in battle. Only for Samuel, the prophet-judge, does the Bible portray the hard work invested in his judicial position, under the grueling conditions prevailing in a nation beset with war along its borders and disputes within its territory:

> Samuel judged Israel as long as he lived. Each year he made the rounds of Bethel, Gilgal, and Mizpah, and acted as judge over Israel at all those places. (1 SAMUEL 7:15–16)

This sort of "circuit judge" or "circuit court" gradually became part of the accepted judiciary system in the Land of Israel and other countries, especially in the Anglo-Saxon judiciary heritage.

In Samuel's old age, the elders of Israel demanded that he appoint a leader and crown him king over Israel, to judge the people and lead them into battle—just as was customary among the surrounding nations, whom they sought to emulate. Samuel's reply to the Elders reflects the bitterness of his heart, and provides a stark contrast to the list of conditions for kingship set down in Deuteronomy.

> He said, "This will be the practice of the king who will rule over you: He will take your sons and appoint them as his charioteers and horsemen, and they will serve as outrunners for his chariots. He will appoint them as his chiefs of thousands and of fifties; or they will have to plow his field, reap his harvest, and make his weapons and the equipment for his chariots. He will take your daughters as perfumers, cooks, and bakers. He will seize your choice fields, vineyards, and olive-groves, and give them to his courtiers. He will take a tenth part of your grain and vintage and give it to his eunuchs and courtiers. He will take your male and female slaves, your choice young men, and your asses, and put them to work for him. He will take a tenth part of your flocks, and you shall become his slaves. The day will come when you cry out because of the king whom you yourselves have chosen; and the Lord will not answer you on that day." (8:11–18)

Despite the severity of Samuel's warning, the People of Israel choose not to heed. Samuel gives in to their repeated demand, and Israel becomes a kingdom. But in future years, the People of Israel would have more than ample reason to "cry out" against their kings, most of whom afflicted them just as Samuel had foreseen, if not more severely.

Before departing from the stage of history, weary of days and full of anger, Samuel sums up his term in office with an emotional speech:

> I have been your leader from my youth to this day. Here I am! Testify against me, in the presence of the Lord and in the presence of His anointed one: Whose ox have I taken, or whose ass have I taken? Whom have I defrauded or whom have I robbed? From whom have I taken a bribe to look the other way? (1 SAMUEL 12:2–3)

With these heartfelt words Samuel hoped to immortalize the unimpeachable ethics of the model judge for generations to come.

From the reign of Saul, first king in Israel, to that of Jeroboam, son of Joash (Jeroboam II) a period of some three hundred years elapsed. During that time the People of Israel learned both the glory and grandeur of kingly rule and the suffering and iniquity that despots could inflict. This was an age of boundless royal treasure—accumulated at the expense of demeaning poverty among the common people, and often with extreme persecution at the hands of the rulers; an age in which the Temple was built in Jerusalem while cruel idolatry flourished in Judea and Samaria; an age that engendered Psalms of praise, in all their beauty; and yet, an age of intrigue, revolt, murder, and assassination. In short, it was an age that echoes the splendor and corruption of the Byzantine era, or the opulence and evil of Shakespeare's *Macbeth*.

It was in the days of Jeroboam, son of Joash, that the period of the Written Prophets began, with Amos. The appearance of these Prophets, and their campaign against corruption and injustice changed the course of history—not only that of the Jews but that of the entire world. We shall continue to follow this marvelous phenomenon, unique in the chronicles of humankind, throughout this book.

Meanwhile, however, even before the emergence of the

Written Prophets, Israel was graced again and again by a succession of courageous Prophets of truth and justice. Some of these have already been mentioned in Chapter 1—Nathan, for example, standing before King David and declaiming his parable of the "poor man's ewe lamb" with its dramatic ending ("That man is you!"); or Elijah, crying out against King Ahab in the vineyard of Naboth, "Would you murder and take possession?"

The less-known Prophet Micaiah, son of Imlah, also confronts King Ahab with the bitter truth—this time, concerning the future of the war with Aram:

> I saw all Israel scattered over the hills like sheep without a shepherd. (1 KINGS 22:17)

The angry king, who had expected encouraging prophecies of victory, is furious at the prophet of truth, and commands his general:

> Take Micaiah and turn him over to Amon, the city's governor, and to Prince Joash, and say, "the King's orders are: Put this fellow in prison, and let his fare be scant bread and scant water until I come home safe." (22:26–27)

Ahab then sets out for war, and he is killed, just as Micaiah had predicted.

This marks the opening scene of what may be termed the great, many-acted drama of "Prophet versus King," with the banner of spiritual ethics raised against the scepter of rule and power. What David and Ahab had not dared do to Nathan and Elijah, Ahab now does by imprisoning Micaiah. Nor will Micaiah be the last of the Prophets to lay down his freedom for the cause of faith and truth.

The campaign of the new Prophets, the Written Prophets, whose greatness lay no less in their capacity as great politicians and social reformers than in their advocacy of truth and justice, was personified by Amos, Written Prophet and champion of social reform.

The wisdom of the Prophets grew and developed over the generations, reaching its zenith in the visions of Isaiah and Jeremiah. To fully understand their teachings, one must thoroughly read the philosophy of Amos, concisely expressed in nine brief chapters. Yet, to benefit from this thorough reading, it is necessary first to understand the political and social background that prevailed at the time of Amos' appearance on the scene. Some of this background is given in the first verse of the Book of Amos:

> The words of Amos, a sheepbreeder from Tekoa, who prophesied concerning Israel in the reigns of Kings Uzziah of Judah and Jeroboam son of Joash of Israel, two years before the earthquake. (AMOS 1:1)

At the time Amos began to prophesy, Judah was ruled by Uzziah, one of the more important kings of the House of David. During his reign, Uzziah considerably expanded and strengthened the borders of Judah, established a strong army, and vanquished numerous enemies.

But Amos prophesied concerning Israel, not Judah, and conducted his ethical campaign against its ruler—Jeroboam, son of Joash.

If military victories and expansion of one's borders are to be considered as criteria for greatness, there can be no doubt that Jeroboam was one of the greatest of Israel's kings. After many years of grueling wars against Aram—Israel's northern foe in those days—it was Jeroboam who succeeded in striking a telling blow against the enemy. In a series of victorious battles, he expanded the borders of the Kingdom of Israel to nearly equal those of the undivided kingdom once ruled by David and Solomon. This is clearly attested to in 2 Kings, with its vivid description of Jeroboam's achievements; yet, interestingly enough, this passage contains a glaring contradiction:

> In the fifteenth year of King Amaziah son of Joash of Judah, King Jeroboam son of Joash of Israel became king in Samaria—forty-one years. He did what was displeasing to the Lord; he did not depart from all the sins that Jeroboam son of Nebat had caused Israel to commit. It was he who restored the territory of Israel from Lebo-hamath to the sea of the Arabah . . . And the Lord resolved not to blot out the name of Israel from under heaven; and delivered them through Jeroboam son of Joash. (14:23–25, 27)

How can this contradiction be resolved? Did Jeroboam, son of Joash, save Israel, or did he cause Israel to sin? The answer is that he did both. He saved Israel from its external enemies by conquering and subduing Damascus and Hamath. The Kingdom of Israel was greatly expanded, and even the Kingdom of Judah became subordinate to it. From the standpoint of territory, the Kingdom of Israel became the greatest nation in the area between the two great powers of that era: Assyria in the north and Egypt in the south.

During Jeroboam II's forty-one-year reign—a very long one for those days—the Land of Israel was, to all appearances, a safe and tranquil place. Trade flourished, cities grew and prospered, and the spoils of war and conquest enriched the royal treasury. This, then, was the "saving" of Israel by Jeroboam, son of Joash.

Yet it was not the saving of Israel that brought the herdsman of Judah to the king's palace in Samaria, but the sin— whose magnitude far outweighed the saving. And what was this sin? Part of it stemmed from the return to idolatry and foreign rites of worship. By far the greater part, however, was the terrible social injustice unleashed in Israel during the days of Jeroboam II. This was the sin against which Amos' soul cried out, irresistibly impelling him to leave his sheep and cattle in Judah and journey north to Samaria, capital of Israel. This was the sin that drove him to lash out at the king, the rulers, and the rich with the most terrible of prophecies— not only rebuking them to their faces for their evil ways but fearlessly invoking their punishment.

The prophecy of Amos, to this day, resonates in its readers' ears like a veritable trumpet of doom, a warning surviving over 2,700 years. Despite the centuries, it still rings clear as this morning's sunrise, relevant as this evening's newscast:

Thus said the Lord: "For three transgressions of Judah, for four, I will not revoke it: because they have sold for silver those whose cause was just, and the needy for a pair of sandals. [Ah,] you who trample the heads of the poor into the dust of the ground, and make the humble walk a twisted course! Father and son go to the same girl, and thereby profane My holy name. They recline by every altar on garments taken in pledge, and drink in the House of their God Wine bought with fines they imposed. (2:6–8)

That is the sin—and this, the punishment:

Ah, I will slow your movements as a wagon is slowed when it is full of cut grain. Flight shall fail the swift, the strong shall find no strength, and the warrior shall not save his life. The bowman shall not hold his ground, and he the fleet-footed shall not escape, nor the horse-man save his life. Even the most stouthearted warrior shall run away unarmed that day—declares the Lord. (2:13–16)

The essence of Israel's sin is sharply and succinctly defined: distortion of justice, persecution of the poor, prostitution, and drunkenness in the guise of religious practice. The punishment is no less clear—the kingdom will have its back broken and lose its physical and military might.

The words of Amos reflect an essential difference from the prophecies and castigations appearing in earlier books of the Bible. The sin condemned by Amos is not the same as that proscribed in the legal code of the Pentateuch. Amos does not cry out against persecution of any one victim by any one robber or murderer—not even against the king alone. The violence here is perpetrated by many against many; or, in a more modern language, by one class against another.

The prophecies of Amos, and those of the Prophets who followed him, are phrased in terms of group phenomena. The "needy" and the "fined" here are not individuals but masses. Amos does not speak of any one poor orphan, or any one starving widow, or of the miserable sick and weak at the edges of any society. The question here is not of those individual unfortunates already protected and defended by the commands of the Pentateuch, but of the *class* of destitute and dispossessed; of many human beings robbed of all they once had—property, riches, dignity, freedom—by a *group* of others. Theirs is the cry that resonates in Amos' words.

The phenomenon of mass dispossession did not exist in the nomadic, tribal society to which the Torah was given. Naturally, that society had its poor, its sick, and its weak;

nevertheless, most of its members retained the basic rights of possession (herds) and status. Such was also the case in the society of free peasants, most of them small landholders, which developed in the days of the Judges and the early years of kingly rule. The sheepherders and cattle tenders (like Amos himself); the vine growers, farmers, and sycamore dressers (another of Amos' occupations); the carpenters and iron-workers—all of these owned property: cattle and sheep, fields and vineyards, workshops and tools. All of these enjoyed the dignity of status in society.

By Amos' time, a new class had arisen. Though admittedly, this did not begin under Jeroboam II, its harbingers were evident as early as the days of the first great kings. This new class was composed of those devoid of property, the op-pressed, and the robbed. These were not poor "by nature," or due to any physical or emotional inability to earn their living. These were persons whose property and rights had been forcibly taken away by another class. This was, one might say, a "collective Naboth," oppressed by a "collective Ahab." And who was (or were) that collective Ahab? The king, the ministers, the officers, the profiteers of war, the black marketeers, and even those priests who peddled im-morality and exploitation in the trappings of religion.

The atmosphere of military victory and economic pros-perity brought to Israel by Jeroboam was an ideal medium for the riotous, malignant growth of this new parasite—the class of corrupt officials; of generals drunk with fame and glory; of cheating, lying bootlickers, toadying their way to favor in the court; of greedy *nouveaux riches* and *arrivistes*; of judges and police who let themselves be bought. And it is Amos who speaks out against them all:

> Gather on the hill of Samaria and witness the great outrages within her, and the oppressions in her midst. They are incapable of doing right—declares the Lord; They store up lawlessness and rapine in their fortresses. Assuredly, Thus said my Lord God: An enemy, all about the land! He shall strip you of your splendor, and your fortresses shall be plundered. . . . I will wreck the winter palace together with the summer palace; the ivory palaces shall

be demolished, and the great houses shall be destroyed—declares the Lord. (3:9–11, 15)

Thus Amos cries challenge and raises the banner of insurrection. The "great outrages" are, simply, riots waged by masses of the destitute and downtrodden, oppressed by those who dwell in palaces, in winter mansions and summer resorts. And, in case the identity of those oppressors is not clear enough to Amos' listeners, he goes on to cite the pampered, perfumed, drunken, and licentious wives—their riches literally squeezed from the starving—who urge their crooked husbands to persecute the lower classes even more. In scorn and anger, Amos terms these women:

> You cows of Bashan, on the hill of Samaria—who defraud the poor, who rob the needy; who say to your husbands, "Bring, and let's carouse!" (4:1)

Now Amos points an accusing finger at another group: the judges. Despite the integrity supposedly required by their very position, the judiciary of Jeroboam II's day habitually perverted justice and accepted bribes, filling their pockets with the pennies of the poor. Or, as Amos puts it:

> [Ah,] you who turn justice into wormwood and hurl righteousness to the ground. . . . They hate the arbiter in the gate, and detest him whose plea is just. Assuredly, because you impose a tax on the poor and exact from him a levy of grain, you have built houses of hewn stone, but you shall not live in them; You have planted delightful vineyards, but shall not drink their wine. For I have noted how many are your crimes, and how countless your sins—you enemies of the righteous, you takers of bribes, you who subvert in the gate the cause of the needy! Assuredly, at such a time the prudent man keeps silent, for it is an evil time. (5:7, 10–13)

Yet, no matter how evil the time, Amos himself cannot keep silent—even though he knows his words will attract the wrath of the authorities. Having reproved the heartless rulers and corrupt judges, Amos turns his attention to another social stratum of oppressors: merchants who bleed their poor customers with dishonest weights and inflated prices. But he

saves his harshest condemnation for the leaders of the society. Amos considers the root of all evil, and the source of all corruption, to lie with the ruling stratum: the king, the nobles, the ministers, and the generals, whose victories and accumulated wealth have overcome sensitivity of spirit, rendering them utterly contemptuous of the laws of justice and righteousness. To them, he cries out:

> Ah, you who are at ease in Zion and confident on the hill of Samaria.... They lie on ivory beds, lolling on their couches, feasting on lambs from the flock and on calves from the stalls. They hum snatches of song to the tune of the lute—they account themselves musicians like David. They drink [straight] from the wine bowls and anoint themselves with the choicest oils—but they are not concerned about the ruin of Joseph. (6:1, 4–6)

And, as always, Amos concludes his scathing description with the terrible punishment in store for this group:

> Assuredly, right soon they shall head the column of exiles.... (6:7)

It is interesting to note that, in this prophecy, Amos includes not only the king and the notables in Samaria, but also those of Jerusalem (Zion), capital of Judah. We will return to describe the social situation then prevailing in Jerusalem as part of our discussion of Isaiah, son of Amoz and a younger contemporary of Amos. For now, it is enough to note that Jerusalem under King Uzziah, from an internal social standpoint, was not all that different from Israel under Jeroboam II: victories, expansion of borders, and internal corruption—a situation known to Amos all too well.

The one thing most hated by the prophet was the unjustified feeling of outward self-confidence and smugness. True, the Kingdom of Israel had grown in area; in spiritual terms, however, it had become a rotten bog, filled with the noxious gases of empty vanity. It is that vanity and false superiority that Amos now attacks, in God's name:

> I loathe the pride of Jacob, and I detest his fortresses. I will declare forfeit city and inhabitants alike. (6:8)

For a destined day was to come when the pretentious gaiety of the ruling class—a gaiety based on the use of force and oppression—would utterly disappear. For the time being, though, the rulers imagined that they and their armies were invincible. Still, on the day of punishment, despite the kingdom's expanded and ostensibly secure borders, it would be entirely overcome by its enemies:

> [Ah,] those who are so happy about Lo-dabar, who exult, "By our might we have captured Karnaim"! But I, O house of Israel, will raise up a nation against you—declares the Lord, the God of hosts—who will harass you from Lebo-Hamath to the Wadi Arabah. (6:13–14)

Amos, though principally a social reformer, here reveals himself as a sagacious politician. He realizes that Israel's expansion had thus far been founded on military victories against small and medium-size neighboring states and kingdoms. Sooner or later, this expansionism was bound to run up against the greatest "nation" of the north—Assyria. That nation (more correctly, superpower) would smash Israel's armies to bits and break its neck.

The very strength and force of these prophecies of anger, boldly proclaimed before masses of people in the Temple courts and opposite the royal palace, hastened Amos' own end as a prophet in Israel. The day finally comes when Amos utters the most terrible of prophecies:

> The shrines of Isaac shall be laid waste, and the sanctuaries of Israel shall be reduced to ruins; and I will turn upon the House of Jeroboam with the sword. (7:9)

This bleak vision was the last straw. In the following tragic and dramatic passage, the high priest, Amaziah, calls for the intervention of King Jeroboam himself to deport the "traitorous" Amos from the Kingdom of Israel; and Amos responds:

> I am not a prophet, and I am not a prophet's disciple. I am a cattle breeder and a tender of sycamore figs. But the Lord took me away from following the flock, and the Lord said to me: "Go, prophesy to My people Israel." And so, hear the word of

the Lord. You say I must not prophesy about the House of Israel or preach about the House of Isaac; but this, I swear, is what the Lord said: Your wife shall play the harlot in the town, your sons and daughters shall fall by the sword, and your land shall be divided up with a measuring line. And you yourself shall die on unclean soil; for Israel shall surely be exiled from its soil. (7:14–17)

—A fearsome and horrifying doom indeed.

Amos then calls to the people to turn aside from their iniquity and choose another way. Even at this "eleventh hour," the prophet pleads with Israel to change course and be saved:

Seek good and not evil, that you may live. . . . Hate evil and love good, and establish justice in the gate; perhaps the Lord, the God of Hosts, will be gracious to the remnant of Joseph. (5:14–15)

Yet no one listens. Amos remains a lone voice crying in the wilderness—the social wilderness and human desolation known as Jeroboam's Kingdom of Israel.

Apparently, Amos bowed to the deportation order and returned to Judah, to his flocks and sycamores. In any event, no word remains of his personal history following his deportation. (Personal fates, as a rule, were not the concern of those who composed the Bible and recorded the chronicles of the Prophets. Like Amos, the fates of Isaiah, Jeremiah, and other Prophets remain unknown to us.)

Nevertheless, we do know the fate of Amos' nine chapters of prophecy. His words, the outcry of an aching heart aimed at the deaf ears of Israel's rulers, became the chief cornerstone of the moral guidelines adopted by Judaism and by humanity in general; the foundation of social reform throughout the course of time. All liberal, progressive, and humanistic/socialist doctrines draw some of their inspiration from Amos, and all human societies characterized by equality and justice owe a debt to the herdsman of Tekoa.

Hosea, Amos' young contemporary, was the last prophet to prophesy in the Kingdom of Israel before its destruction by Assyria. Unlike Amos, Hosea did not arrive in Israel as an adult, but was born and raised there. Like Amos, however, Hosea was aware of the corruption of his people and the betrayal within his home—both his national homeland and his personal household. This is his description of the situation:

> There is no honesty and no goodness and no obedience to God in the land. [False] swearing, dishonesty, and murder, and theft, and adultery are rife; crime follows upon crime! For that, the earth is withered: Everything that dwells on it languishes. . . .
> (4:1–3)

But Hosea's prophecies do not ring with the continuous, burning rage that characterizes those of Amos. In his comforting prophecies, Hosea renews the alliance between Israel and God—a linkage of justice and righteousness, metaphorically depicted as a betrothal:

> And I will espouse you forever: I will espouse you with righteousness and justice, and in goodness and mercy. (2:21)

The personality of Isaiah, also a young contemporary of Amos, encompasses all of the glorious aspects of the phenomenon of prophecy. He is at once a prophet of desolation and of consolation. He is a statesman, predicting from afar the interplay of the major political forces in his area. At the same time, as a member of the nobility, he has an "inside slant" on the kings and courts of Judah.

One facet of Isaiah's manifold nature is as a social reformer, struggling against the moral decadence of his people, his country, and his city. Isaiah "prophesied concerning Jerusalem." He did not have to go as far as Samaria to find corruption. He could see it right before his eyes, on his own doorstep.

Like Amos, who prophesied in Israel in the days of one of its greatest rulers, Jeroboam, Isaiah's first prophecies were delivered during the reign of one of Judah's greatest kings, Uzziah. Like Jeroboam II of Israel, Uzziah of Judah conquered many of his neighboring enemies, considerably expanded his country's borders, reinforced its army and enriched its treasury. This is what the Biblical historians had to say about him:

> He went forth to fight the Philistines, and breached the wall of Gath and the wall of Jabneh and the wall of Ashdod; he built towns in [the region of] Ashdod, and among the Philistines. God helped him against the Philistines, against the Arabs who lived in Gur-baal, and the Meunites. The Ammonites paid tribute to

Uzziah, and his fame spread to the approaches of Egypt, for he grew exceedingly strong. Uzziah built towers in Jerusalem on the Corner Gate and the Valley Gate and on the Angle, and fortified them. He built towers in the wilderness and hewed out many cisterns, for he had much cattle, and farmers in the foothills and on the plain, and vine dressers in the mountains and on the fertile lands, for he loved the soil. Uzziah had an army of warriors, a battle-ready force who were mustered by Jeiel the scribe and Maasseiah the adjutant under Hananiah, one of the king's officers . . . And his name spread far abroad; for he was marvelously helped, till he was strong. (2 CHRONICLES 26:6–11)

At first reading, Isaiah's description of Judah in the days of King Uzziah also seems to reinforce this impression of a valiant, heroic conqueror at the head of a vast, secure, and wealthy kingdom:

Their land is full of silver and gold, there is no limit to their treasures; their land is full of horses, there is no limit to their chariots. (2:7)

Yet, in the very next breath, Isaiah cries out that, for all its riches and power, Judah is anything but an idyllic land:

And . . . their land is full of idols; they bow down to the work of their hands, to what their own fingers have wrought. But man shall be humbled, and mortal brought low—Oh, do not forgive them. (2:8–9)

The writer of the Chronicles indicates that the source of this evil is none other than the pomp and vanity displayed by King Uzziah along with the glory of his military victories. Exhilarated by power, he betrays his God and permits the continuation of idol-worship in his country. Nor does he stop there. Infringing on the rights and duties reserved to the Temple priests, he attempts to burn incense on the altar of the Lord:

When he was strong, he grew so arrogant he acted corruptly: he trespassed against his God. . . . (2 CHRONICLES 26:16)

This "arrogance"—an unjustified sense of superiority over his fellow human beings—was to bring Uzziah suffering for the rest of his days. For his betrayal he is severely punished:

The Lord struck the king with a plague and he was a leper until the day of his death; he lived in isolated quarters. (2 KINGS 15:5)

Nevertheless, the corruption in Judah during those years was not the King's alone. The taint, in fact, was far more profound, affecting the entire ruling circle.

Isaiah was well aware that King Uzziah had built towers in Jerusalem, and that atop those towers roosted instruments of war. He was personally acquainted with the generals, ministers, and officers of the Judean army, with its dazzling display of weaponry. But the prophet's first and foremost concern was: What is happening *inside* the fortified walls of Jerusalem? How do the victorious rulers and heroes treat *their own people*? And Isaiah's answer to this outcry is truly terrible:

Alas, she has become a harlot, the faithful city that was filled with justice, where righteousness dwelt—but now murderers. Your silver has turned to dross; your wine is cut with water. Your rulers are rogues and cronies of thieves, every one avid for presents and greedy for gifts; they do not judge the case of the orphan, and the widow's cause never reaches them. (1:21–23)

Thus, in a few simple sentences, Isaiah lists nearly all of the terrible sins to be found in the Ten Commandments—indeed, in the entire Torah. Isaiah makes no exception for anyone, be he minister, judge, or merchant. Addressing his words to each and every member of the upper classes, he stresses that "every one" is guilty. And, to emphasize this universality even further, he reminds his listeners of the tales of Genesis:

Hear the word of the Lord, you chieftains of Sodom; give ear to our God's instruction, you folk of Gomorrah. (1:10)

The reference is obvious: Just as there was not one righteous human being in Sodom, Isaiah implies that there is no longer a single righteous human being among the notables of Judah—rulers and common people alike. They are all sinners whose iniquity causes others to sin as well.

In our discussion of sacrifices we observed Isaiah's contempt for those who believed that, by slaughtering an animal, they could obtain absolution. In the same speech the prophet denounces the hypocrites who offer frequent and insincere "lip service" to God:

> Though you pray at length, I will not listen. Your hands are stained with crime. (1:15)

Isaiah again attacks the elders and ministers:

> It is you who have ravaged the vineyard; that which was robbed from the poor is in your houses. How dare you crush My people and grind the faces of the poor? (3:14–15)

Continuing the "vineyard" metaphor, he sheds light on the motives that drove the upper classes to oppress small peasants and rob them of their meager land:

> For the vineyard of the Lord of Hosts is the House of Israel, and the seedlings He lovingly tended are the men of Judah. And He hoped for justice, but behold, injustice; For equity, but behold, iniquity! Ah, those who add house to house, and join field to field, till there is room for none. (5:7–8)

This cruel truth exposed, one cannot but wonder what sort of "lovers of husbandry" King Uzziah and his officers were. According to Isaiah, it would appear that their chief delight was not tilling their own lands but confiscating the lands of others. Moreover, the vast resources required for the maintenance of their huge army was drained from the poorest of the people, the workers and peasants brought to the verge of starvation by Uzziah's regime. Isaiah mocks the leaders of the Judean army:

> Ah, those who are so doughty—as drinkers of wine, and so valiant—as mixers of drink! (5:22)

Like Amos, Isaiah does not hesitate to settle accounts with the legislators and judges who, through their perversion of justice, help the rulers to bleed entire strata of the people:

> Ha! Those who write out evil writs, and compose iniquitous documents, to subvert the cause of the poor, to rob of their rights the needy of My people; that widows may be their spoil, and fatherless children their booty! (10:1–2)

Isaiah, then, perceives his country's social situation as exceedingly grim—indeed, as afflicted by a pervasive illness:

> Every head is ailing, and every heart is sick. From head to foot no spot is sound: All bruises, and welts, and festering sores—not pressed out, not bound up, not softened with oil. (1:5–6)

Yet, unlike Amos, Isaiah sees a light at the end of this unsavory tunnel and expresses a fervent hope that better, brighter days will come:

> The people that walked in darkness have seen a brilliant light; on those who dwelt in a land of gloom light has dawned. (9:1)

Although the people will be severely chastised for their corruption, the prophet does not perceive the situation as hopeless. Hope, however, depends primarily on overall ethical reform and on a return to the commandments of righteousness dictated by God. Accordingly, Isaiah appeals to the rulers and oppressors to:

> Cease to do evil; learn to do good. Devote yourselves to justice; aid the wronged, uphold the rights of the orphan; defend the cause of the widow. (1:16–17)

In the future, he assures them, righteousness and truth will again reign in Jerusalem. And over that purified Jerusalem will rule a king whose excellent qualities are attested to in Isaiah's marvelously comforting prophecy:

> He who walks in righteousness, speaks uprightly, spurns profit from fraudulent dealings, waves away a bribe instead of grasping it, stops his ears against listening to infamy, shuts his eyes against looking at evil—such a one shall dwell in lofty security, with inaccessible cliffs for his stronghold, with his food supplied and his drink assured. When your eyes behold a king in his beauty. . . (33:15–17)

In Isaiah's view, it is not the lofty towers erected by Uzziah in Jerusalem and in the desert that will save the king and his people; nor the great herds of sheep and cattle; nor even the mighty army. All of these are founded on iniquity, corruption, and oppression, and so, on the appointed day, they must crumble into dust.

Only moral uprightness can sustain the kingdom. Only if:

> ... a king shall reign in righteousness, and ministers shall govern with justice ... (32:1)

—only then can the kingdom regain its strength, both from within and from without. Only the steadfast bedrock of justice and righteousness can support a firm and lasting structure throughout the turbulent course of history.

Amos, first of the Written Prophets, was followed only by Hosea, who continued the stream of prophecy initiated by his forerunner. Isaiah, however, established a school of disciples in Judah. These disciples were messengers of God who carried the torch of ethics, righteousness, truth, and peace; they set their venerable predecessors' doctrines down in writing and distributed them among the people. A number of them became prophets in their own right. Some, in the strength of their prophecies, even surpassed their masters.

No such "school of prophecy" was established in the Kingdom of Israel. This may be the main reason why the People of Israel were not spiritually strong enough to survive as a people in exile but assimilated into their surroundings and vanished from the stage of Jewish history, remembered only as the Ten Lost Tribes. In Judah, on the other hand, the doctrines of the Prophets prevailed, lending their strength to the people and enabling them to withstand the agonies of exile.

One of Isaiah's young contemporaries and disciples was Micah, a resident of the town of Moresheth-gath. Micah, like Isaiah, realized the extent to which the kingdom and its rulers had been undermined by the rot of depravity. His responses are no less blunt and forceful than those of his predecessor, and often more so. For example, he does not hesitate to cry out against the evil rulers:

> Ah, those who plan iniquity and design evil on their beds; When morning dawns they do it, for they have the power. They covet fields, and seize them; houses, and take them away. They defraud men of their homes, and people of their land. (2:1–2)

This clear and simple accusation is directed against an entire class of land-extorters who deprive another entire class of their homes and heritages. In a peasant society such as that of Micah's Judah, where house and land were virtually the only property owned by the great majority of the people, this mass disinheritance, brutally implemented by despotic rulers and *nouveaux riches*, and condoned by corrupt judges, had the effect of turning vast segments of the population into an utterly destitute class.

Micah adopts a phrase previously used by Amos to define the dreadful social situation of his day, calling it:

> . . . a time of disaster. (2:3)

And if any of Micah's listeners remain unsure of who is to blame, the prophet names them, collectively and explicitly:

> I said: Listen, you rulers of Jacob, you chiefs of the House of Israel! For you ought to know what is right, but you hate good and love evil. You have devoured My people's flesh; you have flayed the skin off them, and their flesh off their bones. And after tearing their skins off them, and their flesh off their bones, and breaking their bones to bits, you have cut it up as into a pot, like meat in a caldron. (3:1–3)

The guiltiest parties, then, are the leaders of the people— the king, his ministers, and his generals. But they are not the only ones: They are assisted by corrupt judges, depraved priests, and false prophets. And the punishment will be fearsome indeed:

> Assuredly, because of you Zion shall be plowed as a field, and Jerusalem shall become heaps of ruins, and the Temple Mount a shrine in the woods. (3:12)

Micah, like Amos and Isaiah before him, scorns the well-to-do who seek to win an easy pardon for their sins by offering impressive-looking sacrifices while their homes are full of treasure stolen from the poor.

In a passage that could as easily have been written about any present-day dictatorship, the prophet depicts the destruction of every healthy fiber in his own society by its depraved rulers, and the permeation of his own environment by the venom of malignant decay:

The pious are vanished from the land, none upright are left among men; all lie in wait to commit crimes, one traps the other in his net. . . . Trust no friend, rely on no intimate; be guarded in speech with her who lies in your bosom. For son spurns father, daughter rises up against mother, daughter-in-law against mother-in-law—a man's own household are his enemies. (7:2, 5–6)

Such was the atmosphere in Jerusalem more than 2,500 years ago; such was the ambience created by George Orwell in his chilling novel, *1984*; such is the nature of any corrupt regime, viewed from within. Yet the amends required by God from the merciless rulers, according to Micah, are comparatively slight: that they act justly, love mercy, and walk humbly with their Lord—a requirement at least as valid and compelling today as it was then.

Isaiah did not find one righteous human soul among the rulers of Judah, whom he termed "rulers of Sodom." Micah, his disciple, also sought a single godly or upright man among them, but searched in vain.

Not many years later another spiritual giant arose in Judah: Jeremiah, son of Hilkiah, a priest from the small town of Anathoth, north of Jerusalem. Arriving in the booming capital, Jeremiah soon becomes aware of its internal and social putrefaction and adds his blazing challenge to those of his forerunners:

Roam the streets of Jerusalem, search its squares, look about and take note: You will not find a man, there is none who acts justly, who seeks integrity—that I should pardon her. (5:1)

Like Amos and Hosea, Isaiah and Micah, Jeremiah foresaw a heavy punishment for his people. There is, however, one great difference. Not only did Jeremiah predict the destruction of Judah and Jerusalem; but he had the unparalleled misfortune of seeing his most dire prophecies become reality. Again and again Jeremiah warned the kings, ministers, and people of Judah, speaking both as a prophet-statesman and as a social reformer. No one heeded him. He was scorned, mocked, beaten, spit upon, and finally handcuffed and thrown into a dungeon.

Jeremiah grieves for society and for the country in his great lamentation for the fate of his people and his land. He, like his forerunners, cries out against the exploitation of the lowly by the newly wealthy. He considers these prosperous oppressors the root of social evil:

> For among My people are found wicked men . . . they set up a trap to catch men. As a cage is full of birds, so are their houses full of guilt; that is why they have grown so wealthy. They have become fat and sleek; they pass beyond the bounds of wickedness, and they prosper. They will not judge the case of the orphan, nor give a hearing to the plea of the needy. An appalling, horrible thing has happened in the land. . . . (5:26–28, 30)

Jeremiah, coming from a priestly family, realizes the extent of his "professional colleagues' " depravity. With his intimate knowledge of the priesthood, he knows how easy it is for priests to become charlatans. And this is no less true of the false prophets, toadying to their rulers and telling them exactly what they want to hear:

> For from the smallest to the greatest, they are all greedy for gain; priest and prophet alike, they all act falsely. (6:13)

Standing before all the thieves, the adulterers, the murderers, the bringers of incense to Baal, who practice their sins in the guise of judges and priests and still dare to serve in the Holy Temple, Jeremiah cries out, in the name of his God:

> Do you consider this House, which bears My name to be a den of thieves? (7:11)

Like Micah, Jeremiah depicts the anatomy of a decayed society in which the judges, via a network of spies and telltales, penetrate the privacy of each individual household and family and hold the entire populace in fear:

> For they are all adulterers, a band of rogues. They bend their tongues like bows; they are valorous in the land for treachery, not for honesty; they advance from evil to evil. And they do not heed Me—declares the Lord. (9:1–2)

In the heat of his rage, Jeremiah denounces the king himself and prophesies his awful doom:

They shall not mourn for him, "Ah, lord! Ah his majesty!" He shall have the burial of an ass, dragged out and left lying outside the gates of Jerusalem. (22:18–19)

This passage brings to mind how, in answer to the people's plea for a king, the prophet-judge Samuel had warned them grimly of the havoc a king would wreak upon them. It recalls how kings of Israel and Judah were beheaded and left for the dogs to lick their blood. And we remember the tragic end that has beset innumerable kings and tyrants throughout the entire world.

Jeremiah, like other great prophets before him, tries his strength at preaching to the rulers, appealing to them to mend their evil ways and return to the path of righteousness. Indefatigably, he pleads with them to repent of their wrongs. He goes so far as to make the continued rule of the House of David contingent upon a revolutionary change of attitude by the king and his ministers. Compelled by God's command, he arrives at the palace and addresses the king, his counselors and advisors, and the royal court:

Thus said the Lord: Do what is just and right; rescue from the defrauder him who is robbed; do not wrong the stranger, the fatherless, and the widow; commit no lawless act, and do not shed the blood of the innocent in this place. For if you fulfill this command, then through the gates of this palace shall enter Kings of David's line who sit upon his throne. . . . But if you do not heed these commands, I swear by Myself—declares the Lord— that this palace shall become a ruin. (22:3–5)

In matters of state as in matters of society, Jeremiah is not heeded. Evil continues to flourish; the rich prosper at the expense of the poor. The prophet himself eventually wearies of preaching to deaf ears and stubborn hearts. In a moment of desperation he complains to God:

You will win, O Lord, if I make a claim against You, yet shall I present charges against You: Why does the way of the wicked prosper? Why are the workers of treachery at ease? (12:1)

This eternal question will be asked again and again by the Prophets, and later by the authors of Job and Ecclesiastes;

later still, by theologians, philosophers, and moralists throughout the ages. Indeed, that question "why" still rings out to this very day.

Despite Jeremiah's vision of destruction, some of his prophecies are comforting. Although destruction must first occur, he does foresee a brighter future. Yet even that future depends upon the righteousness of future rulers. Only a kingdom characterized by internal and social justice can be granted peace and security:

> See a time is coming—declares the Lord, when I will raise up a true branch of David's line. He shall reign as king and shall prosper, and he shall do what is just and right in the land. In his days Judah shall be delivered and Israel shall dwell secure. . . . (23:5–6)

Unfortunately, Jeremiah does not live to see that dream come true; his days are only long enough for him to see the realization of his most ghastly predictions. Nebuchadnezzar, king of Babylon, destroys the Temple, lays waste Jerusalem, and banishes the king and his nobles to exile in Babylon. Jeremiah, too, goes into exile, fleeing with the poorest refugees to Egypt, where he utters the doleful lamentation of the eternal Wandering Jew:

> Remember, O Lord, what has befallen us; behold, and see our disgrace. Our heritage has passed to aliens, our homes to strangers. We have become orphans, fatherless; our mothers are like widows. . . . We are hotly pursued; exhausted, we are given no rest. . . . Our fathers sinned and are no more; and we must bear their guilt. (LAMENTATIONS 5:1–3, 5, 7)

Jeremiah was not the only prophet to experience the destruction of the Kingdom of Judah. Far to the east, across the vast desert and the great river, among those exiled to Babylon with King Jehoiachin about a decade before the final destruction, there arose another prophet: Ezekiel, son of Buzi. Like Jeremiah, Ezekiel had served as a priest in Jerusalem and knew its inhabitants and their way of life. His soul, like Jeremiah's, cried out for his native land. Yet, despite his relative youth, Ezekiel was no less aware than Jeremiah of the dreadful internal situation in Judah and Jerusalem—of the rot and corruption running wild beneath its surface. Accordingly, he too began to prophesy the total destruction of Jerusalem and an additional exile, because:

> ... the land is full of bloody crimes, and the city is full of lawlessness. (7:23)

In a prophecy of terrible rage, Ezekiel describes in minutest detail the harlotries of Jerusalem, the "city that sheds blood," and enumerates those who are responsible, the oppressors and tormentors. No one is spared:

> Every one of the princes of Israel in your midst used his strength for the shedding of blood. Fathers and mothers have been humiliated within you; strangers have been cheated in your midst; orphans and widows have been wronged within you. . . . They have taken bribes within you to shed blood. You have taken advance and accrued interest . . . (22:6–7, 12)

And:

> Her gang of prophets are like roaring lions in her midst, rending prey. They devour human beings; they seize treasure and wealth; they have widowed many women in her midst. Her priests have violated My Teaching. And the people of the land have practiced fraud and committed robbery; they have wronged the poor and needy, have defrauded the stranger without redress. (22:25–26, 29)

Ezekiel joins Amos and Isaiah, Micah and Jeremiah, in the search for a single righteous human being in this crowd of despoilers, but he is no more successful in his search than they in theirs.

In studying the books of the Prophets we observe that, again and again, they condemned an entire social stratum, describing it as completely corrupt with no redeeming graces. There were apparently no exceptions to this group phenomenon; nor, in fact, could there be, as anyone daring to defy the group norm of violence and depravity would have been immediately cast out. Their words are as relevent as ever, with despotic regimes all over the world supported by corrupted military, economic, religious, and political establishments.

Ezekiel learns of the great destruction he had prophesied

from a man fleeing Jerusalem, who tells him that the city was attacked and the Temple destroyed. This news marks a turning point in the prophet's life and chosen mission. From this moment on he considers it his prime duty to lead the hearts of his unfortunate compatriots-in-exile back to goodness. He vows to comfort and guide them and to transform the bitter exile into a furnace of purification, from which, at the appointed time, the exiles would be able to return to their homeland purged of their iniquities and imperfections, and ready to redeem the ruins of their land according to the ways of righteousness and justice.

Obviously, this cannot come to pass unless the future generations are given the chance to make a new, fresh start, free of the stigma of their ancestors' wrongdoings. Thus, Ezekiel—like Jeremiah before him—prophesies an end to cross-generational retribution. Each human being, says the prophet, will be judged on the merit of his or her own deeds:

> Be assured, O house of Israel, I will judge each one of you according to his ways—declares the Lord God. . . . Repent and turn back from your transgressions by which you have offended, and get yourselves a new heart and a new spirit, that you may not die, O house of Israel. (18:30–31)

The words "new heart" and "new spirit" are key expressions, recurring over and over in the great comforting prophecies that gave the people strength to withstand exile.

Describing the new era that would follow the return to Zion, Ezekiel repeatedly emphasizes that the new princes of Israel (not kings, such as ruled over Judah prior to its destruction, but princes; the prophet's term for "prince," *nasi*, is the word now used in modern Israel for an elected president) must be totally different from the old rulers who brought about the cataclysm in Judah:

> Make an end of lawlessness and rapine, and do what is right and just. . . . (45:9)

Justice, then, would be the distinguishing feature of the People of Israel returning to its homeland.

Only after seventy years of the Babylonian exile, with the

rise of Cyrus' kingdom in Persia, did the comforting predictions of the Prophets begin to come true.

Cyrus' declaration in favor of the return to Zion inspired
"Isaiah the Comforter," who we now know as Second Isaiah,
to sing his songs in praise of divine justice. His songs of thanks
and hope for the rebuilding of Jerusalem give a distinctly
different tone to the Book of Isaiah, beginning with verse 40.
This Isaiah envisioned the re-establishment of the royal House
of David as a kingdom of justice in Judah and a beacon of
righteousness for all humankind. Not only the king and the
rulers, announces Isaiah, but the entire People of Israel would
be "a light unto the nations." This, in fact, would be the
justification of God's selection of Israel as the Chosen People
to be a model of all that is good in human society. For the
People of Israel had become "the Lord's servant":

> I the Lord, in My grace, have summoned you, and I have grasped
> you by the hand. I created you, and appointed you a covenant
> people, a light of nations—opening eyes deprived of light, res-
> cuing prisoners from confinement, from the dungeon those who
> sit in darkness. (42:6–7)

The prophet repeatedly demands of those returning to Zion
that they base their new society, to be established in Judah,
on righteousness, far from oppression. By doing so, he promises, they will ensure peace and security for their homeland.
On the eve of return from exile, Isaiah repeats his demand:

> Thus said the Lord: Observe what is right and do what is just;
> for soon My salvation shall come, and My deliverance be re-
> vealed. (56:1)

Yet alas, the reality of the return to Zion proved to be far
different than the prophet had envisaged. There was no mass
reclaiming of the homeland. Those who returned were few,
and their surrounding enemies many. Worse, the new society
was plagued with the same profound social gaps as had afflicted its predecessor. The evil instincts common to all humankind took root and flourished in the small Jewish community. Once again, injustice was rampant in the streets of
Jerusalem. Once again, the rulers exercised tyranny over en-

tire classes of the destitute and helpless. Once again, the poor were oppressed by the rich, and the weak by the strong. The dire wheel had come full circle; the days of predestruction Jerusalem had returned.

Isaiah, who had been so certain of the new leaders' righteousness, cries out once more:

> The watchmen are blind all of them, they perceive nothing. They are all dumb dogs that cannot bark; they lie sprawling, they love to drowse. Moreover, the dogs are greedy; they never know satiety. As for the shepherds, they know not what it is to give heed. Everyone has turned his own way, every last one seeks his own advantage. Come, I'll get some wine; let us swill liquor. . . . (56:10–12)

How fitting a description for leaders whose selfishness and indifference had become their sole characteristics!

The prophet, even as he speaks, knows that his voice will go unheard:

> The righteous man perishes, and no one considers. (57:1)

In Chapter 59 Isaiah draws up a sort of balance sheet, summarizing the state of the nation and its leaders. The bottom line is negative and bleak. The prophet exposes their naked evil, hiding none of their injustice:

> For your hands are defiled with crime and your fingers with iniquity. Your lips speak falsehood, your tongue utters treachery. No one sues justly or pleads honesty; they rely on emptiness and speak falsehood, conceiving wrong and begetting evil. . . . They do not care for the way of integrity, there is no justice on their paths. They make their courses crooked. No one who walks in them cares for integrity. That is why redress is far from us, and vindication does not reach us. We hope for light, and lo! there is darkness; for a gleam, and we must walk in gloom. (59:3–4, 8–9)

The last three Prophets—Haggai, Zechariah, and Malachi—adeptly depict the bitter disappointment following the return to Zion, when all the great hopes for a redeemed society prove vain and void. In fact, the period is a miserable one, beset with economic, social, and moral disaster.

Haggai describes the terrible economic crisis affecting his people in their homeland:

You have sowed much, and brought in little; you eat without being satisfied . . . and he who earns anything earns it for a leaky purse. (HAGGAI 1:6)

Zechariah portrays the social and moral crisis:

Thus said the Lord of Hosts: "Execute true justice; deal loyally and compassionately with one another. Do not defraud the widow, the orphan, the stranger, and the poor; and do not plot evil against one another"—But they refused to pay heed. They presented a balky back and turned a deaf ear. (ZECHARIAH 7:9–11)

Malachi, last of the Prophets of Israel, also foretells the punishment to be dealt to the oppressors and tormentors:

But first I will step forward to contend against you and I will act as a relentless accuser against those who have no fear of Me: Who practice sorcery, who commit adultery, who swear falsely, who cheat laborers of their hire, and who subvert [the cause of] the widow, orphan, and stranger, said the Lord of Hosts. (MALACHI 3:5)

Nevertheless, Malachi, out of true love for Israel, expresses the hope that, despite the grimness of the present, the future will be one of righteousness and justice, and the people will be healed of their afflictions:

But for you who revere My name a sun of victory shall rise to bring healing. (3:20)

The great Biblical chorus of those seeking righteousness for the People of Israel is composed not only of prophets, but also of poets, sages, and philosophers. The poets of the Psalms portray the evil and the righteous in strong contrasting colors, such as this description of an oppressor of the poor:

His mouth is full of oaths, deceit, and fraud; mischief and evil are under his tongue. He lurks in outlying places; from a covert he slays the innocent; his eyes spy out the hapless. He waits in a covert like a lion in his lair; waits to seize the lowly; he seizes the lowly as he pulls his net shut; he stoops, he crouches, and the hapless fall prey to his might. (10:7–10)

The poet goes on to describe a social phenomenon: an entire group within the People of Israel deceitfully taking control of another stratum, robbing it of its last crust of bread, and turning it into a class of destitute and dispossessed.

Both the Prophets and the Psalmists consider the judges—supposed defenders of righteousness and protectors of the weak—as traitors who have abandoned their lofty function to join the ranks of the despoilers. The following appeal to those judges is at once a prayer and a demand:

> How long will you judge perversely, showing favor to the wicked? . . . Judge the wretched and orphan, vindicate the lowly and the poor, rescue the wretched and the needy; save them from the hand of the wicked. (82:2–4)

The wisdom of the Proverbs is also studded with sayings in praise of ethics, righteousness, justice, and the defense of the weak. In the opening sentences of the Book of Proverbs, its author defines his purpose in writing:

> For learning wisdom and discipline; for understanding words of discernment; for acquiring the discipline for success, righteousness, justice, and equity. (1:2–3)

Throughout the book the sage repeats his warnings against charlatans and oppressors, describes the punishment they can expect, and defends the poor and the weak:

> Do not rob the wretched because he is wretched; do not crush the poor man in the gate. (22:22)

Job, perhaps the most tragic figure of the Bible, repeatedly and bitterly asks the eternal question:

> Why do the wicked live on, prosper and grow wealthy? Their children are with them always, and they see their children's children. Their homes are secure, without fear; they do not feel the rod of God. (21:7–9)

Job contrasts the widespread oppression, robbery, theft, and deception practiced by the wicked with his own actions, which he considers according to criteria of justice, integrity, kindness, and mercy. He then asks—or, more correctly, demands—that God take account of the deeds of his life, and weigh him in the balance.

> Did I ever brush aside the case of my servants, man or maid, when they made a complaint against me? . . . Did I deny the poor

their needs, or let a widow pine away. . . . I never saw an unclad wretch, a needy man without clothing; whose loins did not bless me, as he warmed himself with the shearings of my sheep. If I raised my hand against the fatherless, looking to my supporters in the gate. . . . Did I put my reliance on gold or regard fine gold as my bulwark? . . . Did I rejoice over my enemy's misfortune? Did I thrill because evil befell him? . . . (31:13, 16, 19–21, 24, 29)

The answer to all of these rhetorical "ifs" is, of course, a loud and unequivocal "No!" Job committed none of these evils, but rather kept the commandments of righteousness throughout his life; nevertheless, his fate was inescapably sad and bitter. Accordingly, Job challenges his Creator and demands a reply:

O that I had someone to give me hearing; O that Shaddai would reply to my writ. (31:35)

But Job's great question—why righteousness is not rewarded—receives no answer.

Ecclesiastes, the sage renowned for his "vanity of vanities" philosophy, regards the universe, the world, his own country and its inhabitants, with the same utter pessimism. He observes the struggle for truth and righteousness and against evil and oppression from a standpoint of complete despair. Yet his is not the despair of a fighting prophet, seeking to provoke a revolution, but that of surrender and renunciation. Not only does he realize his own impotence; he does not believe that anyone can change the miserable state of his environment. He sums up the shocking, permanent, immutable injustice characterizing human society thus:

And indeed, I have observed under the sun: Alongside justice there is wickedness, alongside righteousness there is wickedness. (3:16)

His words reflect the essence of total despair:

I further observed all the oppression that goes on under the sun: the tears of the oppressed, with none to comfort them; and the power of their oppressors—with none to comfort them. Then I accounted those who died long since more fortunate than those who are still living; and happier than either are those who have not yet come into being and have never witnessed the miseries that go on under the sun. (4:1–3)

Ecclesiastes, too, draws up a balance sheet on humanity—
and his total is just as negative as those of his forerunners:

> For the same fate is in store for all: for the righteous, and for
> the wicked; for the good and pure, and for the impure; for him
> who sacrifices and for him who does not; for him who is pleasing,
> and for him who is displeasing; and for him who swears and for
> him who shuns oaths. That is the sad thing about all that goes
> on under the sun: the same fate is in store for all. Not only that,
> but men's hearts are full of sadness, and their minds of madness
> . . . (9:2–3)

The verdict handed down on humankind in Ecclesiastes—
one of the last books of the Bible—is in full accord with the
initial premise in Genesis:

> How great was man's wickedness on earth, and how every plan
> devised by his mind was nothing but evil all the time. (GENESIS
> 6:5)

But between Genesis and Ecclesiastes, in the full stature of
their dignity, stand the Prophets of Israel, champions of justice
and truth. The Prophets knew, no less than Ecclesiastes, that
"the devisings of man's mind are evil from his youth." Nor
did they hesitate to vividly describe that evil, both in individual human beings and in that melange of human beings
called society. They spared no evildoers, not even kings; and
they deplored collective evil no less vehemently than that of
individuals.

The Prophets' pessimism concerning the evil impulses of
human society was truly great. Time and again they neared
the very edge of ultimate despair and helplessness; many of
them longed to escape their joyless, thankless task. Jeremiah,
most tragic prophet of all, even cursed the day of his birth.
And, for their labors, they were rewarded with stones—both
literal stones thrown at them by angry mobs, and figurative
stones of scorn, mockery, and verbal abuse:

> The prophet was distraught, the inspired man driven mad. (HOSEA
> 9:7)

Yet, though they may have neared the edge of despair, the
Prophets showed their true greatness in never really aban-

doning themselves to it. They truly believed that humankind is capable of change and that each human being is made in the divine image. They saw their own mission in exposing the goodness inherent in humanity. They knew that the root of collective evil lies in individual evil, and that individual evildoers, if given unlimited power over society, are capable of rendering that society utterly evil. They believed that a single good-hearted human being in a position of superiority—a good, just ruler acting as "the Lord's servant"—can exert his beneficial influence on all aspects of his environment: other individuals, large groups, and society as a whole. Therefore, they never lost hope that an entire society could become the true Chosen People and could thereby affect the whole world and improve the overall human condition.

There was not a single prophet who, from the depths of despair engendered by his surroundings, did not nonetheless dredge up comforting prophecies of light; of a new heart and a new spirit for each individual and for all of society; of a new land graced with better and brighter hope.

The Prophets of Israel believed in a future of peace, goodness, blessings, life, grace, kindness, and mercy, for their people and for the entire world. One may, of course, claim that their prophecies and visions were no more than dreams or utopias and that they themselves were merely naive or deluded. In fact, however, they were not only great visionaries, but some of the greatest realistic statesmen the world has ever known. They comprehended and expressed reality on all levels of human civilization: the individual, the group, the society, the kingdom, and the state.

The watchword of the Prophets' struggle was best expressed by Isaiah:

> Cry with full throat, without restraint; raise your voice like a ram's horn. (58:1)

All this they did, and with valor. Again and again they enumerated the sins and transgressions of their people; yet, at the same time, they carried the word of comfort and salvation for that same people and for all the world.

The torch of that struggle was passed on from the Prophets

to the Sages. Rabbi Hillel, who was perhaps the greatest of all, expressed the wisdom of the sages in a single sentence:

> The more study of the Law, the more life . . . the more righteousness, the more peace. (MISHNAH AVOT 2:7)

And Rabbi Eleazar said:

> Whoever does righteously and justly has filled the entire world with lovingkindness, as it is said: "He loves what is right and just; the earth is full of the Lord's faithful care." (SUKKAH 49b/ PSALMS 33:5)

Without justice—in other words, the rule of law—human society would immediately disintegrate into total chaos. In the troubled Israel of today, the courts should be a pillar of great strength.

Following the millennium of the Prophets, the doctrine of truth and righteousness passed to the Sages of the Talmud, who propagated it for a second millennium. Those two millennia were to leave an indelible seal on the People of Israel and the entire world: the seal of freedom, twin of righteousness, which the Prophets sought to set upon the nation of Israel.

CHAPTER THREE

The Longing For Freedom

SINCE THE DAWN OF HISTORY, HUMAN EXISTENCE HAS BEEN linked with labor. People must work to live, to obtain food for themselves and for their households. Only Adam and Eve, in the Garden of Eden, were exempt from having to earn their bread with work. The trees in the garden were beautiful and fruitful; the first human beings had only to stretch out their hands and pluck the fruit. But outside the Garden the land— virgin soil—was waiting, as it were, for Adam to work it and redeem it:

And there was no man to till the soil. (GENESIS 2:5)

Once Adam began to till the earth, he found that work hard, bitter, and exhausting:

By toil shall you eat of it all the days of your life. . . .By the sweat of your brow shall you get bread to eat. (3:17, 19)

Let us note the phrase "all the days of your life." Its meaning is simple: From that day forth, throughout our entire lives, every human being has to work. Thus, humankind became not only masters of the land—as designated in Creation—but its bound slaves.

Yet, also in the dawn of history, human beings became enslaved, not only by the land and its work, but by other human beings. Impelled by human nature, the strong began to conquer the weak by brute strength, to take their personhood away and make them into property, and to set them to forced labor. This occurred both between individual humans and between groups. In the course of wars, strong groups overcame weaker ones. The weak who were left alive by their conquerors—accidentally or intentionally—were taken into servitude.

Thus, from the beginning of civilization, the human race has been afflicted by two kinds of slavery: one to nature, for the sake of survival; the other, of the weak to the strong, out of fear. This dual bondage has been the lot of humankind for countless centuries.

The phrase "to work the land" may certainly include the efforts of those who make their living picking fruit in orchards, from branches far above the ground. Hunters and fishermen, who kill living creatures nourished by nature for their own food, are also "workers of the land," as are shepherds, who raise domestic animals. All of these "work the land," no less than farmers who plow and cultivate the soil.

On these primary occupations, the earliest foundation of humanity, layer after layer of human society was built. After the shepherds and farmers came the makers and users of stone, wooden, and metal plows; the tentmakers; the potters; the bricklayers and carpenters; the founders of villages and cities; the merchants and warriors. And, lower than any of them, the slaves.

When the Torah was given to the Hebrew tribes, they had already known, for many generations, both the toil of hard labor and the bitterness of slavery. Only a few short years before, in fact, they had still been in Egypt, slaves under Pharaoh. Indeed, it was the will to be freed of this dual enslavement that inspired the Biblical lawgivers; for only when people are physically free can they achieve true liberty of spirit.

The lawgivers of Pentateuch times observed the rise of developed societies with complex social structures. Some members of those societies had to work incessantly; others worked less; still others did no work at all. Who but they—so recently freed from slavery in Egypt, the scars of the overseers' whips still fresh upon their backs—realized the full significance of this phenomenon: the peasants' drudging toil on one hand, the indolence of the nobility on the other.

No wonder the Biblical lawgivers adopted, among their lofty goals, the idea of ensuring an interval of rest for each and every member of their people. To this end they established the precept of rest as a divine commandment, pointing out that God Himself had taken a day to rest from the labor of creating the world:

The heaven and the earth were finished, and all their array. On the seventh day God finished the work that He had been doing, and He ceased on the seventh day from all the work that He had done. And God blessed the seventh day and declared it holy, because on it God ceased from all the work of creation that He had done. (GENESIS 2:1-3)

If the Creator Himself could rest after six days of labor, then certainly human beings, made in His image, could and should follow his example.

The question that this brings to mind is whether this does not constitute a diminution and personification of God. Does the Creator of all the universe require rest and relaxation, like any mortal? Is God not above such earthly characteristics? On consideration, however, the day of rest—the Sabbath—appears to imply not a diminution of God, but an elevation of the human image. Those humans who follow the divine example by ceasing from work and resting may perhaps ensure that some portion of divinity will devolve upon them. It was from this rationale that the Sabbath was born.

The importance of the breakthrough achieved by humankind with the enactment of the Sabbath is truly immeasurable. This is a day entirely devoted to rest and recuperation, to human needs above and beyond those achieved by work. Not only is it a day of relaxation for weary bodies, but a day for thought, prayer, reading, pleasure, and enjoyment. Just as God does not work on that day but enjoys His freedom, so should humankind. The connection between rest and freedom is clear. Those who celebrate a periodic day of rest are more free, more liberated. For one day in every week, Moses' Torah commands that each and every human being shall be free.

The precept of the Sabbath, its linkage with divine law and covenant, radically changed the nature and lifestyle of the Hebrews, as individuals and as a nation. This one precept was enough to distinguish the People of Israel from the surrounding nations of the period, whose members worked day in and day out. Other religions and cultures did, of course, have holidays—celebrations of nature and of their various gods, memorial days, and royal feasts. But the uniqueness of the People of Israel lay in their official proclamation of a constant, permanent, weekly day of rest, each week throughout each year of every generation.

The Sabbath as a day of rest should be considered no less than a true social revolution, affecting life and work as a whole. The very calendar is built around the Sabbath; it is the central axis round which the life of Jewish individuals, communities, and society revolves. The declaration of the Sabbath as a workless day for one and all was made with the greatest formality and festivity, as the fourth of the Ten Commandments:

> Remember the sabbath day and keep it holy. Six days you shall labor and do all your work, but the seventh day is a sabbath of the Lord your God: you shall not do any work—you, your son or daughter, your male or female slave, or your cattle, or the stranger who is within your settlements. (EXODUS 20:8–10)

The Torah defines the Sabbath as a perpetual covenant between the People of Israel and their God, for all generations to come.

The Sabbath, as handed down in the framework of the Ten Commandments, embodies several of the elementary concepts of Judaism. In addition to the element of freedom is the idea of equality. All people are equal where the Sabbath is concerned: man and woman, old and young, king and subject, rich and poor—even slaves. Moreover, the Sabbath also embodies the element of brotherhood: Even the stranger—that is, the non-Jew—is excused from work.

Mercy is another element included in the Sabbath. It extends not only toward humans but even toward the domesticated animals that help human beings in their work. They, too, are enjoined to rest from their labor.

Moreover, the Sabbath includes the element of peace. Even the work of war was suspended one day a week, and the Sabbath was observed on the battlefield as a weekly "ceasefire." The enemies of Israel knew that the Jews would not wage war on the Sabbath; some of them exploited that fact to attack them on their day of rest. Only the injunction that the saving of life overrides the Sabbath laws enabled the Jews to bear arms in their own defense on the Sabbath.

All these qualities make the Sabbath the common denominator of freedom, equality, brotherhood, mercy, peace, and justice—justice toward both the working class and society as a whole.

The choice of the seventh day as a holy day of rest was not coincidental. The number seven has historically been held sacred by many civilizations. In Judaism it assumed a significance of manifold sanctity. Seven are the days of the week; the planets known at the time of the Torah; the colors of Noah's rainbow; the seven species of produce mentioned in the Bible as characterizing the Land of Israel (wheat, barley, grapes, figs, pomegranates, olives, and dates); the branches of the candelabra in the Temple; and the seven elements of peace: peace, goodness, blessing, life, grace, lovingkindness, and mercy.

The vital connection between the Sabbath as a day of rest and the concept of freedom is stressed in Deuteronomy, which recapitulates the Ten Commandments. There, as in Exodus, that connection is particularly prominent and has two distinct aspects. The injunction that servants (the Hebrew word used, *'eved*, also means "slave") should rest as well as their masters is coupled with the reminder that the People of Israel had themselves been slaves set free—and, precisely for that reason, should observe the Sabbath.

The Sabbath, then, is a symbol of freedom. In our discussion of justice, we repeatedly mentioned the immutable nature that these elementary Torah concepts had assumed—not only in Judaism, but throughout large segments of humanity. This is no less true of the Sabbath, as a day of freedom enjoined by religious—indeed, by divine—command.

The principle of the Sabbath as a weekly day of rest was passed along from Judaism to Christianity and Islam. The adoption of Sunday by the Christians and Friday by the Muslims as their day of freedom from work helped to propagate the concept of the Sabbath, originated by the Hebrews, throughout the entire world.

With the passage of time, the concept of a day of rest grew beyond its original religious framework. It became a lever for the demands of the working class for time off, and defined freedom as an inalienable right. From this foundation—by virtue of great efforts, sacrifice, agony, and struggle—the working people slowly managed to accumulate more and more rights, such as the right to limit the length of the work-day and the work week; the abolition of child labor; the special rights of working women; the right to strike—all based on the concepts of freedom, dignity, and equality. It may, then, be said that "the Sabbath has kept Israel more than Israel has kept the Sabbath." Furthermore, it might seem that, had Judaism not passed this great asset down to humanity as a whole, humankind would have had to "invent" it, as the touchstone of a free, progressive society.

The legislators of the Bible put the mystic nature of the number seven to good use: not only in the granting of a weekly day of freedom from work, but in the achievement of other worthy goals of freedom, such as the Sabbatical Year. Yet seven is not only a "holy" number but an extremely sensible and appropriate one, as far as the balance between work and rest is concerned. The rhythm of six days' labor to one day's rest takes into account the optimum endurance of the human body. Even today, when the five-day work week has become an established norm in many parts of the world, one of the two days of rest from paid labor is, in practice, devoted to other, unwaged work, such as shopping, errands, sports, and travel.

The Torah was given to a society in which slavery had existed for thousands of years. The first slave of the Bible— Canaan, son of Ham—is mentioned as early as the story of Noah:

> Cursed be Canaan; the lowest of slaves shall he be to his brothers.
> (GENESIS 9:25)

This is a terrible curse indeed: Canaan was the first man to suffer the loss of that great treasure, his freedom. It was this curse that gave rise to the expression "Canaanite slave" as a Biblical metaphor of utter servitude. The Bible also repeatedly mentions the "Egyptian slave," the "Chaldean slave," the "Ammonite slave," and others—including the Hebrew slave. After all, given the fact that all the neighboring nations and cultures considered slavery acceptable and almost natural, it was to be expected that Hebrew slaves, too, would appear within the social stratification of the People of Israel. The Biblical lawgivers were apparently incapable of eradicating slavery—certainly not all at once. Forced to accept its existence, they nevertheless took several decisive steps to lead humanity to a slaveless society.

The Torah—followed by the Prophets—persistently reminded the People of Israel of their own history of terrible slavery in Egypt and the Exodus through which they had been redeemed. The word "remember," frequently repeated in this context, stands out like a huge "Danger" sign, warning the people over and over against the terrors of slavery. The first of these warnings, given by God to Abraham, stresses the terrible fate of those doomed to enslavement:

> Know well that your offspring shall be strangers in a land not theirs, and they shall be enslaved and oppressed four hundred years. (GENESIS 15:13)

The first sentence spoken by God to Moses, out of the burning bush, also deals with the horrors of slavery:

> I have marked well the plight of My people in Egypt and have heeded their outcry because of their taskmasters; yes, I am mindful of their sufferings. (EXODUS 3:7)

The Torah often refers to Egypt as the "house of bondage" because of Israel's slavery there. The festival celebrating the end of that slavery—Passover, the Festival of Freedom—became a major holiday in the life of a people commanded never to forget their servitude:

> Remember this day, on which you went free from Egypt, the house of bondage. (EXODUS 13:3)

The words "house of bondage" are used over and over again, by both the Biblical legislators and the Prophets. Thanks to them, the concept of remembering their slavery penetrated deep into the consciousness of the People of Israel—even more so, in light of their later history of repeated exile, in which, time and again, they were to know the bitter taste of bondage.

A phrase no less harsh, also used in the context of slavery, is "iron furnace":

> But you the Lord took and brought out of Egypt, that iron blast furnace. (DEUTERONOMY 4:20)

The contrast between the torture, agony, and pain of slavery, and the marvelous, uplifting sensation of freedom is effectively delineated by the Psalmist:

> He brought them out of deepest darkness, broke their bonds asunder. Let them praise the Lord for His steadfast love, His wondrous deeds for mankind, for He shattered gates of bronze, He broke their iron bars. (107:14–16)

"House of bondage," "iron furnace," "gates of bronze": all these were apparently well-known synonyms for group slavery at the time of the Torah. Yet there can be no doubt that they also stand as warnings concerning the treatment of individual slaves. In general, the Torah differentiates between the proper treatment of Hebrew slaves and those taken from the surrounding peoples. Nevertheless, several passages in the Bible express an unquestionably and universally humanitarian attitude toward all slaves, irrespective of national origin. Such an attitude is demonstrated by Job in his response to God's "indictment":

> Did I ever brush aside the case of my servants, man or maid, when they made a complaint against me? What then should I do when God arises? When He calls me to account, what should I answer Him? Did not He who made me in my mother's belly make him? Did not One form us both in the womb? (31:13–15)

Job grants his slaves a full measure of equality. Whether Jew or gentile, male or female, they are human beings, no less than he; he and they alike deserve a just trial before the law.

The phenomenon of runaway slaves is one of the most unfortunate of human tragedies. Much has been written on this theme, in Israel and throughout the world. Generally speaking, runaway slaves, if apprehended, were liable to execution or other frightful punishment. But the Torah speaks out in unequivocal defense of runaway slaves, regardless of their origin:

> You shall not turn over to his master a slave who seeks refuge with you from his master. He shall live with you in any place he may choose among the settlements in your midst, wherever he pleases; you must not ill-treat him. (DEUTERONOMY 23:16–17)

The masters of Hebrew slaves were commanded by the Torah to treat them mercifully and refrain from tyrannizing them. They were entreated to care for the poor and to set their servants free at the end of seven years. Hebrew masters and servants alike had been slaves in Egypt. Consequently:

> [Servants] may not give themselves over into servitude. You shall not rule over him ruthlessly; you shall fear your God. (LEVITICUS 25:42–43)

This precept is a combination of the principles of freedom and liberation of slaves, and the concept of equality among the People of Israel in the sight of God. Each and all of the People of Israel are servants of God and are not to be enslaved one by another; Hebrew masters are obligated to treat their Hebrew servants with honor, recognizing their labor potential as that of hired employees rather than beasts of burden. As for the liberation of Hebrew slaves, the Torah found and solemnized a formula with the power to guarantee the release of Hebrew slaves from servitude to freedom.

The relationship forged by the Biblical lawgivers between the sacred number seven and the weekly freedom of the Sabbath given to everyone in Israel—including slaves—carries over into the concept of the Sabbatical Year. The lawmakers draw the authority for this decision from the rest that God was said to have taken on the seventh day of Creation. They then reasoned that if the seventh day is the symbol of universal freedom, why should the seventh year not be a similar symbol of freedom, primarily for slaves? And this is the ruling given:

> When you acquire a Hebrew servant, he shall serve six years; in the seventh year he shall go free, without payment. If he came single, he shall leave single; if he had a wife, his wife shall leave with him. (EXODUS 21:2–3)

The Book of Deuteronomy not only repeats the injunction to liberate Hebrew slaves in the seventh year but adds the obligation to help one's manumitted servants achieve independent status as free citizens. The text goes so far as to specify that slaves not desiring to be set free in the seventh year will be punished physically; for there is nothing more important than one's personal freedom—not even one's dedication to one's master:

> But should he say to you, "I do not want to leave you"—for he loves you and your household and is happy with you—you shall take an awl and put it through his ear into the door, and he shall become your slave in perpetuity. Do the same with your female slave. (15:16–17)

To this day, there is a Hebrew expression, "a pierced slave," stemming from the above passage and designating one who has voluntarily rejected his or her individual freedom.

These two concepts—freedom and the sanctity of the number seven—were expanded by the Biblical legislators to extend not only to human beings, but to the inanimate land itself. Even the land, according to this revolutionary new concept, requires freedom and relaxation. Even the land, servant and master of humankind, does its own kind of labor: Plowed and sown with seed, it gives each day of its very vitals to the crops it grows. It, too, must rest periodically and regain its strength.

Today's agricultural experts and scientists know just how important it is to revitalize the soil. This is the reason for modern crop rotation farming, for improved methods of cultivation, fertilization, and irrigation. Yet this concept was first conceived in the Bible, thousands of years ago, by the decision to establish a periodic year of "holiday" for the land—and what better way to do so than to include the land in the six-years-on, one-year-off cycle established for the people? The seventh, or Sabbatical, year was observed, by Biblical command, as a year of freedom for the land:

> But in the seventh year the land shall have a sabbath of complete rest, a sabbath of the Lord. (LEVITICUS 25:4)

The Sabbatical Year—by no means an easy commandment for the farmers and peasants of Israel to keep—was truly revolutionary in its innovation and modernity. But the legislators of the Bible were not content even with this. Following the laws of the Sabbatical Year, the Torah achieves one of the zeniths of its ambition to combine freedom with justice, equality, and brotherhood. This combination was intended for everyone—human beings, animals, plants, the land and all upon it—in an especially holy year, declared after the completion of seven times seven years, and thus sanctified sevenfold. This is the Jubilee, or fiftieth, year, a year of liberty and freedom for all, most festive and most sacred of years for each generation, which the Prophet Ezekiel called:

. . . the year of release. (46:17)

The proclamation of this most special year is given on the most sacred day of the year, the Day of Atonement.

If the Sabbath constituted a revolution in the lives of the individual, the society, and the People of Israel, then the idea of the Jubilee Year is seven times as revolutionary. Even today, the innovative elements embodied in the Jubilee are no less than amazing: complete liberation for slaves; a redoubled injunction against dishonest dealings; and a divine proclamation that the land can belong exclusively to no one, being God's own, and that, therefore, the celebration of the fiftieth year must include the return to its former owners of land sold by them out of destitution. This is an additional year of total rest and freedom for the land; any fruits it produces are to be given to the poor and not sold for gain.

Adding all these elements, the result amounts to an idealized, nearly utopian society: a society of total justice, charity, and freedom. One should not wonder, then, that the reality was rather different. The real-life society in which the People of Israel lived was incapable of meeting these lofty, idealized demands. The Hebrew society in the Land of Israel was a "normal" society, beset by enemies from without and by bitter conflict from within. It was a polarized society, full of gaps and inequalities, a society whose afflictions were exposed by prophets who fearlessly denounced the corruption of its rulers, judges, and ministers.

In such a society, there was no room for application of the wonderful principles of the Jubilee Year. History indicates that it was apparently not observed in practice. In fact, not even the commandments of the Sabbatical Year—specifically, the liberating of slaves—were fully observed; in many instances, they were not kept at all.

Jeremiah denounces the ruling and prosperous classes for recapturing slaves during the Sabbatical Year, after having set them free for a short time—thus cheating the spirit of the law, while seeming to obey it. The prophet reminds the People of Israel what God had told them:

> I made a covenant with your fathers when I brought them out of the land of Egypt, house of bondage. . . . In the seventh year you must let go any . . . fellow Hebrew . . . but now you have turned back and have profaned My name; each of you has brought back the men and women whom you had given their freedom, and forced them to be your slaves again. Assuredly, thus said the Lord: "You would not obey Me and proclaim a release, each to his kinsman and countryman. Lo! I proclaim your releases"—declares the Lord—"to the sword, to pestilence, and to famine; and I will make you a horror to all the kingdoms of the earth . . . I will make the men who violated My covenant . . . handed over to their enemies, to those who seek to kill them." (34:13–14, 16–18, 20)

This terrible prophecy of destruction was completely fulfilled. Chronicles, the last book of the Bible, recalls the sin of depriving slaves of their liberty, and the fearsome punishment for that sin:

> He therefore brought the king of the Chaldeans upon them, who killed their youths by the sword in their sanctuary; He did not spare youth, maiden, elder or graybeard, but delivered all into his hands. . . . Those who survived the sword he exiled to Babylon, and they became his and his sons' servants till the rise of the Persian kingdom, in fulfillment of the word of the Lord spoken by Jeremiah, until the land paid back its sabbaths; as long as it lay desolate it kept sabbath, till seventy years were completed. (2 CHRONICLES 36:17, 20–21)

Rashi, the medieval sage, gives his commentary on this passage: "Seventy years for the exile of Babylon, in return for seventy Sabbatical Years canceled."

Only after decades of exile came King Cyrus' declaration, permitting the People of Israel to resettle in their homeland. This is a further proof of the profound hold exerted by the tradition of slavery on the People of Israel, and of the great difficulty they had in extricating themselves from its bondage. Even the commands of the Torah were of no avail at the time.

Nevertheless, we must remember that, in their struggle against the institution of slavery, the Torah and the Prophets were many generations ahead of their environment. Just as the Prophets had woven splendid visions of peace and justice for Israel and the entire world, they also proclaimed visions of total freedom and equality for all of humankind—including, of course, the slaves. Here, for example, is the vision of Joel:

> After that, I will pour out My spirit on all flesh; your sons and daughters shall prophesy; your old men shall dream dreams, and your young men shall see visions. I will even pour out My spirit upon male and female slaves in those days. (3:1,2)

"Those days," as foreseen by the prophet, were a long time coming. Human societies of East and West alike—the Greeks, the Romans, the Babylonians, the Egyptians, the Persians, and many other large empires, medium-sized nations, and small peoples—were based on slavery. This grim institution, in a myriad of forms, has accompanied humanity throughout nearly its entire history.

The age-old course of human history has witnessed not only the servitude of individuals, but group enslavement of peoples. Such was the fate of the People of Israel, captured by Egypt and set to the forced construction of the great temples at Peethom and Rameses. Only a few generations ago did those who fought for freedom—priests, politicians, and common people, mainly in democratic countries such as Britain, France, and the United States—arise and dedicate their bodies and souls to the struggle against the slave trade, especially the sale of black slaves from Africa. Not in vain did many of these crusaders adopt the Biblical slogan, "Proclaim liberty throughout the land, unto all the inhabitants thereof!" as their battle cry in the war on human beings' limitless cruelty to human beings. Yet, despite their efforts, the cruelty still exists and the struggle is still going on.

But, as in mass murder and genocide, the record for mass slavery—millions of souls deprived of their basic freedom by cruel rulers—is held by our own twentieth century. Hitler's Third Reich conquered millions and set them to forced labor in the nightmare of the Nazi concentration camps, and Stalin imprisoned millions in the dreadful Gulags of frozen Siberia.

To this day, clandestine and semi-clandestine slavery are to be found in many parts of the world. Young girls and boys are turned into human mules by dealers in deadly drugs. Arrests and detainments, often accompanied by torture, are the lot of many whose opinions and beliefs differ from those of their rulers. Forced labor and concentration camps exist in scores of countries, fully and horribly described in Amnesty International's annual reports. In Israel, too, there are major violations of human rights, but impartial jurists and civil libertarians consistently fight against this trend.

The day when the prophetic visions of freedom will be fulfilled is still far in the future. Nevertheless, we must not abandon our struggle, nor yet our hope. We must adopt and maintain the goal set by Isaiah:

> To unlock fetters of wickedness and untie the cords of the yoke to let the oppressed go free; to break off every yoke. (58:6)

In the course of some two thousand years of exile and wandering, Jews were put into "houses of bondage" again and again: as individuals, as groups, and occasionally as an entire people. There were the exiles in Babylonia; the bearers of the seven-branched candelabra in the Emperor Titus' triumphal procession in Rome; and all the agonies of two millennia of exile, culminating in the Holocaust when those Jews not murdered by the Nazis were forced into slave labor to support the German war machine.

No wonder, then, that throughout those twenty centuries, the longing for freedom was so strong as to make the departure from Egypt into a symbol of liberty and freedom, and the Passover festival into a time of prayer and hope for freedom. The ancient Haggadah, the Passover book retelling the Exodus story, is recited in praise of freedom, with the transition from slavery to liberty spoken and sung in Jewish homes throughout the world. Always, the story begins with the solemn declaration:

> This is the bread of affliction, which our fathers ate in the Land of Egypt. Let all who are hungry come and eat. Let all who are needy come and celebrate Passover. This year, here; next year, in the Land of Israel. This year, as slaves; next year, as free people.

The Haggadah contains a commandment valid for Jews and for all of humanity alike:

> In every generation a man must so regard himself as if he came forth himself out of Egypt. (MISHNAH PESACH 10:5)

Here again, the signpost of our history admonishes us all not to re-enter slavery: neither as slaves to our own evil impulses, nor as the slaves of other peoples; nor yet indeed as the masters of other human beings. Let us not permit the great treasure of our freedom to be taken from us; and let us not steal the freedom of others, born to liberty, for we who knew the pains of subservience for centuries, should never become masters of another people.

But, freedom alone is not enough. Without equality, freedom cannot be whole. The Prophets of Israel knew this, and they venerated equality no less strongly than they revered freedom.

CHAPTER FOUR

Equal in the Sight of God

T HERE IS NO EQUALITY IN NATURE. THE MOSS ON THE WALL is not "equal" to the cedars of Lebanon, nor are minnows "equal" to whales. Nor is there equality even within a single species: The circumstances of our birth, life, and death make each of us different from all others. Some of us are old, others young; some are women, others men. We are darker or fairer, shorter or taller, stronger or weaker, in better or worse health— an endless list of differences.

In human society, as throughout the living world, there can be no absolute equality. Society is composed of human beings, no two of whom are the same; therefore, there can be no true and complete equality among humankind.

Yet strong desire prevails among the better elements of humanity to reduce inequality as far as possible. For inequality is one of the composite elements of social injustice. Most men are physically stronger than most women; therefore, many men attempt to subjugate women and force their will upon them. Similarly, those in a position of strength often enslave those in a position of weakness. Those whose color is considered "preferable" by society often humiliate those of other skin tones. A society in which "might is right" is a society of merciless cruelty, with no place for the poor, the sick, or the stranger.

No small number of such societies have existed throughout human history. Yet champions of justice and ethics have come forth throughout the generations to oppose the exploitation of natural inequalities, and to create a system of rules that would reduce the share of inequality among humankind.

An echo of a mythical universal society characterized by true equality, and the power inherent in such a society, has come down to us in the story of the Tower of Babel. The opening sentence of that story is full of wonderful symbolism. Speaking of an extremely ancient society that apparently comprised all human beings, the first line emphasizes the common language spoken by all:

> Everyone on earth had the same language and the same words.
> (GENESIS 11:1)

Language, then, is a factor unparalleled in its capacity to equalize and to unite.

The story goes on to illustrate that those of "one language" were, in fact, all "one people"; and that, given its equality in the framework of a single people with a common tongue, humankind is potentially capable of achieving whatever marvels it desires.

But according to the story, that primeval equality did not last long. God confounded the language of human beings and scattered them throughout the earth. Not only did inequality then become characteristic of human society, but humanity itself was unevenly distributed into larger and smaller, stronger and weaker, tribes and peoples.

Nevertheless, the Prophet Zephaniah had the courage to foresee that, once the peoples of the world had adopted ethics and mended their ways, they would return to speaking a single language:

> For then I will make the peoples pure of speech, so that they all invoke the Lord by name and serve Him with one accord. (3:9)

This vision, like Isaiah's and Micah's visions of international and cosmic peace, is an early foretelling of international equality, with one language linking all of humankind.

In our day and age we are still quite far from equality, either among or within peoples. There can, however, be no doubt that the factor of a common language remains vital to the development of humanity. In practice, there has almost always been an "international" language, a worldwide medium of communication: first Greek and Latin, then French, and now English. There have also been attempts to achieve the goal of one language by inventing a synthetic one, such as Esperanto. Unfortunately, these attempts have enjoyed no great success.

As the century draws to a close, "computer language" is beginning to assume a decisive role throughout human society. Modern technological advances are bringing humankind closer and closer to the adoption of a single language— that of technology. Yet, by its very nature, no language of machines, sophisticated though it may be, can contain the elements of ethical and moral values. Those are the very elements that give "one language" its unifying power, and they can only be found within the human heart.

The ancient Hebrew society was not, and could not have been, egalitarian. Accordingly, the lawgivers of the Bible did not try to advocate a goal that they themselves considered unnatural and impossible. But they did give the status of divine commands to laws intended to reduce the inequality of their society and to narrow its social gaps as far as possible.

We know, or can assume with a high degree of probability, the nature of the citizens within the early Israelite society. At first they were a society of wandering shepherd tribes; later, following the conquest of the Land of Israel, they developed into a society of peasants. According to the law of those days, all citizens enjoyed an equal status. They were given the same rights and the same responsibilities, judged by the same judges, and obliged to follow the same commandments. Naturally, some of them were poor or otherwise afflicted by fate. Those citizens not so unfortunate were legally enjoined to help them.

As the generations passed, many of the citizens became rich—some of them very rich indeed—and a vast number of less fortunate persons were persecuted and robbed by these rich citizens, thus becoming poor and destitute. This oppression and the resultant social gap evoked the bitter protests of the Prophets. Yet, even as destitute citizens, those who were not sold into slavery to pay their debts still retained their equality in the eyes of the law (at least in theory, if not always in practice).

In addition to the Hebrew citizens, the Land of Israel was inhabited by another class of people: the "stranger" (Hebrew, *ger*). Who were these "strangers" living in the Land of Israel? Although they are often mentioned in the Pentateuch and the books of the Prophets, the Bible gives no exact definition of their nature; they apparently included several classifications of people. The very word *stranger* may be understood as one living outside his or her homeland. Strangers, then, are members of a certain people, native to a certain land, who, for whatever reasons, live as a minority among another people, in a land not their own.

The Hebrews were themselves strangers in Egypt; the Torah repeatedly reminds them of this fact when dealing with the status of non-Hebrew strangers in the Land of Israel. Moses, the great lawgiver, calls his son by the symbolic name of Gershom (literally, "stranger there"):

He said: "I have been a stranger in a foreign land." (EXODUS 2:22)

Apparently, most of the strangers in the Land of Israel were originally refugees who had attached themselves to the People of Israel in several ways. One group of refugees—some of whom had almost certainly been slaves—were those who took advantage of the Exodus from Egypt to make their own escape from the Egyptian "house of bondage" and follow the Hebrew camp through the wilderness. A second category was composed of various peoples who had inhabited the Land of Israel before its conquest and chose to remain there under Hebrew rule, as tolerated aliens. A third group included the refugees, who, for different reasons—social persecution, economic suffering, or war—fled from their own homelands and came to settle in the Land of Israel.

All of these refugee and remnant groups were "noncitizens," devoid of property, and (one would think) devoid of protection and legal recourse as well. The Torah, however, makes truly impressive provisions to ensure aid and shelter for these unfortunates. Three times, in three books of the Pentateuch, clear and precise commands are handed down by the Hebrew legislators concerning the equality of strangers and citizens: All shall be governed by "one law"*(Exodus 12:49)*, "one standard" *(Leviticus 24:22)*, and "one statute" *(Numbers 9:14)*—what could be clearer?

The Torah then goes on to demand that strangers be treated with justice and decency, again reminding the People of Israel not to do to the strangers what others—in this case, the

Egyptians—had done to them when they themselves had been "strangers in a foreign land."

In a moving passage, the Biblical legislators not only reaffirm the prohibition against maltreatment of strangers but also demonstrate a profound understanding of the emotional distress suffered by defenseless minorities among a majority foreign to their own lifestyle:

> You shall not oppress a stranger, for you know the feelings of the stranger, having yourselves been strangers in the land of Egypt. (EXODUS 23:9)

Nor does the Torah content itself with demanding justice for strangers; it insists that they be treated lovingly. Mere formal equality is not enough, nor is even mercy; strangers must be shown real love, as if they belonged to one's own tribe and family:

> . . . you shall love him as yourself. (LEVITICUS 19:34)

The Biblical legislators repeatedly include strangers in the precepts dealing with protection of the weak, the orphans, the widows, and the poor. All of the "shall" and "shall not" precepts that citizens must observe in their treatment of these groups, such as the Sabbath rest and the right to glean in the fields, are also required of them in relation to strangers. The attitude toward strangers propounded throughout the Torah is summed up and explained in one short biblical phrase:

> For the Lord your God . . . upholds the cause of the fatherless and the widow, and befriends the stranger, providing him with food and clothing. (DEUTERONOMY 10:17–18)

Thus, according to the Bible, if God Himself loves and preserves strangers, the People of Israel must certainly do the same.

In reality, this precept was not generally honored. Stronger members of the Hebrew society often tyrannized the weak, thus incurring the bitter anger of the Prophets. Among those so oppressed were the strangers against whose persecutors Ezekiel cries out:

And the people of the land have practiced fraud and committed robbery; they have wronged the poor and needy, have defrauded the stranger without redress. (22:29)

Nevertheless, the purely egalitarian, ethical attitude toward strangers remains perfectly preserved in the commandments of the Pentateuch, as a light to guide the footsteps of the righteous throughout the generations. One of the greatest righteous souls of all time, Job, emphasizes this attitude when recounting his good deeds before God:

No sojourner spent the night in the open; I opened my doors to the road. (31:32)

The Bible teaches that not only strangers but all refugees must be treated with justice and mercy. Isaiah showed understanding and compassion for the unfortunate refugees forced to flee their homeland at swordpoint—even those whose own people were hostile to the Land of Israel. Speaking in God's name, the prophet demands special treatment for refugees.

In his Moab Pronouncement, which prophesies disaster for the nation of Moab—usually counted among Israel's enemies—Isaiah compares the refugees of that nation to "wandering birds," appealing to "the daughter of Zion" for help:

Conceal the outcasts, betray not the fugitives. Let Moab's outcasts find asylum in you; be a shelter for them against the despoiler. (16:3–4)

His Desert of the Sea Pronouncement, too, seeks to enlist aid and comfort for the Arabian refugees wandering in the desert, saying those fleeing from war should be met with bread and water.

Ezekiel was another prophet who defended the stranger. In a truly revolutionary move, he demanded that, upon the return to Zion following the exile in Babylon, strangers be given plots of land, subject to the same laws of inheritance as those governing the Hebrew tribes:

This land you shall divide for yourselves among the tribes of Israel. You shall allot it as a heritage for yourselves and for the strangers who reside among you. . . . (47:21–22)

Another expression given by the Bible to the value of equality is its reiterated insistence that all human beings, irrespective of class, are equal in the eyes of the Creator: rich and poor, generals and common soldiers, ministers and simple people. An impressive example of this equality may be found in the story of David, greatest of the kings of Israel. On the day when David and his men, accompanied by a great crowd, returned the Ark of the Covenant to Jerusalem—a day on which a lesser king could well have sought to aggrandize himself in the eyes of his people—David's behavior before the Lord is depicted as strikingly simple, humble, and egalitarian. Accompanied by "all the house of Israel," he:

...whirled with all his might before the Lord ... [brought] up the Ark of the Lord with shouts and with blasts of the horn. And ... Michal daughter of Saul looked out of the window and saw King David leaping and whirling before the Lord; and she despised him for "... exposing himself today in the sight of the slavegirls of his subjects, as one of the riffraff might expose himself!" David answered Michal: "It was before the Lord who chose me instead of your father and all his family and appointed me ruler over the Lord's people Israel! I will dance before the Lord and dishonor myself even more and be low in my own esteem; but among the slavegirls that you speak of I will be honored." (2 SAMUEL 6:14–16, 20–22)

Equal in the sight of God, then—as David sharply and scornfully reminds Michal—are the king and the least of his slaves, the queen and the least of her handmaids.

The Prophets of Israel, on numerous occasions, demand exemplary behavior of their country's rulers: kings, ministers, and other leaders. This demand not only refers to their personal deportment but frequently includes stipulations that the wealth of their kingdom must be distributed justly and equally among their citizens. Those who fail to live up to the Prophets' exacting standards are severely called to account.

As an example, let us take the Prophet Ezekiel's reproach of the leaders of Israel, in which he compares them to shepherds who, instead of treating their flock justly, discriminate against them:

Ah, you shepherds of Israel . . . you partake of the fat, you cloth yourselves with the wool, you slaughter the fatlings; but you do not tend the flock. You have not sustained the weak, . . . but you have driven them with harsh rigor. (34:2–4)

The above passage is an example of a nonegalitarian attitude displayed by the shepherd to his flock. Yet the lines that follow this passage depict stronger animals within the flock, seen by the prophet as mercilessly afflicting their fellow sheep. This is Ezekiel's *Animal Farm*, uncannily echoed in George Orwell's phrase: ". . . but some animals are more equal than others":

And as for you, My flock, thus said the Lord God: "I am going to judge between one animal and another. To the rams and the bucks: Is it not enough for you to have grazed on choice grazing ground, but you must also trample with your feet what is left from your grazing? And is it not enough for you to drink clear water, but you must also muddy with your feet what is left? And must My flock graze on what your feet have trampled and drink what your feet have muddied?" Assuredly, thus said the Lord God to them: "Here am I, I am going to decide between the stout animals and the lean. Because you pushed with flank and shoulder against the feeble ones and butted them with your horns . . . I will rescue My flock and they shall no longer be a spoil; I will decide between one animal and another." (34:17–22)

This prophecy, though uttered in reference to the People of Israel, is universal in nature. Attempts by "rams and bucks" to oppress and crush "lean cattle" are common to every human society. The Prophets demand that the national leadership institute a maximally egalitarian division of pasture land and water, as well as a policy of protection toward those who are sick, broken, driven away, or lost.

An extraordinary attitude is exhibited in the literature of wisdom and ethics comprising the last books of the Bible. This attitude is one of contempt for material wealth, which does not guarantee happiness. Excessive wealth is held to be just as disagreeable as excessive poverty; in the end, rich and poor will suffer the same fate. Or, as Agur, son of Jakeh, puts it:

Two things I ask of you; do not deny them to me before I die: Keep lies and false words far from me; give me neither poverty nor riches, but provide me with my daily bread. (PROVERBS 30:7–8)

And Ecclesiastes, who describes his own youth as having had every material advantage that money could buy, sums up the insufficiencies of wealth:

A lover of money never has his fill of money.... A worker's sleep is sweet, whether he has much or little to eat; but the rich man's abundance doesn't let him sleep. Here is a grave evil I have observed under the sun: riches hoarded by their owner to his misfortune, in that those riches are lost in some unlucky venture; and if he begets a son, he has nothing in hand.... As he came out of his mother's womb, so must he depart at last, naked as he came.... (5:9, 11–14)

The Bible calls for increased equality among human beings, not only within the same society and the same people, but between peoples. The Prophet Amos, observing the rot and corruption afflicting the Kingdom of Israel, realizes the connection between these afflictions and the vain, contemptuous, and showy behavior of the country's rulers, whose conquests and military victories have led them to believe that they are exalted above other nations—and, worse, that this superiority is part of their nature, a gift from God. He predicts that the Kingdom of Israel will be destroyed because of its wicked and oppressive rulers, and that it will not rise again unless it can be ruled in righteousness and justice.

The Prophet Malachi appeals to all of the People of Israel— priests, Levites, and common folk alike—to consider themselves equal in the sight of their Creator, and to adopt the doctrine of truth, life, and peace:

Have we not all one Father? Did not one God create us? (2:10)

This moving, dramatic appeal, over the years, became the watchword of all those seeking equality: not only among Jews, but throughout the world. Its echoes can still be heard today in the struggle against racism and discrimination.

The Psalmist, too, sings of equality between nations and classes:

Hear this, all you peoples; give ear, all inhabitants of the world, men of all estates, rich and poor alike. (49:2–3)

The conditions of the early Hebrew society made each step in the direction of equality extremely difficult. Even those societies of that day and age considered as more egalitarian than Israel—such as Greece and primarily the democracy of Athens—were based on a sizable slave population, who literally bore the democracy upon their backs.

Israel, always small in area, and its people, always small in number, have consistently been subject to the influence of strange and cruel religions, the yoke of imperial conquest, and the pollutant effect of neighboring societies guided by "principles" of enslavement, occupation, and the supremacy of force. It is truly wondrous that, even under those conditions, the lawmakers and Prophets of Israel—faced with a stubborn, conservative people fighting for its existence—never ceased to propagate revolutionary breakthroughs, the greatest of which was monotheism, followed by the Sabbath, the Sabbatical and Jubilee Years, and the egalitarian attitude toward strangers. From the seeds of these laws and precepts sprouted some of the fairest fruits of peace, justice, freedom, equality, and brotherhood, both in the Jewish world and throughout all humanity. Perhaps the finest fruits of all have grown from this small but highly significant seed:

Love your neighbor as yourself. (LEVITICUS 19:18)

This precept—phrased with exceptional brevity and surrounded by an array of easier and more mundane rules and precepts in Leviticus—has been the foundation of great ethical structures, erected by the spiritual builders of Israel and by many later societies.

In those few simple words, the Torah adjures its followers to ascend to the highest moral plane attainable in human life, the summit of social equality. The equality at issue is not that between fathers and sons, or husbands and wives, but that between comrades. And the key word, of course, is "love."

The love of self is a natural rule of life. In humankind's ascent from this basic level of self-love to the love of others, the requirement to love one's family members as oneself is a relatively easy first step. Family members, after all, are "one's own flesh and blood," an extension of one's own personhood. The commandment to "Honor your father and your mother" is easily understood and observed, as is that of love for one's own children. Indeed, the love of parents for their offspring is not an exclusively human characteristic, but one common to large portions of the animal kingdom. And a profound love for one's siblings—born of the same womb and suckled on the same milk—is equally natural.

"Love your neighbor as yourself," however, requires an extension of this love to those who share no bond of blood, but merely the much looser tie of friendship or geographical proximity. This is a degree of love attained by comparatively few; one of its more famous Biblical manifestations in the friendship of David and Jonathan, is praised by David:

> Your love was wonderful to me, more than the love of women.
> (2 SAMUEL 1:26)

This equality of comradely love exists; yet it is rare. There are and have always been those willing to lay down their very lives for their friends—chiefly in time of trouble, distress, and war. Unfortunately, though, these are only exceptions that prove the rule.

The Sages of Israel knew the value of "Love your neighbor as yourself." Rabbi Akiba says:

> It is a great rule in the Torah. (SIFRA KEDOSHIM/LEVITICUS 19:18)

And Hillel the Sage replies to the heathen's request to teach him the entire Torah while standing on one foot:

> What is contemptible to you, do not do to your friend—that is the whole Torah, and the rest is commentary. Go and learn!
> (SHABBAT 31a:1)

Hillel's formula is a slightly softened paraphrase of "Love your neighbor as yourself." This attenuated version of equality is one that moral human beings can observe.

The Sages of Israel, in their determination of basic moral precepts toward non-Jews, repeatedly had to address the subject of equality. Are the great "You shall" and "You shall not" precepts concerning behavior between human beings equally applicable if one of the human beings is not a Jew? Let us consider some of their opinions in this great and complex issue.

The circumstances of the closed Jewish society, more than occasionally exposed to the alienation and hatred of its gentile neighbors, might well have given rise to the "natural" tendency to interpret vaguely phrased precepts to mean that some offenses ethically forbidden to perpetrate upon Jews—such as theft, robbery, and cheating—may be used against non-Jews. This tendency incurred vehement opposition by the sages, whose ruling unequivocally states:

> Anyone who steals from a Gentile must make restitution to the Gentile. Stealing from a Gentile is more serious than stealing from an Israelite, because of the profanation of the Name. (TOSEFTA BAVA KAMMA 10:16)

The severity of this ruling is striking: Stealing from a Gentile is a greater offense than stealing from a Jew. It constitutes no less than profanation of the Name of God, a comparison that would be deemed to apply to all similar breaches of negative ("you shall not") precepts.

Equally egalitarian is the sages' attitude toward the positive ("you shall") precepts dealing with aid to fellow human beings in distress. The sages termed this aid "saving of souls," and made it clear that the saving of a single human life is equal in merit to the saving of "an entire world." This ruling exists in two versions. In the Babylonian Talmud it is ethnically limited:

> He who causes the loss of one soul among the People of Israel is deemed to have caused the loss of an entire world, and he who saves one soul among the People of Israel is deemed to have saved an entire world. (MISHNAH SANHEDRIN 4:15)

But the original version of the same ruling, as recorded in the (Jerusalem) Talmud, embraces all humanity:

> He who causes the loss of one soul is deemed to have caused the loss of an entire world, and he who saves one soul is deemed to have saved an entire world. (SANHEDRIN 22a)

Anyone who saves one life—of any human being, Jew or Gentile—has saved an entire world; accordingly, this precept must be held supreme. The formula for this ruling in the Jerusalem Talmud contains the essence of Jewish humanism in all its beauty.

The egalitarian observation of other practical precepts toward Jews and non-Jews alike, particularly those dealing with protection of the weak and sick, may be found in many places throughout the Talmud. The sages frequently link the observation of these precepts toward non-Jews with the theme of peace and neighborly relations with the surrounding nations:

> The poor Gentiles are to be supported along with the poor of Israel, and the sick Gentiles are to be visited along with the sick of Israel, and the dead Gentiles are to be buried along with the dead of Israel, to preserve the ways of peace. (GITTIN 71a:1)

Maimonides reinforces this ruling with passages from the Bible:

> As it is written: "The Lord is good to all, and his tender mercies are over all his works;" and "Her ways are ways of pleasantness, and all her paths are peace." (MAIMONIDES, HILKHOT MELAKHIM 80:12)

The repeated word "all" stands for universal equality in the observance of Jewish ethical precepts.

And the sages conclude:

> I call heaven and earth to witness: Whether Gentile or Israelite, man or woman, slave or handmaid, the Holy Spirit abides in each according to his deeds. (TANNA DEBE ELIYAHU RABBA 8)

Equality is part of the essence of freedom. Without it, freedom becomes discriminatory. But the combination of freedom and equality leads to an even higher level in the values of human society: brotherhood.

CHAPTER FIVE

Brothers Dwelling Together

THE WORD "BROTHERHOOD" APPEARS IN THE BIBLE ONLY once. The Prophet Zechariah, speaking of internal relationships within his people, mentions:

... the brotherhood between Judah and Israel.... (11:14)

The origin of the term lies in the close emotional ties between brothers (or siblings). The primary meaning of the term "brothers" in the Bible is simply a biological one: sons of the same mother and/or the same father. But a brother may also be a friend, a comrade, a loved one, or a member of the same tribe or even the same people.

Brotherhood, then, is a feeling of togetherness which, by its very nature, is reciprocal. The Psalmist expresses this feeling beautifully:

How good and how pleasant it is that brothers dwell together. (133:1)

However, if we review some of the better-known relationships between brothers in the Bible, in the majority of cases brotherhood does not prevail. The first brothers in the Bible are, of course, Cain and Abel; their "relationship" terminates with the world's first murder. The second pair of brothers discussed in any depth are Isaac and Ishmael. Here, too, little brotherhood is evident—neither between the mothers, Sarah and Hagar, nor between their sons. Each brother goes his own way and seeks his own fate. In time, the children of Isaac will establish the People of Israel, and those of Ishmael, the Arab peoples.

Next are the twins, Esau and Jacob; they too are far from brotherhood. They are said to have contended with each other even within their mother's womb, with one taking hold of the other's heel during the birth process. The feelings that develop between them, with the passage of time, are not brotherhood, but vengeance and jealousy, and this enmity is passed down from generation to generation.

The story of Joseph and his brothers also begins with emotions of jealousy and hatred, and progresses to acts of cruelty and deception on the part of the brothers. True brotherhood between them comes but many years later, when Joseph dramatically reveals himself to his brothers, who have come to beg for food in Egypt—and even this is preceded by his act of "sweet revenge."

By contrast, the brothers Moses and Aaron—the great prophet and the great priest who work together, each complementing the other—exhibit true cooperation. One a leader and legislator, the other a pursuer of peace, together they achieve a marvelous display of brotherhood.

The story of Abimelech, son of Jerubbaal, who slaughters his seventy brothers on one stone, is one of unparalleled cruelty.

The sons of King David, their eyes on their father's throne, entrap and seek to kill each other. No two of them show even the slightest sign of brotherhood; on the contrary, their relationship is characterized by greed, intrigue, and unbridled ambition. From this point, the history of the kingdoms of Judah and Israel is filled with bitter, dark, and often bloody struggle between sons and brothers contending for inheritance. Even the glorious Hasmonean royal house was not free of cruel internecine rivalry. The endless power struggles of its brother-members only hastened the collapse of the last Jewish kingdom.

Many of the renowned Biblical conflicts between brothers actually gave rise to decisive events in the history of the People of Israel. Nevertheless, in individual and social life, love and brotherhood are the rule, and the exceptions to that rule only prove its general validity.

To give brotherhood the validity and force of a divine command, the Torah stipulates:

You shall not hate your kinfolk in your heart. (LEVITICUS 19:17)

This stipulation is both deep and broad. Not even in the innermost depths of one's heart may one hate one's brother. Step by step, the concept of brotherhood expanded into greater and greater circles of society.

Following a dispute over grazing land in Abraham's extended family, the patriarch calls on his nephew, Lot, to find a compromise acceptable to both sides:

> Let there be no strife between you and me, between my herdsmen and yours, for we are kinsmen. (GENESIS 13:8)

In later years, the tribal structure developed in Israel. The backbone of this structure was constituted by a dozen brothers and their children, descendants of the dynasty of founding fathers. The structure itself was beset with constant tension, especially in the period when the Land of Israel was divided among the tribes. The books of Joshua and Judges include descriptions of many facets of these relationships—some depicting cooperation and mutual consideration, especially in time of trouble, when some or all of the tribes united against a common enemy; and others illustrating quarrels and disputes, which often ended in intertribal bloodshed. The most severe rivalry was that prevailing between the tribes of Ephraim in the north and Judah in the south, with each battling the other for control of the emerging people.

The People of Israel reached a period of splendor in its unification under the rule of King David and King Solomon. However, immediately after Solomon's death, the kingdom was torn and the people divided into two separate parts: the Kingdom of Israel and the Kingdom of Judah. These two kingdoms had a love/hate relationship. At times they fought, each allying itself with foreign powers in its struggle to dominate the other; yet, between periods of strife they achieved reconciliation and peaceful coexistence.

This great national tragedy—the separation of the descendants of Abraham, Isaac, and Jacob—haunted the Prophets, who longed to heal the rift and to forge a new and peaceful union of the divided brothers. In their comforting prophecies, they repeatedly foresee a new covenant between Israel and Judah, a homecoming of all the exiles, and a common effort to rebuild the united homeland. Isaiah, for example, speaks of a vision where:

> Each one helps the other, saying to his fellow, "Take courage!"
> (41:6)

The Psalmist, too, sings of a renewed period of brotherhood, of tribal unity under the peaceful rule of the House of David. And the Prophet Hosea, who worked within the Kingdom of Israel and predicted its destruction, also considered brotherhood to be the vision of the future:

> The people of Judah and the people of Israel shall assemble together and appoint one head over them; and they shall rise from the ground—for marvelous shall be the day of Jezreel. Oh, call your brothers "Ammi" (that is, "My People"); And your sisters, "Ruhamah" (that is, "Lovingly Accepted!"). (2:2–3)

Again, the Torah does not limit itself to biological or tribal brothers. The word *brothers* may also refer to friends, companions, or fellow citizens, with no familial or tribal bonds. They, too, must help one another and treat each other like sons of the same parents; they must refrain from hating each other; and especially they must extend a hand to those of them who are in need:

> Let him live by your side as your kinsman. (LEVITICUS 25:36)

This mandate, like "Love your neighbor as yourself," is a great rule. While the literal reference is to all brothers, and indeed to all citizens, the Biblical legislator makes it clear that it is especially pertinent to one's weaker brothers, those whom the Bible calls the "waxen poor." These are the ones who must be helped; the ones from whom it is forbidden to take interest or usury. This is more than a mere expression of the need for righteous action. By denoting the poor and humble with the appellation "brother," the Torah seeks to apply to them as well a dimension of brotherhood equal to that required of real siblings.

In the wisdom of the Proverbs, we find an additional definition of the nature of relationships that should exist between human beings:

There is a friend more devoted than a brother. (18:24)

And:

A close neighbor is better than a distant brother. (27:10)

Love, friendship, and neighborliness, then, are even stronger than family ties. Brotherhood can exist between lovers, friends, and neighbors as it does between siblings.

Ecclesiastes, too, in his own special way, speaks of the brotherhood of friends:

Two are better off than one, in that they have greater benefit from their earnings. For should they fall, one can raise the other; but woe betide him who is alone and falls with no companion to raise him! Further, when two lie together then they are warm; but how can he who is alone get warm? Also, if one attacks, two can stand up to him. A threefold cord is not readily broken. (4:9–12)

Even pessimistic, skeptical Ecclesiastes can appreciate the brotherhood of friends, and the strength within that brotherhood.

We find in the Bible an amazing development: a form of relationship that the Torah and the Prophets seek to cultivate between Israel and foreign nations near and far. Yet "the brotherhood of nations" is a modern, not a Biblical, phrase. The Torah was handed down in a period when the Tribes of Israel repeatedly had to defend themselves by force of arms against larger and smaller belligerent nations. Admittedly, the Torah commanded no small number of wars for the sake of revenge; and, in the case of Amalek, the war ordered was one of annhilation. Yet that same Torah also calls for quite another kind of relationship to other nations.

Concerning Edom, for example, the Torah states:

You shall not abhor an Edomite, for he is your kinsman. (DEUTERONOMY 23:8)

This command is no less than astonishing. True, the Edomites—descended from Esau—are, technically speaking, brothers of Jacob's descendants, the Israelites. But Esau was certainly no model brother to Jacob: He sought to kill him and constantly harassed him. Moreover, Esau's children, the Edomites, were bitter enemies of Israel. Nevertheless, the Pentateuch actually forbids the People of Israel to abhor the Edomites. And if the reason for this prohibition is that the Edomites are brothers to Israel, then Edom, too, must be treated with brotherhood. In fact, this commandment characterized the subsequent relationship between the Kingdom of Edom and those of Israel and Judah: a relationship of hatred and love, of conquest and liberation, of repulsion and attraction.

One of many examples of this ambivalent relationship may be found in Amos' prophecy of rage against Moab:

> Thus said the Lord: "For three transgressions of Moab, for four, I will not revoke it: because he burned the bones of the king of Edom to lime." (2:1)

Amos was well aware that both Moab and Edom, during considerable periods, were sworn enemies of Israel. Why, then, should he care that the king of Moab acted with terrible cruelty and burned the bones of the King of Edom? Is it any of Amos' business? Or is it a crime so terrible that the God of Israel must Himself cry out against it?

The answer to the last question is a thundering "Yes!"— not only because Amos and his fellow prophets considered the God of Israel to be a righteous judge among all peoples, but because of Israel's ambivalent attitude toward Edom, its sister nation.

The culmination of the strange relationship between Edom and Israel came in the days of the half-Edomite, half-Jewish King Herod, who was both a great builder and a terrible, cruel ruler; and in the Great Revolt against the Romans, when regiments of Edomites fought and died alongside the desperate Jewish rebels.

No less surprising than the Torah's command regarding Edom is the second half of that same verse:

> You shall not abhor an Egyptian, because you were a stranger in his land. (DEUTERONOMY 23:8)

Edom, after all, is descended from Esau, brother of Jacob. So the Edomites are relatives, and not to be abhorred. But what of the Egyptians? Was it not they who tortured and afflicted the People of Israel in captivity? Was Egypt not a "house of bondage"? Did the Egyptians not seek to wipe out the Hebrews, by commanding that all male Hebrew infants be thrown into the Nile? Did the Egyptians not pursue the People of Israel following the Exodus to the point where only a divine miracle saved them from the sword of Pharoah's army?

The answer lies in two great qualities, reflected precisely here, in this seemingly incomprehensible command. The first is the quality of mercy—even to one's bitterest enemies. The second is that of gratitude—to that earlier Pharoah who had raised Joseph to a position of honor and allowed his brothers and their families to settle as strangers in Goshen, thus saving them from famine and extinction; to the daughter of the later Pharoah, who rescued Moses and raised him as a prince in her own palace; and perhaps even to the great civilization of Egypt, whose influence contributed to Israel's own.

During the centuries of ceaseless warfare, throughout the times of Joshua, the Judges, Samuel, Saul, and David, the People of Israel was too busy fighting for its survival to have time to foster brotherhood with neighboring peoples. With the establishment of Solomon's kingdom and the building of the First Temple, however, Israel entered a period of peace. Solomon, in his wisdom, concluded treaties with the surrounding nations, married an Egyptian princess, and forged a covenant of brotherhood with Tyre and other neighbors.

Solomon turned his country into an international crossroads of trade. The port of Ezion-geber on the Red Sea became a gateway to far-off, mysterious lands. From the harbors of the Mediterranean, the sailors of Tyre and Israel made their way to Tarshish. Jerusalem was visited by kings and ministers—including the lovely, worldly Queen of Sheba.

Small wonder, then, that Solomon's Israel could permit itself to practice brotherhood with nearby nations. In fact, Solomon's prayer, at the dedication of the First Temple, emphasized this brotherhood:

> Or if a foreigner who is not of Your people Israel comes from a distant land for the sake of Your name . . . when he comes to

pray toward this House, oh, hear in Your heavenly abode and grant all that the foreigner asks you. (1 KINGS 8:41–43)

Solomon's prayer did not refer to converts to Judaism, or even to strangers willing to settle within the Land of Israel. It explicitly refers to non-Jews who become convinced of the greatness of Israel's God, come to Jerusalem to pray to that God, and return, as non-Jews, to their own countries and peoples. It is the first intimation of what, in the Prophets, becomes a repeated, reinforced theme: a belief that the God of Israel is indeed a God of "all the peoples of the earth"— that is, of all the nations of the world—and that He will, in time, cause a covenant embracing all humanity to be concluded in Jerusalem.

Amos, considered first of the Written Prophets, discusses the brotherhood of nations in his very first prophecy. There he speaks of the "brotherly covenant" concluded between King Solomon and King Hiram of Tyre, and of Tyre's breach of the covenant and joining of forces with Israel's enemies. The furious prophet foresees a terrible punishment for Tyre for having rejected covenant and brotherhood in favor of betrayal of a brother nation:

I will send down a fire upon the wall of Tyre, and it shall devour its fortresses. (1:10)

Isaiah, the great statesman-prophet, was well aware of the geopolitical situation affecting his people and country, caught between the hammer of the Egyptian great power to the south and the anvil of the Assyrian great power to the north. This situation—which left Israel always uncertain of whether the next blow would be struck from north or south—haunted the country for many generations.

In both his Egypt Pronouncement and his words to other nations near and far, great and small, Isaiah brings one so-lution to the international quagmire of his time—a solution appropriate to his unshakable faith in his God: If and when those nations, including Egypt and Assyria, begin to believe in the One God of Isaiah and his people, the prevailing sit-uation will change. The small, oppressed nation of Israel, trodden by the imperial armies of the Egyptian and Assyrian great powers, will become a bridge linking its great northern and southern neighbors. Its role will be not only that of a worldwide religious and spiritual center, but that of a cornerstone for an entirely different kind of international relations:

> For the Lord will make Himself known to the Egyptians, and the Egyptians shall acknowledge the Lord. . . . In that day, there shall be a highway from Egypt to Assyria. The Assyrians shall join with the Egyptians, and Egyptians with the Assyrians, and then the Egyptians with the Assyrians shall serve [the Lord]. In that day, Israel shall be a third partner with Egypt and Assyria, as a blessing on earth; for the Lord of Hosts will bless them, saying, "Blessed be My people Egypt, My handiwork Assyria, and My very own Israel." (19:21, 23–25)

Isaiah certainly conveys a shining international vision. It is, perhaps, not as deeply imbued with pathos as "And they shall beat their swords into plowshares" in his prophecy of "the days to come." Nevertheless, it is more firmly rooted in the reality of the area—thus proving that the Prophets were not merely sublime utopian universalists, but worthy statesmen, capable of believing and proclaiming that God would call Egypt "My people" and Assyria "My handiwork."

This is a vision of true brotherhood of nations, bringing peace and blessing to the entire area. Isaiah obviously believed that such a vision was really possible. In fact, the dream of Israel as the linchpin of a tripartite confederation in the Middle East holds great appeal to this day. Once peace comes, Israel, the Palestinians, and Jordan may create a common market. Such a bond could lead to further amity in a region tragically plagued by war.

The Prophets—some more so, others less—considered themselves to be God's messengers to both the People of Israel and all of humanity. They sought to bring redemption to Israel, both by renewing their people's persistent faith in God and by reforming its criminal and evil ways. Yet they also believed that, along with the redemption of Israel, the dawn of redemption would come for all nations—indeed, for all of humankind. Such an advent would require the Gentiles to recognize the God of Israel as the One God, Creator of Heaven and Earth, to mend their ways and values, and to adopt a life of brotherhood and peace.

Amos considered his God to be truly egalitarian in His treatment of peoples. Isaiah, in his vision of the "end of days," achieved the spiritual height of universal peace and supreme brotherhood of nations. His young disciple, Micah, followed in his footsteps.

Jeremiah, at the awesome moment of his consecration as a prophet, became a messenger bearing tidings not intended for his own people alone:

> And the Lord said to me: "Herewith I put My words into your mouth. See, I appoint you this day over nations and kingdoms: To uproot and to pull down, to destroy and to overthrow, to build and to plant. (1:9–10)

Jeremiah was to become a prophet of rage and reproof, prophesying visions of destruction for his people—yet also a comforting prophet for the remnant surviving the cataclysm. His words, addressed to many peoples and kingdoms, eventually made his name a metaphor, or even a synonym in many languages, for one who foresees and warns against impending disaster, yet remains unheard.

Zephaniah, who prophesied at about the same time as Jeremiah, speaks to the nations:

> For then I will make the peoples pure of speech, so that they all invoke the Lord by name, and serve Him with one accord. (3:9)

Among the prophecies concerning Israel's universal mission and role among the nations, the greatest are those of the "comforting" Isaiah. He was the prophet who witnessed Cyrus' victory and the building of the vast Persian Empire, encompassing scores of peoples and states, religions and cultures; the prophet who saw the beginning of the Return to Zion fulfilled. This prophet also foresaw that the new Zion, located in the center of the geographic world known to him, would also be a spiritual center for all nations:

> I will also make you a light of the nations, that My salvation may reach the ends of the earth. (49:6)

The People of Israel, then, has been assigned a new and great task: to be "a light of the nations"—a human lighthouse, whose beams of God-fearing, justice, and peace would reach the ends of the earth and guide all nations in their splendor. Israel is to be a source of light, inspiration, and hope for all peoples.

According to Isaiah, Israel will be redeemed specifically to serve as a source of light and glory to the peoples of the world:

> Arise, shine, for your light has dawned; the Presence of the Lord has shone upon you! Behold, darkness shall cover the earth, and thick clouds the peoples; but upon you the Lord will shine, and His Presence be seen over you. And nations shall walk by your light, kings, by your shining radiance. (60:1-3)

In the last chapter of his prophecies, Isaiah impressively describes the process by which the hearts of all nations, even the most remote, will be rendered good, and he predicts how all humanity, without exception, will observe the principal commandments and make Jerusalem their focal point:

> [The time] has come to gather all the nations and tongues; they shall come and behold My glory. I will set a sign among them. . . . For as the new heaven and the new earth which I will make shall endure by My will, so shall your seed and your name endure. And new moon after new moon, and sabbath after sabbath, all flesh shall come to worship Me—said the Lord. (66:18-19, 22-23)

Let us note the key words of this prophecy: "the new heaven" and "the new earth." This, then, is a whole new world in which the laws of truth and justice, so long perverted by mankind, will finally prevail. In this new world, under these new heavens, the People of Israel will have a vital role: that of example to "all flesh"—that is, to all humanity.

The later Prophets—those who prophesied following the Return to Zion—also clung to this goal with all their might. Even faced with the grayness of everyday life, the unfinished city wall, the painfully slow rebuilding of the Temple, the diminutive nation of Judah surrounded by large and greedy enemies, and the resurgence of oppression and violence among the People of Israel returned to the homeland—despite, and possibly because of, all these, they repeatedly predicted that this tiny state, could it but mend its ways, would yet become a spiritual crossroads for the entire world.

Zechariah, in nearly all of his prophecies, emphasizes the worldwide extent of the future faith in the One God, Who will lead all the nations in His light and in the light of the people chosen to guide humanity:

> Thus said the Lord of Hosts: "In those days, ten men from nations of every tongue will take hold—they will take hold of every Jew by a corner of his cloak and say, 'Let us go with you, for we have heard that God is with you.' " (8:23)

In his description of the future Jewish king—a king depicted both as poor and righteous—the prophet states:

> The warrior's bow shall be banished. He shall call on the nations to make peace. (9:10)

And he concludes with an apocalyptic prophecy, ending in the great and world-embracing proclamation:

> And the Lord shall be king over all the earth; in that day there shall be one Lord with one name. (14:9)

Malachi, last of the twelve Prophets, maintains the vision of the People of Israel and the Holy City as a focal point for all peoples:

> For from where the sun rises even to where the sun sets, My name is honored among the nations. (1:11)

What could be more natural than for the Psalmists—who, in the days of the Prophets, sang their hymns of praise in the Temple courts—to use the exciting content of the sublime idea that the God of Israel is also God of all the nations; that all peoples would one day live together in brotherhood and peace; that Jerusalem would become an international spiritual center; and that all this would take place under a rule characterized by righteousness and justice for all.

These lines, sung by joyful voices, accompanied by violins and psalteries, harps and flutes, drums and cymbals, sound like a wonderful symphony:

But the Lord abides forever; He has set up His throne for judgment; it is He who judges the world with righteousness, He rules the peoples with equity. The Lord is a haven for the oppressed, a haven in times of trouble. (PSALMS 9:8–10)

The "new song" of Psalm 96 echoes the prophetic theme of new heavens, a new earth, a new heart, and a new spirit:

Sing to the Lord a new song, sing to the Lord, all the earth. . . . Tell of His glory among the nations, His wondrous deeds among all the peoples. . . . Ascribe to the Lord the glory of His name, bring tribute, and enter His courts. Bow down to the Lord majestic in holiness; tremble in His presence, all the earth. Declare among the nations, "The Lord is King!" . . . Let the heavens rejoice, the earth exult; let the sea and all within it thunder, the fields and everything in them exult; then shall all the trees of the forest shout for joy at the presence of the Lord, for He is coming, for He is coming to rule the earth; He will rule the world justly and its peoples in faithfulness. (96:1, 3, 8–10, 11–13)

And the last Psalm of all—the last chord in the divine symphony of the Book of Psalms—ends in a crescendo in which the breath of life, of all humanity, is joined in one great song of praise:

Hallelujah. Praise God in His sanctuary; praise Him in the sky, His stronghold. Praise Him for His mighty acts; praise Him for His exceeding greatness. Praise Him with blasts of the horn; praise Him with harp and lute. Praise Him with timbrel and dance; praise Him with lute and pipe. Praise Him with the resounding cymbals; praise Him with the loud-clashing cymbals. Let all that breathes praise the Lord. Hallelujah. (150:1–6)

No wonder that, of all the holy writings, the Psalms, with their unique musical rhythm, became perhaps the most popular, both in Israel and throughout the world. They are all-embracing: songs of one and many, the human and the divine, the national and the international, the persecuted and the victorious. They are equally enjoyable to young and old, sick and well. They include songs of love and songs of nature. They are appropriate to all periods, all human beings, all nations.

The relationship of Judaism to brotherhood—both between individuals and between peoples—may be summed up in a saying of the Sages of Israel:

> Who is a hero of heroes? He who makes his enemy into his friend. (AVOT DE-RABBI NATAN^A CH. 23)

The Sages of the Jerusalem Talmud drew a parallel between the brotherhood of nations and the passage "My beloved has gone down to his garden" in the Song of Songs:

> "My beloved has gone down to his garden"—"my beloved" is the Holy One, blessed be He, "is gone down to his garden"— that is the world. . . "to feed in the gardens"—that is the nations of the world, and "to gather lilies"—those are the righteous among them. (P. BERAKHOT 5b–c)

Thus the sanctity of life is linked with justice, justice with freedom, and all three with equality and brotherhood. Corresponding to all of these is a human quality far above the normal reckoning of stages in human ethics, and encompassing all of these stages: the quality of mercy.

CHAPTER SIX

Tender Mercies

T HE QUALITY OF MERCY IS MORE THAN A HUMAN TRAIT. AC-
cording to the Bible, it is primarily a divine quality. Nevertheless, mercy is to be found throughout the animal kingdom.
Like its opposite, cruelty, it is embedded within the very fibers
of our world. Mercy may be said to be one facet of the
biological instinct of self-preservation and species preservation. It may also be described as a sort of reflex command—
one of many reflexes included in the genetic code—to protect
one's offspring.

Human beings, created in the image of God, are granted
some measure of God's great mercy. A poetic expression of
the nature of that divine quality is given by the Psalmist:

> The Lord is gracious and compassionate, slow to anger and
> abounding in kindness. The Lord is good to all, and His mercy
> is upon all His works. (145:8–9)

The passage emphasizes the all-encompassing nature of
mercy, and gives a number of synonymous expressions describing the merciful God of Israel: "gracious," "compassionate," and simply "good."

God, then, is merciful to all. To rule out any possibility of
error on this point, the Psalmist echoes: "His mercy is upon
all His works"—that is, over all living creatures. In fact, "all
His works" may be considered to include the plant and even
the mineral kingdom; the command "You shall not destroy"
may be applied to all unnecessary destruction: trees, flowers,
and all other creations in nature.

In human beings, the clearest, strongest, and most direct
form of mercy is that within the family. The mercy of mothers
is perhaps the most moving and most conspicuous of all.
However, the mercy of fathers and brothers is also powerfully
stressed in the Bible. Joseph, for instance, is moved to tears
at the sight of his little brother Benjamin:

He was overcome with feeling toward his brother and was on the verge of tears. (GENESIS 43:30)

A dramatic example of a mother's mercy is given by a harlot, the true mother of the child in Solomon's famed judgment, at the moment of truth:

And the king said, "Cut the live child in two, and give half to one and half to the other." But the woman whose son was the live one pleaded with the king. . . . "Please, my lord," she cried, "give her the live child; only don't kill it." (1 KINGS 3:25–26)

The "comforting" Isaiah, seeking for an incomparably strong expression of God's mercy for His exiled, unfortunate people, compares it to that of a mother:

Zion says, "The Lord has forsaken me, My Lord has forgotten me." Can a woman forget her baby, or disown the child of her womb? Though she might forget, I could never forget you. (49:14–16)

By contrast, the Psalmist chooses to liken God's mercy to that of a father:

As a father has compassion for his children, so the Lord has compassion for those who fear him. (103:13)

The quality of all-embracing divine mercy is portrayed in the Biblical story of the Flood and Noah's Ark. The Flood, according to that story, was brought down upon the earth because of the evil of humankind—of humankind, and not of the animals. Accordingly, when God rescues Noah the Righteous and his family and thus saves the human race, He naturally has mercy on the animals and saves them too. A phrase that may describe God's thought at the time appears in the Bible as spoken centuries later, by King David:

. . . but these poor sheep, what have they done? (2 SAMUEL 24:17)

The actual sign of God's mercy on living creatures—His gift of new life, following the recession of the flood waters— is depicted in the Torah as having been entrusted to an animal, the dove:

The dove came back to him toward evening, and there in its bill a plucked-off olive-leaf! Then Noah knew that the waters had decreased on the earth. (GENESIS 8:11)

No wonder that, ever since, the dove and the olive branch have been known as symbols of hope and peace.

The Torah's attitude regarding mercy toward animals is fascinating. The author of the lovely "Give ear, O heavens" passage in the Book of Deuteronomy illustrates God's mercy and care for His people with the following simile:

Like an eagle who rouses his nestlings, gliding down to his young. (32:11)

And if animals have mercy on their own cubs and fledglings, humans too must have compassion on them and not mistreat them unnecessarily. This is the underlying principle of a number of beautiful commands regarding animals. First of all, as mentioned earlier, the Torah imposed the Sabbath— the weekly day of rest—not only on humankind, but on the beasts of burden in the service of humanity, who, by the sweat of their brow, help to bring forth bread from the earth. They too are worthy of rest—as it is written:

Six days you shall do your work, but on the seventh day you shall cease from labor in order that your ox and your ass may rest, and that your bondman and the stranger may be refreshed. (EXODUS 23:12)

This verse constitutes a revolution within a revolution: the application of the rule of kindness to animals as an integral part of a more just and more egalitarian system of human society, granting a day of freedom to human and animal alike.

Another Pentateuchal command combines the principles of mercy toward animals, mutual aid, and refraining from hatred of one's enemies.

When you see the ass of your enemy lying under its burden and would refrain from raising it, you must nevertheless raise it with him. (EXODUS 23:5)

And again, in the Book of Deuteronomy, the Torah returns to the same theme:

If you see your fellow's ass or ox fallen on the road, do not ignore it; you must help him raise it. (22:4)

The rules of mercy and kindness to animals are most explicitly expressed in the following prohibition:

If, along the road, you chance upon a bird's nest, in any tree or on the ground, with fledglings or eggs, and the mother sitting over the fledglings or on the eggs, do not take the mother together with her young. Let the mother go, and take only the young, in order that you may fare well, and have a long life. (22:6–7)

This command indicates a sort of mystical connection between the continuity of human life and the continuation of existence in the animal kingdom. One generation passes away, and another generation comes; and life continues on.

The quality of mercy to animals is beautifully expressed in the following saying:

A righteous man knows the needs of his beast, but the compassion of the wicked is cruelty. (PROVERBS 12:10)

The Pentateuchal command "You shall not destroy" applies to trees as well:

When in your war against a city you have to besiege it a long time in order to capture it, you must not destroy its trees, wielding the ax against them. You may eat of them, but you must not cut them down. Are trees of the field human to withdraw before you into the besieged city? (DEUTERONOMY 20:19)

This command may, of course, be given the practical interpretation that fruit trees must not be cut down because they supply food to humankind. However, it seems to this author that the motives of the legislators must have included a measure of mercy toward the tree itself.

One of the books of the twelve Prophets, the Book of Jonah—a short book, only four concise chapters in length—takes the entire range of mercy and transforms it into a literary jewel. Jonah is guided and controlled by a compassionate and merciful God. The entire book is filled with mercy for all: Jews and non-Jews, old and young, simple sailor and mighty king, and even animals and plants.

Jonah the Jew is commanded by God to go to Nineveh, capital of a great foreign empire, and prophesy destruction. Jonah knows the nature of his God:

> You are a compassionate and gracious God, slow to anger, abounding in kindness, renouncing punishment. (4:2)

He knows that, if the people of Nineveh turn aside from their evil ways, God will have mercy on them and pity them. In such a case, Jonah himself will appear to be a false prophet, as his warning of destruction will not be fulfilled. Accordingly, he seeks to evade his mission. But his God and his destiny pursue him, even into the sea itself. The ship on which he had attempted to escape is caught up in a mighty storm. Its sailors believe Jonah to be the cause of the tempest. Although they have pity on him, he commands them to cast him into the sea. Once this is done, God has mercy on the sailors; and the ship is not wrecked. Meanwhile, Jonah himself is swallowed by a huge fish. He prays to God to save him from the fish's belly. God, in His compassion, does so.

Eventually, Jonah reaches Nineveh and prophesies upheaval and destruction. At his words, the entire population of Nineveh (which is, of course, not Jewish)—including the king and his ministers—repent of their evil deeds, fast, and beg for absolution. A striking passage describes how every single denizen of Nineveh—humans and animals alike—fast and put on the garments of penitence:

> And he had the word cried through Nineveh: By decree of the king and his nobles: "No man or beast—of flock or herd—shall taste anything! They shall not graze, and they shall not drink water! They shall be covered with sackcloth—man and beast—and shall cry mightily to God. Let everyone turn back from his evil ways, and from the injustice of which he is guilty. Who knows but that God may turn and repent? He may turn away back from His wrath so that we do not perish. (3:7-9)

Of course, as Jonah had predicted, God has mercy on the human and animal population of Nineveh. He forgives them for their evil deeds and lets them live. Jonah, who had known that this would happen, is nevertheless irritated. In his shame, he flees from the city that God saved from the destruction he had foreseen, and sits alone in the blazing desert. God again has pity on him and makes a gourd vine grow up out of the soil to give him shade. Jonah, naturally, rejoices in the gourd. Yet, in order to demonstrate the power of mercy, God causes the gourd to dry up. When Jonah, again afflicted by the savage heat and dehydration, expresses his willingness to die, God answers:

> . . . You cared about the plant, which you did not work for and which you did not grow, which appeared overnight and perished overnight. And should not I care about Nineveh, that great city, in which there are more than a hundred and twenty thousand persons who do not yet know their right from their left, and many beasts as well! (4:10–11)

This, then, is the universal essence and message of mercy. True mercy must be shown to every human being and every living thing. True mercy must be shown even to the most cruel of criminals and oppressors. The one prerequisite for mercy is simple:

> Let everyone turn back from his evil ways and from the injustice of which he is guilty. (3:8)

The opposite of violence is righteousness, and the wonderful levers capable of changing creatures of violence to creatures of righteousness are repentance and mercy.

If the story of Jonah covers the entire gamut of mercy, the Book of Genesis reveals a marvelous example of mercy carried beyond the bounds of family or tribe, and applied to every human being—Hebrew or foreigner. This is the moving dialogue between Abraham and God concerning the sinful city of Sodom, which, with its sister city of Gomorrah, had gone far astray and committed dreadful sins.

Abraham, aware of God's decision to punish Sodom by destroying the city and all its inhabitants, is no less aware than Jonah of God's merciful and compassionate nature. Unlike Jonah, Abraham does not attempt to escape, but stands before God and begins to argue, or—perhaps more accurately—to bargain:

Abraham came forward and said: "Will You sweep away the innocent along with the guilty? What if there should be fifty innocent within the city; will You then wipe out the place and not forgive it for the sake of the innocent fifty who are in it? Far be it from You to do such a thing, to bring death upon the innocent as well as the guilty, so that the innocent and guilty fare alike. Shall not the Judge of all the earth deal justly?" And the Lord answered, "If I find within the city of Sodom fifty innocent ones, I will forgive the whole place for their sake." (GENESIS 18:23–26)

Abraham continues the dialogue, bargaining the number of righteous down below twenty:

"Let not my Lord be angry if I speak but this last time: What if ten should be found there?" And He answered, "I will not destroy, for the sake of the ten." (18:32)

Above and beyond the awesome idea of a mere human being daring to debate, and even to reprove, his God ("Far be it from You to do such a thing"); above and beyond God's willingness to accept Abraham's proposals, the key sentence of this dialogue is God's declaration that "If I find within the city of Sodom fifty innocent ones, I will forgive the whole place for their sake." This passage emphasizes the duty of the righteous—even if they represent lone individuals or a small minority within an evil society—to maintain the struggle for righteousness and justice. It is for their sake and the sake of their perseverance that the "whole city"—that is, the entire society—will be saved.

This thesis recurs in various places throughout Jewish tradition. In the story of the Flood, God saved all of humanity and the entire animal kingdom for the sake of Noah, the one "righteous and blameless" person of his society. In the tale of Sodom, the wicked city would have been saved for the sake of ten righteous inhabitants, had such existed. In the Book of Jonah, the city of Nineveh was saved by the repentance of its king and people. And—so the legend states—the entire world continues to exist for the sake of thirty-six hidden righteous.

In other words, the quality of mercy will always prevail

over that of justice. Yet, to enable it to serve as a lever powerful enough to deflect pronounced judgment, even the quality
of mercy requires a fulcrum. This fulcrum is the righteous
soul, or group of righteous souls, small as that group may
be. In today's world there is a built-in contrast between the
"paper walls" of immigration laws and the moral duty of
giving haven to refugees fleeing the sword.

Let us note that, in none of the three biblical stories cited—
Noah and the Flood, Abraham and Sodom, and Jonah and
Nineveh—are the righteous ones Jews (in Noah's day, of
course, the human race was not yet divided into nations).
They are, first and foremost, human beings; and their cities
and countries are saved from destruction for their sake.

Similarly, the story of the infant Moses in his basket illustrates the mercy of Pharaoh's daughter—a righteous woman
of Egypt, whose compassion saved the life of one who was
to become the greatest legislator of Israel and humanity. She
saw that "this is one of the Hebrews' children," and she felt
compassion for him.

The Bible, as the Great Book of the People of Israel, focuses
its description of mercy on that shown by God to His people,
even beyond the universal examples of mercy already discussed in this section.

But even before the People of Israel existed as a nation,
God showed mercy to both of Abraham's sons: Isaac, son of
Sarah, and Ishmael, son of Hagar the Egyptian. In the latter
case, Hagar and her son are cast out into the desert with only
bread and a bottle of water, but:

> God heard the cry of the boy, and the angel of God called to
> Hagar from heaven and said to her, "What troubles you, Hagar?
> Fear not, for God has heeded the cry of the boy where he is.
> Come, lift up the boy and hold him by the hand, for I will make
> a great nation of him." (GENESIS 21:17–18)

The divine quality of mercy saved little Ishmael—who, in
the course of time, was to become the father of the Arab
peoples. And it was that very same quality of mercy, in the
next chapter of Genesis, that saved young Isaac from his
father's knife. Isaac later became the father of the People of

Israel. Both of the sons of Abraham—and all of their descendants—thus owe their lives to mercy.

In God's mysterious and glorious revelation to Moses, within the burning bush on the mountain of God in Horeb, Moses asks God for His name, so that he could identify the Lord to the children of Israel. God's answer, more occult than open, may be considered as a sort of code:

> God said to Moses, "Ehyeh-Asher-Ehyeh." He continued, "Thus shall you say unto the Israelites, Ehyeh sent me to you." (EXODUS 3:14)

In another revelation of God to Moses—after Moses breaks the Tablets of the Law, at sight of the golden calf—Moses again asks:

> Now, if I have truly gained Your favor, pray let me know Your ways, that I may know You and continue in Your favor. (33:13)

And the answer is:

> I will make all My goodness pass before you, and will proclaim before you the name of the Lord, and the grace that I grant and the compassion that I show. (33:19)

This is perhaps the key to the code of God's ways and nature: The same God who stated that His name is "Ehyeh-Asher-Ehyeh" now replies that His way is to show "grace" and "compassion." This, then, is God's great attribute: mercy—which is equivalent to "all His goodness."

This mercy had to be applied again and again throughout the history of the People of Israel: a small people, constantly oppressed by numerous enemies, and almost always in a state of sin. Sometimes Israel committed sin through error, but often did it deliberately, confessing and repenting only to return to its evil ways again and again. This evil quality, unfortunately, was one of the distinguishing traits of the emergent People of Israel.

The giver of the Torah, from the very beginning, illustrates the measure of mercy applied to the sins of the People of Israel, the repeated attempts to ignore the elaborate nature of those sins and to ascribe them to human error—which, by its nature, can and must be forgiven:

> The whole Israelite community and the stranger residing among
> them shall be forgiven, for it happened to the entire people through
> error. . . . For the citizen among the Israelites and for the stranger
> who resides among them—you shall have one ritual for anyone
> who acts in error. (NUMBERS 15:26, 29)

In this passage, the Torah applies the full measure of mercy,
and, while doing so, mentions yet again the equality of home-
born and strangers in the eyes of the law.

The establishment of the cities of refuge is founded on the
same principle: to allow those who sin through error the
chance to enjoy the benefit of the doubt until they can be
tried:

> You shall provide yourselves with places to serve you as cities
> of refuge to which a manslayer who has killed a person unin-
> tentionally may flee. The cities shall serve you as a refuge from
> the avenger, so that the manslayer may not die unless he has
> stood trial before the assembly. (35:11–12)

If the "Give ear, O heavens" passage in Deuteronomy lik-
ens God's attitude toward His people to that of an eagle
compassionately protecting its young, the Prophets often
compare God to a shepherd mercifully tending his flock—
the People of Israel. A wonderful expression of this simile
appears in Ezekiel:

> As a shepherd seeks out his flock . . . so I will seek out My flock,
> I will rescue them from all the places to which they were scattered
> on a day of cloud and gloom. . . . I Myself will graze My flock,
> and I Myself will let them lie down—declares the Lord God. I will
> look for the lost, and I will bring back the strayed; I will bandage
> the injured, and I will sustain the weak. . . . (34:12, 15–16)

One after another, in comforting prophecies, the Prophets
emphasize God's mercy on His people, despite its sins. Skilled
as the Prophets were in castigating the people for its crimes
of oppression, violence, and robbery, the quality of mercy
nevertheless breaks through even their prophecies of rage.

Amos, in the midst of a bitter passage foretelling destruction for Israel, halts to ask for mercy for the same people
which he so angrily chastises:

I said, "Oh Lord God, pray forgive. How will Jacob survive? He is so small." (7:2)

Jeremiah, great prophet of rage, between prophecies of ruin intersperses a song of mercy and love for his unfortunate people:

> Truly, Ephraim is a dear son to Me, a child that is dandled! Whenever I have turned against him, My thoughts would dwell on him still. That is why My heart yearns for him; I receive him back in love—declares the Lord. (31:20)

The same prophet, who repeatedly warns the people and the king against the Babylonians and their terrible power, now calls upon the mercy of God to save them from that might:

> Do not be afraid of the king of Babylon, whom you fear; do not be afraid of him—declares the Lord—for I am with you to save you and to rescue you from his hands. I will dispose him to be merciful to you; he shall show you mercy and bring you back to your own land. (42:11–12)

The "comforting Isaiah" describes the process by which anger is changed to mercy, mercy to forgiveness, and forgiveness to redemption:

> [The Lord] says: "Build up, build up a highway! Clear a road! Remove all obstacles from the road of My people . . . For I will not always contend, I will not be angry forever: Nay, I who make spirits flag, also create the breath of life. For their sinful greed I was angry; I struck them and turned away in My wrath. Though stubborn, they follow the way of their hearts, I note how they fare and will heal them: I will guide them, and to the mourners among them, heartening, comforting words. (57:14, 16–18)

Toward the end of his prophecies, Isaiah returns to the same theme, summing it up in one all-inclusive sentence:

> For in anger I struck you down, but in favor have I taken you back. (60:10)

From mercy for all, for the entire people or the entire public, it is but one step to mercy for the weak and poor— who, after all, are most in need of mercy. As Isaiah says:

For the Lord has comforted His people, and has taken back His afflicted ones in love. (49:13)

And the Psalmist sings:

The Lord supports all who stumble, and makes all who are bent stand straight. (145:14)

Mercy toward the weak—over and above simple justice—constitutes the underlying principle for a long series of Biblical laws. Among these are the laws of gleaning the corners of the field, the laws protecting slaves, and the laws dealing with strangers. One of the most beautiful of the laws protecting the poor appears in the Book of Deuteronomy, and has to do with pledges and wages:

When you make a loan of any sort to your countryman, you must not enter his house to seize his pledge. You must remain outside, while the man to whom you made the loan brings the pledge out to you. If he is a needy man, you shall not go to sleep in his pledge; you must return the pledge to him at sundown, that he may sleep in his cloth and bless you; and it will be to your merit before the Lord your God. You shall not abuse a needy and destitute laborer, whether a fellow countryman, or a stranger in one of the communities of your land. . . . (24:10–14)

This passage illustrates the sensitivity of the Biblical law-makers to both the needs and the dignity of poor persons and hired laborers.

The Psalms, too, emphasize the quality of mercy toward the poor and helpless:

For He did not scorn, He did not spurn the plea of the lowly; He did hide His face from him; when he cried out to Him, He listened. (22:25)

The Book of Proverbs demands mercy for the hungry who steal bread to assuage their hunger:

A thief is not held in contempt for stealing to appease his hunger. (6:30)

This theme is frequently repeated in the world's great literature. It is enough to mention the compelling character of

Jean Valjean in Victor Hugo's *Les Misérables*, imprisoned for many years, and despised by all of his society, for the sole crime of stealing a loaf of bread to keep his starving soul alive. Another phrase coined by the Book of Proverbs is a sort of motto for the value of mercy, which provides a gateway back to repentance and the good life:

He who confesses and gives them up will find mercy. (28:13)

The Prophets were well aware of what wrong had been done to Israel by some of its nearer or more distant neighbor nations. Moreover, that awareness did not stem solely from history lessons, describing the fate of the People of Israel in its wanderings through the desert and in the days of Joshua and the Judges; it was strengthened and reinforced by the events of their own reality. During most of the Prophetic period, the relationship prevailing between Israel and the surrounding nations was one of hostility and battle, sometimes to the point of all-out war. The feelings of rage and frustration experienced by the Prophets toward those nations were naturally expressed in prophecies of doom.

Marvelously enough, the Prophets were nonetheless able to raise themselves above those feelings, to take pity on many of those nations, and to utter—despite the bloody score still to be settled between them and Israel—prophecies of comfort. These comforting messages to the nations are like pearls, hidden away within the iridescent shell of prophecy in Israel.

In his Moab Pronouncement, Isaiah predicts a terrible destruction for Moab, Israel's eastern neighbor and traditional enemy. Yet, in the midst of this description of ruin, the prophet has pity and proclaims:

My heart cries out for Moab. (15:5)

Later, following additional portrayals of collapse and destruction, the prophet is again stricken with compassion. He sheds tears over the fate of Moab and its cities, just as he repeatedly weeps for the downfall of his own people. His mercy overflows the national banks and washes over every people in need and every city in distress.

We have already mentioned Isaiah's compassion to the Arab refugees in his In the Steppe Pronouncement:

> For they fled before swords, before the whetted sword, before the bow that was drawn, before the stress of war. (21:16)

The prophet continues by appealing to neighboring nations to help these unfortunate refugees, wandering through the desert, beaten and thirsty.

Jeremiah was especially consecrated by God to be "a prophet concerning the nations," and was commanded to speak both to Israel and to other kingdoms, prophesying both a forecast of doom and destruction, and the hope of mercy and reconstruction. This mission is admirably fulfilled in Jeremiah's great prophecies to the various nations.

After describing how the proud kingdom of Egypt will be laid waste and conquered, and its pharoahs will fall into the hands of their Babylonian enemies, Jeremiah concludes with words of comfort to Egypt:

> But afterward she shall be inhabited again as in former days, declares the Lord. (46:26)

Even Egypt, according to the prophet, will regain its former glory and attain a shining future.

In his prophecy to the Philistines, enemies of Israel for many generations—the same Philistines who blinded Samson, captured the Ark of the Covenant, killed Saul and Jonathan, conquered some of the Hebrew tribes, and endangered the existence of the entire People of Israel—Jeremiah predicts a terrible fate. Yet immediately after pronouncing the fateful words "Baldness has come upon Gaza, Ashkelon is destroyed," he cries out:

> O sword of the Lord, when will you be quiet at last? Withdraw into your sheath, rest and be still. (47:6)

In his prophecy to Moab, the pattern is repeated: prophecy of destruction, exile, and agony—suddenly interrupted, at the climax of doom, by the prophet's piercing outcry:

> Therefore I will howl for Moab, I will cry out for all Moab. . . . Therefore, My heart moans for Moab like a flute; Like a flute my heart moans for the men of Kir-heres. . . . (48:31, 36)

Jeremiah repeats, almost word for word, Isaiah's outcry in his Moab Pronouncement *(Isaiah 16:9, 11)*. Both prophets "wail," both "cry out," and both "weep" at the catastrophe befalling Moab.

Jeremiah continues his message to the nations with a prophecy to the Ammonites. Knowing full well the bitter score Israel has to settle with the Ammonites, he prophesies that their capital, Rabbah, will become "a desolate mound," and that their king will go into captivity along with his priests and princes. (Ammon, today's Jordan, is still in conflict with the children of Israel.) Yet, as in his prophecy to Egypt, Jeremiah concludes with words of comfort:

But afterward I will restore the fortunes of the Ammonites— declares the Lord. (49:6)

The phrase used by the prophet for the return of the Ammonites from captivity is exactly that which he uses for his own beloved, unhappy People of Israel. In other words, the return of the Ammonites may also be considered their redemption.

Now Jeremiah addresses Edom. The account between Israel, descendants of Jacob, and the Edomites, descendants of Esau, was long and frequently bloody; despite the Biblical prohibition of "You shall not abhor an Edomite," reality dictated near-incessant strife and turmoil. Edom too, says Jeremiah, will drink of the bitter cup of war and utter ruin. Yet once again, immediately after pronouncing that Esau's "offspring is ravaged," he is overcome by mercy and pity for the orphans and widows of Edom; overcoming his anger for a moment, he adds:

Leave your orphans with Me, I will rear them; Let your widows rely on Me! (49:11)

In his prophecy to Elam, this amazing phenomenon recurs. Jeremiah first prophecies Elam's doom and destruction and then follows these harsh words with a vision of comfort, return, and redemption for the very same nation:

And I will dispatch the sword after them until I have consumed them. And I will set My throne in Elam, and wipe out from there

kings and officials—says the Lord. But in the days to come I
will restore the fortunes of Elam—declares the Lord. (49:37–39)

Ezekiel, too, creates a parallel between Israel and the surrounding nations in some of his prophecies—both in the
description of sins and in the promise of mercy. In his prophecy to Jerusalem, Ezekiel compares the city to a harlot. Indeed,
he goes so far as to say that the sins of Jerusalem are worse
than those of Samaria, and even worse than those of Sodom.
Yet, after describing the severe punishment to be imposed by
God on Jerusalem, Samaria, and Sodom, he adds that they
will:

. . . return to their former state. (16:55)

The extent of mercy necessary to promise Sodom a return to
days of goodness, repentance, and reconstruction is even more
amazing in light of the terrible image that the city retained
in the consciousness of the People of Israel.

Another of Ezekiel's prophecies of rage concludes in just
as surprising a manner. In his prophecy to Egypt, he foresees
war, destruction, and exile; he phrases these visions of wrath
in the very same terms that he uses for the fate of Israel:

And I will scatter the Egyptians among the nations and disperse
them throughout the countries. (29:12)

Yet here is the surprise:

Further, thus said the Lord God: After a period of forty years I
will gather the Egyptians from the peoples among whom they were
dispersed. I will restore the fortunes of the Egyptians. (29:13–14)

Admittedly, following its return, Egypt, according to Ezekiel,
"shall be the lowliest of all the kingdoms, and shall not lord
it over the nations again;" yet it will nevertheless be a kingdom. Notable is Ezekiel's use of the words "gather" and
"restore": in Hebrew, the very words denoting the ingathering and return of Israel from exile.

If we examine more closely what may be termed "outbursts
of comfort for the nations," as voiced by Amos, Isaiah, Jeremiah, and Ezekiel—outbursts occurring in the midst of

prophecies of rage, generally directed toward Israel's enemies—we will observe two common denominators.

The first of these is their brevity and terseness. The words
of comfort to Moab or Ammon, Egypt or Edom, are expressed in one Biblical verse, or two at the very most. In this
sense, there is no comparison between these messages and
those of comfort to Israel. In speaking to or of their own
people, the Prophets go into great detail—both in the por-
trayal of crime and punishment and in the description of
repentance, with its attendant rewards: comfort, return, reconstruction, flourishing, and complete redemption.

The second common denominator is very interesting: the
lack of any contingency in the comforting of the nations.
While for Israel, redemption is contingent on abandonment
of evil, this does not seem to be the case for other nations;
they are given unconditional comfort. All the Prophets, except
for Jonah, do not ask Ammon, or Moab, or the Philistines,
or even Sodom, to return from their wicked ways. Although
it may be assumed that the Prophets and their God very much
want these nations to repent, this is not explicitly specified
in any comforting passage.

It seems that precisely this unconditional comfort repre-
sents the shining essence of mercy. For mercy—unlike righteousness, justice, and repentance—is unlimited and un-
bounded. Mercy seems to have blazed up in the Prophets'
hearts, affording them no rest, driving them to speak—even
in the midst of their fury—a word of comfort and sympathy
to the very nations they reproach.

Thus, in a kind of heartfelt sigh, the Prophets mourn for
Moab, weep for the Philistines, cry out for the refugees of
Arabia, and demand life for the orphans of Edom. This is a
sort of lamentation, an "Ah, brother! Ah, sister!" for peoples
that, although not Jews, are certainly composed of human
beings, created in the image of God and thus entitled to mercy,
which devolves even upon the least of living things.

The greatness of mercy is praised by the Sages of the Talmud:

> He who asks for mercy for his friend . . . is first given mercy for
> himself. (BAVA KAMMA 92a)

And:

He who has mercy on his fellow creatures—Heaven has mercy on him. (SHABBAT 151b)

And:

Charity and good deeds are equal in weight to all the precepts of the Torah. (P. PEAH 16b)

Through the centuries, the Jews have been the victims of human cruelty culminating in the horrors of the merciless Holocaust. In their own state, the value of mercy should have special significance. In the spirit of the Prophets, who wept even for Israel's worst enemies, today's Israelites should not rejoice in the fall of their enemies but should strive for peace.

CHAPTER SEVEN

The Pursuit of Peace

Is HUMANKIND, BY ITS VERY NATURE, TO BE RECKONED AMONG the beasts of prey? There is no clear answer to this question, neither in the Bible nor in modern research. It is, however, obvious that human beings have found it necessary to kill other animals and eat their flesh from time immemorial, for the sake of their own continued existence.

The primary motives for the aggregation of human beings into herds and groups—a process which led to the socialization of humankind—were both the advantages to be gained from joint pursuit of food and the desire to defend themselves against stronger predators. Primitive humans were prepared to kill not only animals outside their own species, but even their brother humans. Such killing is murder. When murder is organized by a group of people, it becomes a severe social problem. When several groups clash with each other in order to murder, this is known as war.

The history of war is as long as that of humanity. In the beginning, the wars of humankind—like those of the animal kingdom—were wars of survival: wars waged over the food required to sustain one's family, group, or tribe. These "simple" wars mutated into wars over territory where food was to be found: hunting grounds, or pastureland and fields where crops were grown. From then until today, the principal motive for the wars of humankind has been the desire of one group of people to acquire, by force of violence, territories belonging to other groups, or to defend territories held by the group.

What have human beings waged war over, throughout history and prehistory? Over territory? Certainly and frequently. Over religion? Of course—with the God of the tribe or people leading the hosts of warriors.

And wars have been waged over women, race, skin coloring, language, honor, prestige, interests, vengeance, xenophobia, revenge, inheritances, dynasties, ideology, greed, gold, trade, natural resources, slaves, freedom, equality, enslavement, independence, control of land, sea, and air space, the whims of rulers and the madness of leaders. Thus, war became a permanent phenomenon in human social life. No period of history or archaeology is without its wars. This is true throughout the world, on every continent and in every era.

The instinct of survival, coupled with the "devisings of man's mind (which) are evil from his youth," has led to wars among human beings. Even when the instinct of survival is satisfied and the fear of hunger has dissipated, the powerful impulses of evil and destruction remain. Moreover, many wars have been given further "justification": if not war over food, then war over principles; if not war over survival, then war over "honor"; if not war over physical territories, then war over ideological areas.

From these facts, a deadly equation may be deduced: the instinct for survival + the instinct for evil = war. This equation has remained constant throughout the ages, with the exception of a single variable: the means by which wars among humans are actually waged. While this variable—weapons and war technology—continues to "develop" and "improve" with time, the purpose of war has never changed: slaughter of the enemy.

The earliest, most primitive, most animal means of war involved the use of parts of the body for fighting and defense. Arms and fists were used for hitting, fingernails for scratching and tearing, feet for kicking and trampling, and teeth for biting.

Somewhere in the fog of the distant past, humankind "developed" an additional, revolutionary technology of war, based on the combination of brains, eyes, and hands wielding instruments of destruction. The latter began as clubs, followed by sharp-pointed stones thrown at the target—that is, at the enemy. This was done through the joint efforts of brains that thought and planned, eyes that spotted the target and measured the range, muscle energy that moved the throwing arm, and the stone missile that (if all went according to plan) struck and killed the enemy.

Today, at the end of the twentieth century, the most sophisticated technological armament is the intercontinental ballistic missile with hydrogen warhead. The difference between this missile and the primitive pointed rock is quantitative only. The human brain has been augmented by computers; the eyes, by optical instruments that home the missile on its target. Muscle energy has been replaced by powerful fuel energy. And instead of the stone or arrow, which struck and killed one human enemy at a time, the hydrogen missile can strike and destroy an entire city, killing hundreds of thousands of people and all animal and plant life adjacent to the target zone. The quantitative ratio is 1:1,000,000—and the difference in principle is precisely zero.

Is this the balance of humanity? Is this the sum total of thousands of years of culture, religion, and civilization? Are the smokestacks of Auschwitz and the mushroom cloud over Hiroshima to be the criteria? Are they to be the thundering answer that, indeed, "man has no preeminence above a beast"; that the sum total of humanity is equal to the sum total of its wars and nothing more?

Yet there is another criterion: the desire to cease making war—in other words, the desire for peace. This desire is the potential for good within human society—a potential that humankind has never stopped striving to fulfill.

In this connection, let us note a verse from the Book of Isaiah, describing God:

I form light and create darkness, I make peace and create evil. (45:7)

The noteworthy point of this passage is the contrast drawn between peace and evil—denoting that war is evil. Peace, then, may be equated to light and goodness; war, to darkness and evil—and these opposites have been linked in our world throughout time.

The inevitable struggle of good against evil, which has characterized human culture throughout its existence, means that peace must struggle against the warlike, murderous instincts with which humankind and society are imbued. Furthermore, in this struggle, the balance of forces is unequal. The instinct of war is primordial: Darkness existed before light, war before peace. The struggle against war is the struggle against the evil element of human nature. At best, peace is achieved as an interlude between wars, a pause to gather strength and weapons in preparation for the war to come.

At first glance, human history seems to be on the side of evil: Such peaceful interludes as have occurred have been short and inevitably washed away by renewed rivers of blood. Nevertheless, the proponents of light and hope for peace have never given up—not even those whose own generations were not graced with peace.

Let us follow this struggle in the Bible. Amazingly, the terms *war* and *peace* are not mentioned in the first eleven chapters of the Book of Genesis, which supposedly sum up all human history up to the time of Abraham. These chapters deal with the creation of the world; the "devisings of man's mind"; the fate of humankind on earth; the division of early human beings into hunters, shepherds, and farmers; the establishment of settlements. The concepts of war and peace apparently did not yet exist.

The account of Noah and the Flood, though, states:

> And the earth was filled with lawlessness . . . for all flesh had corrupted its ways on the earth. (GENESIS 6:11–12)

It is quite probable that this lawlessness and corruption included incessant warfare among human beings.

The first sign of peace in the Bible is that of the olive branch brought back by the dove to Noah's Ark. This is a message of peace between God and humanity, God's promise that, although "the devisings of man's mind are evil from his youth," humankind will not be wiped off the face of the earth. God makes a covenant with humanity and with the entire living world, and gives them a second sign, seemingly also a sign of peace: the rainbow.

The actual words *war* and *peace*, however, do not appear until the first Biblical dispute occurs in the time of Abraham: a dispute between Abraham and Lot, uncle and nephew, both heads of large families of shepherds. This is a classic dispute over territory—in this case, grazing land:

> So that the land could not support them staying together; for their possessions were so great that they could not remain to-

gether. And there was quarreling between the herdsmen of Abram's cattle and those of Lot's cattle. (GENESIS 13:6–7)

This is a dispute, a strife; it is not yet war. No blood has been spilled, no humans killed. Abraham finds a way to settle this territorial dispute, which could so easily have become a war: the way of compromise. This, the first compromise mentioned in the Bible, is a signpost pointing to a highway of non-violent solutions in conflicts between individuals, groups, and peoples. Abraham says to Lot:

Let there be no strife between you and me, between my herdsmen and yours for we are kinsmen. Is not the whole land before you? Let us separate: if you go north I will go south; and if you go south, I will go north. (13:8–9)

The principle of compromise, then, is: I will not have it all, and neither will you. We will make an equitable settlement between us and keep the peace.

The first real war described in the Bible *(Genesis 14:1–2)* also takes place in Abraham's time. The opposing sides in this war are actually two coalitions: one of four kings, headed by the king of Shinar; the other of five, headed by the king of Sodom. Here we already find a listing of the procedures of war—conquerors and rebellious conquered, battles "set in array," victors and vanquished. Here the victors already take spoils and prisoners; and, as a result, there are refugees:

[The invaders] seized all the wealth of Sodom and Gomorrah and all their provisions, and went their way. They also took Lot, the son of Abram's brother, and his possessions, and departed; for he settled in Sodom. (14:11–12)

Yet—and this may, perhaps, be considered symbolic— Abraham the Hebrew does not take part in this war. Only after one of the refugees informs him that his nephew Lot and his family have been taken prisoner by the victors does he lead forth his 318 "trained men" in pursuit of the victors, to free his relatives from captivity. In a night battle, he attacks the enemy and restores his nephew, his family, and their property to their hometown, Sodom.

In this war, Abraham does not try to acquire anything from

anyone, neither territory nor property. All he wants to do is to perform the humanitarian action of redeeming prisoners. When the king of Sodom proposes to pay Abraham for his assistance, he refuses categorically—he did not engage in warfare to become rich.

The concept of *war* and *warrior*, therefore, remained inapplicable to Abraham; nor, with the passage of time, did it apply to Isaac or to Jacob. Admittedly, these founding fathers did defend themselves when necessary. Jacob went so far as to prepare for a violent struggle with Esau. Yet they waged no actual war and shed no blood.

Immediately following the story of the first war and Abraham's involvement therein comes the first Biblical mention of the word *peace*. This occurs when God concludes a covenant with Abraham and informs him that his seed will inherit the Promised Land:

> You shall go to your fathers in peace. (15:15)

However, the meaning of the word "peace" here is simply quiet, tranquility, security. "Peace," in this context, does not yet denote the opposite of war.

Peace, in the full meaning of the word, is only mentioned in the days of Isaac, following his severe dispute with the Philistines and their king, Abimelech. Once again, the dispute is based on pastureland, and also on wells that Isaac's shepherds had dug and the Philistines' shepherds had stopped up. Yet the Bible adds another reason for the strife: the Philistines' jealousy of Isaac and his property.

This severe dispute also ends without bloodshed: Isaac simply moves out of the areas of contention and finds new grazing grounds and water sources for his flocks in Beersheba, east of the disputed areas. The Philistines, headed by King Abimelech and his captain Phicol, come to Isaac and ask to conclude a covenant with him, reminding him that they had previously treated him peacefully and done "nothing but good" to him. The two rivals conclude a covenant of peace:

> Early in the morning, they exchanged oaths. Isaac then bade them farewell, and they departed from him in peace. (26:31)

This is a true peace, anchored in an oath and a covenant. In the generations that followed the descent of the Hebrew tribes into Egypt, they became slaves. For many years their entire lives were limited to the bitter taste of enslavement and the pain of their oppressors' whips. Only after the Exodus from Egypt and the decades of wandering in the desert did the tribes begin the difficult and complex process of transformation into a nation with the goal of acquiring land by force.

Even before reaching Canaan, the Hebrews began to clash and fight with peoples on the East Bank of the Jordan River: the Amalekites, the Amorites, the Moabites, the Midianites, and others. These were wars in the full sense of the word— bloody, cruel, and merciless. Indeed, in some of them, each side vowed to annihilate the other.

These wars were only a forerunner of the wars that the Hebrews would have to face en route to conquering the Land of Canaan and its peoples, on the West Bank of the Jordan. Slowly, through one war after another, the People of Israel began to acquire an attitude toward war *per se*, and to formulate a sort of code of war, including martial procedures and customs. Bearing this code, Joshua led his army across the Jordan and launched the conquest of the land in blood and fire.

From that conquest until Bar-Kochba's revolt about 1,500 years later, the Jews inhabited their own land, in an atmosphere of near-incessant war. War, in fact, became accepted as the status quo, and periods of calm were considered exceptional. Concerning those short periods, which were not even real peace, the Book of Judges states: "And the land had rest forty years"—meaning four decades of remission between one war and the next.

The Jews fought many wars. They fought against the peoples of Canaan: the Canaanites themselves, the Hivites, the Jebusites, the Perizzites, the Amorites, the Girgashites, and the Hittites. They fought war after war with the Amalekites and the Edomites, the Moabites and the Midianites to the east, and with the Philistines to the west. They fought with the Zidonians and the Arameans to the north; with the great empires of the ancient East—Egypt, Assyria, and Babylonia; and with the great empires that came out of the West—the Greeks and Romans. And, as if this was not enough, they fought each other, time and time again, in cruel civil wars, in the days of the Judges and the Kings.

These wars of the Jews were no different, either in nature or in course, from the wars fought by other peoples in corresponding periods. Most of them, like wars in general, were cruel, bloody territorial wars, making use of the weapons, tactics, and strategies common to the times. Innumerable dead and wounded were left on the field, with many captives taken and sold as slaves. These wars exposed all of the major characteristics of human nature: brotherhood of arms and individual courage—alongside the cunning and trickery of war; self-sacrifice, perseverance, consistency, and sometimes even mercy—alongside the bestial instincts of cruelty, murder, torture, rape, robbery, looting, torment of the living, and desecration of the dead. And always the cries of the victors and the howling of the vanquished; always the fear and terror, the moans of the wounded, and the bitter weeping of the widows and orphans. All of these are described in the Bible, in powerful images of plot and narrative.

Yet these wars were but little different from the wars of the Greeks as depicted by Homer, or from the wars of the Assyrians and the Babylonians recounted in the epic of Gilgamesh. These wars scarcely differed from the wars of the pharoahs engraved on the temple columns at Luxor, or from the wars of India and China—or, indeed, from any wars at any time and place throughout history.

In most every war, battle is waged in the name of some God—of the God of each side's tribe, or city, or kingdom, or faith. So it was with the Hebrews. They considered their God to be a God of war, and frequently referred to Him as "the Lord of hosts." They waited for a sign from Him before engaging in combat. They sang songs of battle and songs of victory, bewailed defeat and destruction, eulogized the fallen, and mourned the dead. In all of this, they were no different from other nations.

The authors of the Great Book were well aware of the

horrors of war. Many of them experienced such horrors personally. A passage vividly expressing these horrors in the form of a dreadful curse appears in the Book of Leviticus:

> I will bring a sword against you to wreak vengeance for the covenant; and if you withdraw into your cities, I will send pestilence among you; and you shall be delivered into enemy hands. . . . I will make the land desolate, so that your enemies who settle in it shall be appalled by it. And I will scatter you among the nations, and I will unsheath the sword against you. Your land shall become a desolation and your cities shall become a ruin. . . . As for those of you who survive, I will cast a faintness into their hearts in the land of their enemies. The sound of a driven leaf shall put them to flight. . . . (26:25, 32–33, 36)

The books of the Prophets include a number of chilling passages on war and its destiny. Here is one, given by Jeremiah:

> For death has climbed through our windows, has entered our fortresses, to cut off babes from the streets, young men from the squares. Speak thus—says the Lord: The carcasses of men shall lie like dung upon the fields, like sheaves behind the reaper, with none to pick them up. (9:20–21)

This, then, is war. But what was the Jews' attitude toward peace, and how did it develop, during the Biblical period? The Torah does not discuss the subject to any great extent. The people wandering in the desert readies itself for war, conquest, and settlement of the conquered lands. Its leaders and lawgivers know that war will be cruel indeed and prepare the people to face this fact. Yet the very code of war contains the seeds of the concepts of mercy and peace. In Deuteronomy *(20:5–8)* the legislator of this code allows for the release of several kinds of warriors from military service: one who has built a new house, or planted a vineyard without reaping its fruit, or betrothed a wife.

Even the naturally harsh laws of war include a note of consideration and mercy for individuals, of admission and acceptance of human weaknesses and fears. And, in those same laws, appears for the first time a note of peace:

> When you approach a town to attack it, you shall offer it terms of peace. (DEUTERONOMY 20:10)

The Biblical legislator thus calls the warriors' attention to an entirely different kind of alternative. Instead of besieging the city, attacking it, destroying it, and killing its population, the besiegers offer the besieged a chance to stay alive—though, admittedly, not much more than that, as the next verse shows:

> If it responds peaceably and lets you in, all the people present there shall serve you at forced labor. (20:11)

This is not yet true peace, and is certainly not peace between equals. Nevertheless, it is the first step on a road that leads to something other than a war of out-and-out annihilation.

Deuteronomy tells us that the Hebrews, in their approach to King Sihon, did precisely this:

> Then I sent messengers from the wilderness of Kedemoth to King Sihon of Heshbon with an offer of peace, as follows, "Let me pass through your country. I will keep strictly to the highway, turning off neither to the right nor to the left. What food I eat you will supply for money, and what water I drink you will furnish for money; just let me pass through." (2:26–28)

The messengers tell King Sihon that similar appeals of peace toward the Edomites and the Moabites were answered in the affirmative, allowing the People of Israel to pass through their countries in peace. Sihon, however, does not agree, and war breaks out.

Naturally, the Torah also expresses longing for peace in the future. Immediately following the blessing of plenty that God promises the People of Israel, provided only that the people observe His laws and commandments, appears the blessing of peace:

> I will grant peace in the land, and you shall lie down untroubled by anyone; I will give the land respite from vicious beasts, and no sword shall cross your land. (LEVITICUS 26:6)

And the Priestly Blessing—a very important part of the Jewish prayer service—says:

> The Lord bestow His favor upon you and grant you peace. (NUMBERS 6:26)

This blessing is given both to every individual and to the entire people. Here, the longed-for peace is the antithesis of war; peace is the desired state of goodness and blessing.

The westward crossing of the Jordan River by the Hebrew warriors, led by their general, Joshua son of Nun, ushered in a period devoted to conquest and settlement. This period, with its ups and downs, its victories and defeats, went on until the time of King David—and even then, wars did not cease.

The period, which lasted many generations, was dominated almost entirely by war, with hardly any breathing space for peace. The war was very cruel, with neither mercy nor refuge, and captives were rarely taken. That was how the Hebrews treated their enemies in the days of Joshua and the Judges. This attitude was apparently quite mutual, with the various enemies giving precisely the same treatment to the Hebrews. It was war without compromise, war of annihilation.

With horrifying simplicity, the Bible relates the initial phases of the conquest of the Land of Israel, and what occurred following the collapse of the wall of Jericho and the taking of the city by Joshua and his troops:

> They exterminated everything in the city with the sword: both man and woman, young and old, ox and sheep and ass. (JOSHUA 6:21)

Joshua and his army continually wage war. The enemy casualties in those wars are summed up by the historian:

> They cut down their populations with the sword until they exterminated them; they did not spare a soul. (11:14)

Only in one exceptional case does Joshua make peace with a delegation from a Canaanite people—the Gibeonites; and even then, that peace results from the Gibeonites' trickery. Disguising themselves as if they came from a far country, they ask Joshua to make peace with them:

> Joshua established friendship with them; he made a pact with them to spare their lives, and the chieftains of the community gave them their oath. (9:15)

From this and the following verses, we learn that, just as there are laws of war, there are also laws for making peace, and that a sworn covenant of peace cannot be broken. In this instance, several days after swearing peace with the Gibeonites, the People of Israel realize that the Gibeonites had deceived them, and that they were living among them—in other words, that the Israelites should have fought and destroyed them. The Israelites complain to the elders of the community for having concluded peace with the Gibeonites; but the elders answer:

> We have sworn unto them by the Lord, the God of Israel; therefore we cannot touch them. (9:19)

Joshua saves the Gibeonites from the People of Israel, who would have killed them; but the sort of peace and life that he and the elders grant the Gibeonites is far from desirable:

> And they became hewers of wood and drawers of water for the whole community. (9:21)

In the period of the Judges, the conquests went on. The settlement did not always take place according to plan. Enemies to the west, east, north, and south repeatedly attacked the Tribes of Israel with much bloodshed on all sides. Wars broke out among the tribes themselves. The land was "empty, and void, and waste," with only brief cease-fires and truces interspersed between wars.

Only a few times throughout the period of the Judges did the light of peace shine forth. One of these occurs after God reveals Himself to Gideon and commands him to save his people from Midian. God promises:

> . . . All is well; have no fear, you shall not die. So Gideon built there an altar to the Lord and called it "Adonai-shalom" (that is, the Lord is peace). . . . (JUDGES 6:23–24)

This juxtaposition of the name of God with the word *peace* was later adopted by the Sages of Israel as one of the foundations of their great doctrine of peace:

> Peace is great, as the name of the Holy One, Blessed be He, is called peace. (LEVITICUS RABBA 9:9)

Peace is mentioned again in the Book of Judges, as a solution to cruel internecine war. Following the incident of the concubine in Gibeah and the subsequent war launched against the Tribe of Benjamin by the other tribes, the People of Israel tires of war and proclaims peace with the children of Benjamin.

In the days of Samuel, judge and prophet, the People of Israel was still afflicted by wars, the most difficult and severe of which was that with the Philistines. Yet, for the first time following the period of Joshua and the Judges, we read that a covenant of peace was concluded between Israel and one of its old enemies, the Amorites *(2 Samuel 7:14).*

Naturally, that peace was temporary, partial, and separate. Not much later, the People of Israel cried out to Samuel, asking him to appoint a king, to lead them and fight their wars. That king, Saul, ushered in the period of kingly rule in Israel.

Yet the wars did not cease. Saul fought through all his life and died in battle. Moreover, a bitter war of inheritance was instituted in his day when Saul, one of the tragic figures of the Bible, was stricken with unbridled jealousy of the young David. This war—called "the long war" in the Bible—between the progressively stronger House of David and the progressively weaker House of Saul continued even after the elder's death.

In one of the battles of that war, Abner, the great and glorious captain of the House of Saul, kills Asahel, younger brother of Joab, David's captain. Joab and his men pursue Abner and the dreadful war goes on. The two camps eventually confront each other, one camp on one hill and the other on a hill opposite, ready to continue the bloodshed. And then Abner, the tough veteran soldier, calls to his comrade-and-enemy Joab:

> . . . Must the sword devour forever? You know how bitterly it's going to end! How long will you delay ordering your troops to stop the pursuit of their kinsmen? (2 SAMUEL 2:26)

With Abner's appeal, the war comes to a halt—but, alas, not for long. The Biblical tragedy soon continues, with the sword of revenge not returning to its scabbard until Abner is treacherously killed by Joab. Years later, Joab is killed by the sword of Benaiah, son of Jehoiada, the captain of King Solomon. Yet the cry of "Must the sword devour forever?", first sounded by Abner, becomes the clarion call of the Prophets of Israel in their challenge against all forms of war.

The first of these prophets is Nathan—the same Nathan who dared call out "That man is you!" against King David, accusing him of having arranged the death of Uriah the Hittite in battle. This prophet, years later, is again summoned to King David. By now the king has had enough of war and victory. His throne is secure; his tribes are united; he has attained most, if not all, of his objectives:

> The Lord had granted him safety from all the enemies around him. (2 SAMUEL 7:1)

Now the king is eager to achieve his most fervently desired aim: To establish a beautiful temple to the God of his people, in his capital, Jerusalem.

To this end, the king consults the prophet, and the prophet consults his God. God's answer, however, is completely negative: God does not wish David to establish His house. Accordingly, speaking through Nathan, He informs the king that not he, but his son, will build the temple.

In the Book of 2 Samuel, where we first read of this astonishing refusal, the narrator gives no reason for it. However, in 1 Chronicles, David himself tells his son Solomon why Nathan, in God's name, refused him this privilege:

> My son, I wanted to build a House for the name of the Lord my God. But the word of the Lord came to me, saying, You have shed much blood and fought great battles; you shall not build a House for My name for you have shed much blood on the earth in My sight. But you will have a son who will be a man at rest for I will give him rest from all his enemies on all sides; Solomon will be his name and I shall confer peace and quiet on Israel in his time. He will build a house for My name.... (22:7–10)

It is a dramatic turning point in the faith of Israel, and in its prophets' attitude to the concepts of war and peace. God prefers the "man of peace" to the "man of war," even though the latter is the greatest of Israel's kings: David, the admired hero and "sweet singer of Israel." The reason for this preference is utterly clear: The shedding of blood and the waging of war have rendered David unfit to establish the house of God. Thus, for the first time, war—any and all war, even those of David himself—is perceived as essentially evil, and peace as essentially good. Moreover, this perception is given validity by the word of God.

This solitary dove of peace, with a fresh olive leaf in its beak, is sent out by Nathan the Prophet over a cruel, "hawkish" world. It does not yet presage a spring of peace—neither for Israel nor for the surrounding nations. It will be shot at, and wounded, again and again for many years. Yet, only a few generations later, Nathan will be joined by a mighty chorus of prophets proclaiming peace to Israel and to the world.

Solomon, meanwhile, fulfills the hope of the prophet and the people. With great sophistication and success, he manages to combine military, economic, and commercial power with peace-oriented diplomacy, even to the extent of marrying the daughters of near and distant kings. Thus, he succeeds in preserving the united kingdom of Judah and Israel left him by his father, David:

> And he had peace on all his borders roundabout. All the days of Solomon, Judah and Israel from Dan to Beersheba dwelt in safety, everyone under his own vine and under his own fig tree. (1 KINGS 5:4–5)

Solomon makes peace with his great neighbor, Egypt, and marries the pharaoh's daughter. He does the same with his important neighbor to the north, the leader of trade and shipping, mighty Tyre. A covenant of peace and trade is concluded between Solomon and Hiram, King of Tyre. The two monarchs launch ships to the ends of the Mediterranean and Red seas. Solomon develops land and marine trading on a large scale, and reaches a zenith of international peace and brotherhood with the visit of the Queen of Sheba from southern Arabia.

Naturally, Solomon also carries out his great aim: the construction of a Temple in Jerusalem. On the night of the dedication of the Temple, God appears to Solomon and says:

Ask, what shall I grant you? (2 CHRONICLES 1:7)

Solomon's beautiful answer is:

Grant me then the wisdom and the knowledge to lead this people, for who can govern Your great people? (1:10)

And the Lord replies:

Because you want this, and have not asked for wealth, property, and glory, nor have you asked for the life of your enemy, or long life yourself, but you have asked for the wisdom and the knowledge to be able to govern My people over whom I have made you king, wisdom and knowledge are granted to you, and I will grant you also wealth, property, and glory, the like of which no king before you has had, nor shall after you have. (1:11–12)

Note that, because Solomon does not pray for the death of his enemies, he is given to attain the exalted status of "man of rest" and "man of peace."

Obviously, historians and scholars should not indulge themselves in guessing or wondering "What would have happened if. . . ?" Nevertheless, we others may yet ask ourselves: "What would have happened if Rehoboam, the foolish son, had not ascended to the throne after the death of King Solomon?"

As the Bible has it, members of the people approached Rehoboam after his coronation and asked him to lighten the tax burden (as citizens have asked their rulers to do from time immemorial). Instead of dealing pleasantly with them, he threatened to impose additional taxes and "to chastise them with scorpions." Ten of the Twelve Tribes, led by Jeroboam, rebelled against the king; the united kingdom was divided into the kingdoms of Israel and Judah. Yet, had Solomon been succeeded by a wiser, more farsighted, and more peace-loving king—a king more skilled at strengthening the loosened links between the northern and southern tribes—the kingdom would have remained strong and united, and the course of Jewish history could well have been unrecognizably altered.

As it was, the united kingdom was split in two. The People and Tribes of Israel were divided. For the next two centuries, they lived in two neighboring Jewish kingdoms: the Kingdom of Israel in the north, with Samaria as its capital; and the Kingdom of Judah in the south, with its capital of Jerusalem. The two parts of the people, each with its own royal house, developed different—and frequently divergent—interests. At times, they fought bloody wars between themselves; in other periods, they allied themselves to strike at a third party. The Kingdom of Israel, larger in land area, was more conspicuous in its social instability and frequent changes of government, marked by intrigue, rebellion, and murderous wars of inheritance.

In the time of Jeroboam, son of Joash—that is, Jeroboam II, king of Israel, one of that nation's greatest king-conquerors—a comet appeared on the spiritual and social horizon. That comet was Amos, the herdsman and dresser of sycamores from Judah who came to Israel to prophesy.

Amos had no interest in the conquests of King Jeroboam and his army. He was, rather, appalled at the terrible oppression of the poorer classes at the hands of the king, his generals and ministers, and the wealthy. Unimpressed by the apparently good state of foreign affairs, he cried out for internal social justice. To him, the prevailing customs of violence, robbery, and theft heralded the destruction of the kingdom; accordingly, he prophesied its utter ruin unless it mended its ways.

The word *peace* appears in none of Amos' prophecies. As far as he was concerned, the most important social value was that of justice as we have discussed in the chapter on that subject. To Amos, any society devoid of justice and ruled by evil, no matter what its status—even the largest, richest, and mightiest of kingdoms—was a society rotten from within and doomed to collapse and be overthrown.

Hosea, the next prophet after Amos, also prophesied in the Kingdom of Israel. Like Amos, he saw the awful distortion of his society and prophesied the terrible punishments of destruction and exile. Yet Hosea also pronounces words of comfort for his unfortunate people, whom he compares to a treacherous loved one. In the future, prophesies Hosea, the nation will repent of its evil ways and return to ways of righteousness and justice, lovingkindness and mercy. Then, he promises in God's name, peace will come:

I will also banish the bow, the sword, and war from the land. Thus I will let them lie down in safety. (2:20)

The furious prophecies of Amos and the punishment foreseen by Hosea came true within a very few generations. The Assyrian great power descended upon Israel in battle. Ephemeral alliances concluded between Israel and neighboring nations proved to no avail, as did attempts to form an alliance with the Egyptian great power. All of the small, inconsequential "games of kings" in Samaria could not withstand the onslaught of the Assyrian War. The kingdom was destroyed and its population exiled, and the doom of the Kingdom of Israel was sealed.

The Kingdom of Judah was now the solitary kingdom representing the People of Israel in its homeland. But it was a dismembered kingdom, small by all criteria: area, population, military strength, and economic power. Even when this or that king managed to conquer an extra bit of land and annex it to Judah, the kingdom remained small. In the eyes of the great powers—Assyria and Babylonia, Egypt and Persia—it was no more than a statelet, a sort of city-state, composed of Jerusalem and its surrounding towns and villages, not much different from Ashdod or Gaza or Edom.

At times, Judah was somewhat of a nuisance to these powers in their vast, sweeping movements to the north and south. At times, it was a thorn in their flesh—a thorn that had to be pulled out by the roots. The name of Judah appears in inscriptions of victory, engraved in the temples of the pharaohs and the palaces of Nineveh and Babylon, as one of a list of similar miserable nations that various monarchs had happened to conquer, destroy, and send its king and nobles into exile.

Nor was the lot of the Kingdom of Judah improved by the

quality of its rulers, descendants of the House of David, who ascended to the throne after Solomon. Most of them were mean and narrow-minded petty tyrants whose wars had neither purpose nor object. They concluded short-lived alliances in unfortunate attempts to sow discord between the great powers. They were alternately bribed by their great neighbors to the north and south—who, when unsuccessful in bribing them, would periodically overrun their kingdoms. Through most of this period, the kingdom was in fact controlled by corrupt ministers and rotten nobles who sucked the very marrow of the poor and lower classes.

True, there were some exceptional kings who "did that which was good in the sight of the Lord," and who attempted to achieve social reform and to act with some measure of good statesmanship. These, however, were only the exceptions that proved the rule.

And yet, over only a few generations, the Kingdom of Judah gave rise to spiritual giants who set their indelible seal on the People of Judah—the Jewish People. These were difficult and bitter generations for Judah; yet, for prophecy, they comprised a Golden Age. From Isaiah to Malachi, last of the Prophets, these seers lifted their reproofs, songs, proverbs, and discourses to heights unparalleled before or since, to this very day.

These Prophets influenced not only their own generation, but the ethics of generations far into the future—both among the Jewish People and throughout the world—more than any other group of persons in world history. Who would have remembered the Judean kings Uzziah, Jotham, Ahaz, and Hezekiah, mentioned in the Book of Isaiah, as having ruled in Jerusalem during that prophet's time? Yet today, millions of people read and study about those kings—for no other reason than that they lived and reigned in the days of Isaiah. Who would have noticed the Judean ministers Elnathan, son of Achbor, and Gemariah, son of Shaphan, had they not been mentioned in the Book of Jeremiah as having had a share in that prophet's bitter fate?

From the earliest days of the Kingdom of Judah, from the time of David himself, we know that there were prophets in

Jerusalem. We have mentioned Nathan; we read of Gad the Seer and Huldah the Prophetess; and we know that Amos, although he prophesied in Israel, was born in Judah. But it was Isaiah who led the first rank of prophets of Judah. In Isaiah, we see a new kind of prophet.

The common denominator of all of Israel's Prophets was a fervent belief in One God, Creator of heaven and earth, who revealed Himself to the Prophets and entrusted each of them with a mission to their people—a message that must be transmitted to the people. Jeremiah describes this message in these words:

> But [His word] was like a raging fire in my heart, in my bones. (20:9)

Yet nevertheless, the attitudes reflected in the words and actions of the various prophets differ widely. The Prophets may be classified into four categories: prophet-legislators, prophet-judges, prophet-social reformers, and prophet-statesmen. For example, Moses, father of prophets, was also the Great Legislator; Deborah and Samuel were prophet-judges; Amos and Hosea were social reformers. And Isaiah was prophet-statesman *par excellence.*

Naturally, this definition is somewhat of a generalization. Moses, for example, was a leader and a social reformer as well as a statesman; but, first and foremost, he was a legislator.

Isaiah, perhaps the greatest of the Written Prophets, was, of course, also a social reformer. However, he was primarily a great statesman, in the most modern meaning of the word. The finest politician of his people and time, he was blessed with vast knowledge, great understanding, and correct judgment, not only concerning the state of his own society but also regarding the entire political world of his day—both the courts of the kings of Judah and the deeds and intentions of the surrounding rulers and great powers. Moreover, Isaiah, by virtue of his status, also intervened actively in advising and guiding the kings who ruled Judah in his time. Not always—in fact, hardly ever—did those kings listen to him and act according to his counsel. Yet his words had some influence in fateful state decisions.

In the first two chapters of his book, Isaiah sums up the main points of his doctrine. Chapter 1 is a short and frightening summation of the injustice, corruption, and social wrongs existing in Judah, and the dreadful punishment due to that country. Chapter 2, by contrast, is a vision of national and universal peace in the future:

> In the end of days, the Mount of the Lord's House shall stand firm above the mountains and tower above the hills; and all the nations shall gaze on it with joy. And the many peoples shall go and say: "Come, let us go up to the mount of the Lord, to the House of the God of Jacob; that He may instruct us in His ways, and that we may walk in His paths." For instruction shall come forth from Zion, the word of the Lord from Jerusalem. Thus He will judge among the nations and arbitrate for the many peoples, and they shall beat their swords into plowshares and their spears into pruning hooks: Nation shall not take up sword against nation; they shall never again know war. (2:2–4)

All at once, dramatically and with no warning to the listener or reader, the prophet launches himself out of Zion, his capital city and that of his people, to a lofty height, from where he can look down on the entire world and all humanity and predict the future of all humankind.

This is a sort of return to the days of Genesis, to the age of the most ancient ancestors of the human race. Isaiah's prophecy foresees a sort of return to the charmed past, when all of humanity spoke one language. In those legendary days, all humankind was united; there were no tribes or races. The world was:

> . . . one people with one language for all. . . . (GENESIS 11:6)

All these persons were united in their will to build themselves:

> . . . a city, and a tower with its top in the sky. . . . (11:4)

Moreover, they actually began to implement this mighty plan, in Babel. Only God, who did not want to give unlimited control of His world to human beings, was able to stop them, by confounding their language and scattering them abroad upon the face of the earth.

Thus it was at "the beginning of days"; and now Isaiah prophecies that, "in the end of days" there will once again be a city to which "all nations will flow"—the city of Jerusalem. Once again there will be a tower. But, this time, it will be a tower of light and justice; not a Tower of Babel, but a Tower of Zion:

... a light of nations. (49:6)

This worldwide wonder will, of course, come to pass only after the inhabitants of Zion and Jerusalem have cleansed and purified themselves and have learned to seek justice—in other words, after their light has first begun to shine upon themselves, their society, and their people.

Thus, Isaiah became a universal prophet, a prophet for all who dwell throughout the world. For when Isaiah, one of the noble scholars of Jerusalem, speaks of "all nations," he means precisely that. He is well acquainted with the location, size, and importance of the nations of his time. When he speaks of all nations and peoples, his reference is to all of humanity, irrespective of language, race, or culture.

And what is the most important message—in essence, the only message—that God will teach all nations and peoples? What are God's ways and paths, along which all humankind must walk? The message is simple: peace, peace for all, peace for all time. If it is true that God:

... imposes peace in His height (JOB 25:2)

—then the vision of the future is that peace will also prevail throughout the entire earth.

War is considered by Isaiah to be the root of all evil. When the weapons of war, which destroy the earth and its peoples, are transformed into tools that work and fertilize the land; when the doctrine and ways of war will no longer be learned and so will cease to be a permanent phenomenon in human life—then the light will overcome the darkness, and good will vanquish evil.

If we return to the question "Must the sword devour forever?", Isaiah's vision provides a thundering answer—and the answer is "No! Not forever!" And, even if the day of peace is far away, it will surely come—for this is the will of God, as foreseen by His prophet.

So, more than 2,500 years ago, in a small state surrounded by enemies from without and corroded with discord and corruption from within, the first glimpse arose of a new and beautiful sight, a new vision of international peace, centered upon the capital of that state and that nation, once it has purified itself of sin and adopted peace as its great goal.

From the time of Isaiah's vision until this very day, the sentence beginning "And they shall beat their swords into plowshares" has stood as the watchword and the banner of all those who long for peace throughout the world. Those great words have been carved in stone and inscribed on scrolls; painted, illustrated, and sung; proclaimed by statesmen and shouted by battle-weary soldiers.

It would appear that today, at the end of the twentieth century, we are still as far from Isaiah's vision as our ancestors were in the day when it was first voiced. Humankind has not followed the paths of the Torah, of which the Book of Proverbs states that:

> Her ways are pleasant ways and all her paths, peaceful. (3:17)

Isaiah, following the crescendo that opens his words, does not abandon the subject of peace. In a prophecy concerning the future of the House of David, he foresees a king of Judah who will carry the torch of peace in his country and throughout the world:

> For a child has been born to us, a son has been given to us. And authority has settled on his shoulders. He has been named "the Mighty God is planning grace; the Eternal Father, prince of peace"—In token of abundant authority and of peace without limit, upon David's throne and kingdom, that it may be firmly established in justice and in equity.... (9:5–6)

Again and again, the prophet stresses the indissoluble link between peace on one hand and justice and righteousness on the other. Once more, he thrusts upward from his first words, "For a child has been born to us," to a height of vision, from where he can observe a new world, a world of peace, encompassing not only humankind, but all that lives:

But a shoot shall grow out of the stump of Jesse, a twig shall sprout from his stock. The spirit of the Lord shall alight upon him: A spirit of wisdom and insight, a spirit of counsel and valor, a spirit of devotion and reverence for the Lord. He shall sense the truth by his reverence for the Lord: He shall not judge by what his eyes behold, nor decide by what his ears perceive; thus he shall judge the poor with equity, and decide with justice for the lowly of the land. He shall strike down a land with the rod of his mouth and slay the wicked with the breath of his lips. Justice shall be the girdle of his loins, and faithfulness the girdle of his waist. The wolf shall dwell with the lamb, the leopard shall lie down with the kid; the calf, the beast of prey, and the fatling together with a little boy to herd them. . . . The earth shall be filled with devotion to the Lord as water covers the sea. In that day, the stock of Jesse that has remained standing shall become a standard to peoples—Nations shall seek his counsel and his abode shall be honored. (11:1–6, 9–10)

Isaiah reaches an additional zenith when he comforts all of humanity and all nations, prophesying a shining future for all peoples, when God:

. . . will destroy death forever. (25:8)

And when death has ceased—it seems that the prophet's reference here is to murder and war, rather than death in the strictly biological sense—tears will be wiped from all faces; for the tears of all who weep are identical in composition and saltiness. The tears of bereaved fathers, of widows and orphans, of everyone who mourns, will all be wiped away.

One might think that Isaiah was a sort of utopian prophet, with his head in the clouds and his eyes on the end of days. In fact, however, he was an incomparably realistic statesman, with his political feet firmly rooted in the soil of his day's political reality. More than kings and ministers, Isaiah was aware of the international situation prevailing in his region, with the crushing might of the Assyrian Empire to the north and the treacherous intrigues of the Egyptian Empire to the south. He knew that both those empires yearned to overrun the surrounding small nations and kingdoms, and that Judah, located between the two great powers, was one of those kingdoms. He realized that each of those empires sought to gain control of this strategic buffer zone—whether directly, by conquest, or indirectly, by bribery and diplomacy.

Sooner than the kings and advisors of Judah, Isaiah knew the utter worthlessness and unimportance of the temporary, ephemeral covenants and alliances forged between the small nations against the great powers. He knew that once the mighty armies of Assyria or Egypt appeared on the horizon, none of the little kings and their ineffectual forces would be able to withstand them.

To keep Judah from being wiped out—like its sister-nation Israel, which was destroyed precisely because of such a petty, fumbling policy—Isaiah demands absolute non-intervention in the game between the great powers. He demands that Judah concentrate on its own internal weaknesses and diseases, and that it make sure that these are cured before branching out into international relations. In his opinion, a government of internal justice and a strong faith in the One God are the best guarantee for peace—and peace, according to Isaiah, is security. If the people and its ministers preserve justice, they will be able to appeal with pure hearts and ask for peace:

> Lord! May you grant peace for us, since you have also requited all our misdeeds. (26:12)

According to Isaiah, social justice and peace are interrelated. There can be no real peace without justice, and no real justice without peace:

> For the work of righteousness shall be peace, and the effect of righteousness, calm and confidence forever. Then my people shall dwell in peaceful homes, in secure dwellings, in untroubled places of rest. (32:17–18)

Over and over again, Isaiah emphasizes that the preservation of internal and international peace is the best guarantee for security. Yet he is well aware that the road to peace— not only the worldwide peace of the end of days, but even peace in the present—is long and tortuous. He knows that no one listens to his advice, that corruption continues to flourish; and what of peace? On this, the prophet states:

> The messengers of peace weep bitterly. (33:7)

Toward the end of King Hezekiah's reign, after Jerusalem is miraculously saved from the sword of Sennacherib, king of Assyria, the Judean king again begins to get involved in international intrigue. This time, the king of Babylon, in revolt against Assyria, attempts to bribe the king of Judah to take up the banner of rebellion against Assyria. Isaiah warns the king against this course, prophesying that a day will come when Hezekiah's descendants will be exiled as slaves of Babylonia. The king accepts Isaiah's counsel, adding:

It means that peace is assured for my time. (39:8)

The effect of Isaiah's prophecies on the history of Judah is immeasurable. Whereas Amos and Hosea were "lone stars" in the skies of the Kingdom of Israel, appearing and disappearing with meteoric suddenness, Isaiah established a school of disciples to propagate his ethical and political doctrine as a dominant tide in the roaring river of prophecy.

Micah was Isaiah's model pupil and young contemporary. His prophecies, too, recall a pendulum swinging back and forth between rage directed at Zion, his city, which he saw as being built on blood and evil, and comfort addressed to his people and all of humankind. With only minor changes, Micah *(4:1–4)* repeats Isaiah's vision of the end of days; like his great master, he too foresees world peace, when everyone, all of humanity, will sit unafraid under their vines and fig trees.

Only two or three generations later, Jeremiah, son of Hilkiah, of the priests in Anathoth, came to Jerusalem to pass unprecedented judgment on the city and its rulers. Jeremiah, the prophet of doom, was also a true prophet-statesman. Yet, unlike Isaiah, who—even if his prophecies often went unheard—was himself always respected in the king's court and among the people, Jeremiah was known from the beginning as:

. . . a man of conflict and strife with all the land. . . . (15:10)

Jeremiah fought on two fronts at once: against the corruption that had spread throughout the people, and primarily throughout the rich and ruling classes; and against the mean, destructive policy practiced by the kings of Judah and their advisors. He repeatedly warned, shouted, and pleaded for them not to involve themselves in regional and great power politics.

On this score he went even further than Isaiah. Realizing that the rising power in the East of his day was that of Babylonia, which had overwhelmed its predecessor, Assyria, he understood what kings and false prophets failed to understand: that Judah had no chance of rivaling Babylonia. No alliance with Egypt would avail; no loose-knit coalition of small nations could succeed. The only way to prevent ruin and exile was to make peace with the Babylonians, while at the same time maintaining a government of strict internal freedom and social justice. According to Jeremiah, making and preserving peace with Babylonia was vital, even if it meant incorporating Judah into the Babylonian Empire. That was the price to be paid, if Judah wished to survive.

Jeremiah summons Judah before the palace of King Zedekiah:

> Put your necks under the yoke of the king of Babylon; serve him and his people, and live! (27:12)

But Jeremiah is considered a traitor in the eyes of the rulers. They accuse him of frightening the people, and even of being a spy in the service of Babylon: one who has "fallen away to the Chaldeans"—that is, gone over to the enemy camp. Jeremiah is arrested, tortured, thrown into solitary confinement, and finally almost put to death in a pit of mire. Nevertheless, though beaten and humiliated, Jeremiah does not recant. He continues to prophesy death to the king, destruction to the city, and exile to the people.

Yet here and there, between prophecies of rage and lamentation, he appears as a comforting prophet to his beloved, blind, and unfortunate people, who did not wish to listen to his voice. In these comforting prophecies, he predicts that, following the disaster and the ruin, other days will come upon the defeated people, whose souls are as weary as Jeremiah's own:

> I am going to bring her relief and healing. I will heal them and reveal to them abundance of peace and truth. And I will restore the fortunes of Judah and Israel, and I will rebuild them as of old. . . . And she shall gain through Me renown, joy, fame and glory above all the nations on earth. . . . (33:6–7, 9)

Here we see that Jeremiah, too, sees in his mind's eye the day when all the nations will take glory in the new and purified Jerusalem. This prophecy, in a certain respect, echoes the "end of days" prophecies of Isaiah and Micah. Yet this echo of a distant future peace is swallowed up by the noise of war, death, and destruction, which take place before the prophet's despairing eyes.

The torch of prophecy passed from Jeremiah's weary hands to those of Ezekiel, the prophet of the Babylonian exile. Ezekiel's main purpose was to strengthen the spirit of his fellow expatriates; to give them hope that they—"those dry bones"—would yet be covered with flesh and sinew, and breath would come into them, and they would return to the united Land of Israel.

Ezekiel foresees the future reunion of Judah and Israel, and maps out a plan for this reunited people returned to its homeland. The plan, of course, centers on not regressing into the sins of the past, but on rebuilding the land on a foundation of faith, righteousness, and justice. This could be accomplished only if the people underwent a revolutionary process, investing it with a new heart and a new spirit.

Ezekiel considers peace to be both an aim and a prerequisite for the building of the People and Land of Israel:

> And I will grant them a covenant of peace. I will banish vicious beasts from their land. . . . They shall no longer be a spoil for the nations, and beasts of the earth shall not devour them; they shall dwell secure and untroubled. (34:25, 28)

Not many years later, the comforting prophecies of Jeremiah and Ezekiel seem to start coming true. Cyrus, king of Persia, overthrows Babylonia, founds a mighty empire and issues a declaration to the exiled Jews, recognizing their right to resettle and rebuild their ruined homeland and re-establish their Temple.

Carried on the wings of this great hope, the "comforting Isaiah" begins to prophesy. He lifts up his great voice in a song of thanks and rejoicing, of faith in the splendid future of the people returning to its homeland. True, he does not fail to see the poverty and difficulties involved in the return; nor does he overlook the renewed outbreak of corruption. Relentlessly, he rebukes the people and its leaders, demanding that they mend their ways. Yet nonetheless, he does not despair, and all his prophecies are dominated by songs of praise for the future of his people and of the entire world.

The importance of peace is central to Isaiah's prophecies. The herald of peace is also the herald of goodness; peace mingled with justice is like a river or sea of beauty and power; peace brings the distant exiles closer to their brothers in Zion; peace is the best guardian of Jerusalem's walls and gates:

> How welcome on the mountain are the footsteps of the herald announcing peace, heralding fortune, announcing victory. . . .
> (ISAIAH 52:7)

And:

> Peace, peace, to the far and the near—said the Lord—and I will heal them. (57:19)

Like his teachers before him, the comforting Isaiah also bears a vision of world peace, which will arrive with the redemption of Israel, when Zion and its people will be a light of the nations:

> And nations shall walk by your light, kings, by your shining radiance. (60:3)

And:

> I will extend to her peace like a river, the wealth of nations like a wadi in flood. (66:12)

The prophet reaches a new height in his song of the future, whose theme is that of new heavens and new earth:

> For behold! I am creating a new heaven and a new earth; the former things shall not be remembered, they shall never come to mind. . . . For I shall create Jerusalem as a joy, and her people

as a delight. And I will rejoice in Jerusalem and delight in her people. Never again shall be heard there the sounds of weeping and wailing. . . . The wolf and the lamb shall graze together, and the lion shall eat straw like the ox, and the serpent's food shall be earth. In all My sacred mount nothing evil or vile shall be done—said the Lord. (65:17–19, 25)

This sublime vision blends well with Ezekiel's vision of "a new heart and a new spirit." Both have to do with the great new biological and cosmic change that will occur throughout the world following the change in the heart of humankind—that is, following the overcoming of evil impulses by good. Let us note that the "new heaven" and "new earth" in Isaiah's prophecy are symbols of a truly universal renewal.

As in the prophesy of Ezekiel, Isaiah's vision includes a change in the nature of the animal kingdom: On the new earth under the new heaven there will be no more predators and no more prey. It is quite possible that, as in the preceding vision, the prophet means that there will be no more predatory peoples and no more victimized peoples—in other words, that the old proverb *Homo homini lupus est* will no longer be true in the new world.

The three last prophets—Haggai, Zechariah, and Malachi—lived during the time of the Return to Zion from exile in Babylonia and the building of the Second Temple. By contrast to the lovely vision of the great comforting prophets, the reality in Judah in the years following the return was gray, difficult, and often miserable. The hostility and jealousy of neighboring nations, the assimilation and corruption among the returned Jews, the suspicion of the Persian administration—all these led the people to disappointment, and sometimes to despair. The role of these three prophets was to encourage the gloomy and depressed people. Accordingly, their prophecies reflect the hope of better days and of peace. Haggai, for instance, says:

The glory of this latter House shall be greater than that of the former one, said the Lord of Hosts; and in this place will I grant peace. (2:9)

Zechariah foresees future harmony and peace between the descendants of the royal House of David and the priestly caste. He considers the state of peace to be the seed of life and fertility for humans, animals, and plants. Only when peace has come to the remnant of Israel can they experience complete redemption:

> For as the seed of peace, the vine shall produce its fruit, the ground shall produce its yield, and the skies shall provide their moisture. I will bestow all these things upon the remnant of this people. (8:12)

But, like the great Prophets before him, Zechariah also links peace with social justice and fair trial: He calls for truth, honesty, and peace.

The future king of Zion, following the arrival of redemption and peace, is envisioned by Zechariah not as a war hero, returning to his capital bedecked with the honors of battle, riding on a noble horse at the head of a glorious procession of cheering soldiers and chained prisoners, but:

> ... riding on an ass, on a donkey foaled by a she ass. ... The warrior's bow shall be banished. He shall call on the nations to make peace. (9:9–10)

Malachi, last of the Prophets, with whom the written record of prophecy in Israel is concluded, defines the essence of the concept of peace in one short, decisive sentence:

> I had with him a covenant of life and peace. . . . (2:5)

Life and peace are a single entity. Without peace, life cannot be complete.

The 150 Psalms are a highly concentrated collection of the song of Israel: songs for solo and for chorus; sad, lyric songs recalling the sobbing of violins, and ringing songs of praise, echoing as drums and cymbals; the flourish of trumpets of victory, and the weeping of the soul bereaved. All these— and with them love and hatred, hope and despair, and, first and foremost, faith in God—are blended into a marvelous work, in which anyone, on any occasion, can always find verses appropriate to his or her feelings.

No wonder that the Psalms became an entity in their own right among the Holy Writings—and, over the generations, an asset that many Jews carry in their hearts (and quite a few on their persons), memorize avidly, and study and repeat on every conceivable occasion. No wonder that, of all the Holy Writings of the Old Testament, the Psalms were transmitted by Christianity to the world at large and won the hearts of untold millions. No wonder that the Psalms, which were sung in the Temple and accompanied by ensembles of many instruments, found their way into the music of the Jews and of the world.

Among the Psalms, to be sure, are songs of war and battle; war, after all, was a nearly quotidian facet of the Psalmists' lives. Yet, throughout the Book of Psalms are scattered notes of longing, yearning, and hope for peace—peace for individuals, for the People of Israel, and for all humankind. The silver bells of peace resound in the Psalms. In Psalm 29, the songster combines strength—the power of the people—with the blessing of peace achieved by moral as well as physical strength:

> May the Lord grant strength to His people; may the Lord bestow on His people peace. (29:11)

In Psalm 125, the Psalmist coins a short, simple, yet meaningful phrase:

> Peace be upon Israel. (125:5)

And in Psalm 128, this phrase is repeated, along with the other side of the coin—the good of Jerusalem, and the good of the individual and the general population in the redeemed Zion:

> May the Lord bless you from Zion; may you share the prosperity of Jerusalem all the days of your life and live to see your children's children. Peace be upon Israel! (128:5-6)

"Peace be upon Israel" became a slogan carried in the heart of the sword-ridden, war-harried People of Israel for more than 2,000 years. Again and again, the slogan was and still is repeated—as a request, a plea, a prayer; indeed, it has become a focal point in the Jewish prayer service.

The Psalmists—like the great Prophets, their sources of inspiration—also linked peace with goodness, righteousness, lovingkindness, and justice:

But the lowly shall inherit the land, and delight in abundant peace. (37:11)

And:

Mark the blameless, note the upright, for there is a future for the man of peace. (37:37)

Again, in Psalm 85, the songster creates a marvelous metaphor, portraying the principal ethical values in terms of love and nature:

Faithfulness and truth meet; justice and peace have kissed each other. Truth springs up from the earth; justice looks down from heaven. (85:11–12)

A new definition of peace, linked with safety and security, is given in Psalm 147:

For He made the bars of your gates strong and blessed your children within you. He endows your realm with peace, and satisfies you with choice wheat. (147:13–14)

Peace, then, is the best and most secure of borders. It is important that Zion's gates be strong, but it is no less important that peace prevail along its borders. It is this combination of strongly barred gates and quiet borders that blesses the People of Israel with confidence and the Land of Israel with fertility. A promise of this peace, and an echo of the vision of the "end of days" may be found in Psalm 146—a song of victory, in which the Psalmist thanks God for having saved his people and his country:

He puts a stop to wars throughout the earth. (46:10)

One of the wonderful and special concepts wrought by the Psalmists is the notion that peace must be pursued. In general, the term "pursuit" is linked with war and battle. In Psalm 34, however, we find that peace, too, must be pursued if it is to be won:

Guard your tongue from evil, your lips from deceitful speech. Shun evil and do good, seek peace and pursue it. (34:14–15)

War is simply begun: Once the king or his general has decided to wage war, it bursts into flame at once, consuming everything in its path. By contrast, peace is fleet-footed as a deer in the field; one must run after it, in order to attain it and force it upon the combatants.

On this concept—the active pursuit of peace—the Sages of Israel later built a large and impressive structure, developing it into an entire theory of life. Aaron the High Priest, brother of Moses, is depicted in the legends of the sages as the prototype of one who loves and pursues peace. Aaron is crowned with a halo of marvelous legends proving the great lengths to which he was prepared to go in his pursuit of peace.

The Book of Proverbs and other Holy Writings also direct us in the pleasant paths of peace, contrasting them with the evil ways of war:

> Deceit is in the minds of those who plot evil; for those who plan peace there is joy. (12:20)

The Proverbs also warn against vanity and pride following victory in war, which often lead to insouciance and oversights:

> Pride goes before ruin and arrogance before failure. (16:18)

If generals throughout the history of humankind—including that of Biblical and modern-day Israel—had kept the above verse in mind, many terrible defeats and disasters could well have been prevented.

An original and incomparably wise definition of the concept of might appears in the Proverbs. True might, according to that book, is composed of patience and self-control:

> Better to be forbearing than mighty, to have self-control than conquer a city. (16:32)

The Proverbs teach us ethics and mercy in prescribing the proper attitude toward a broken and defeated enemy:

> If your enemy falls, do not exult. If he trips, let your heart not rejoice. (24:17)

And:

> If your enemy is hungry, give him bread to eat; if he is thirsty, give him water to drink. (25:21)

From here, it is but a single step to the saying of the Sages of Israel: "Happy is he who makes his enemy into his friend."

Ecclesiastes draws a fascinating parallel on peace in the couplets of his "A season is set for everything" passage:

> A time for slaying and a time for healing. . . . A time for war and a time for peace. (3:3, 8)

War is killing; peace is healing. It is impossible to contrast killing—that is, individual murder—with "and a time to restore to life," as it is beyond our power to revive those who have been murdered. But war, which is collective killing, can be healed by peace.

This idea of peace as a healing remedy for war is not new to prophecy. Isaiah says:

> And the light of the moon shall become the light of the sun, and the light of the sun become sevenfold, like the light of the seven days, when the Lord binds up His people's wounds and heals the injuries it has suffered. (30:26)

And what are these strokes and bruises, if not wars? The identification of peace with healing is even more conspicuous in this comforting prophecy of Isaiah:

> Peace, peace to the far and the near—said the Lord—and I will heal them. (57:19)

And in Jeremiah:

> I am going to bring relief and healing. I will heal them and reveal to them an abundance of peace and truth. (33:6)

Yet how easy it is to strike and bruise—and how hard to heal!

Thus, over more than a thousand years, the Bible developed a doctrine of peace perhaps unique in the history of ancient peoples and civilizations. To be sure, the Bible also includes a doctrine of war, cruel by its very nature. (". . . You shall not let a soul remain alive." *Deuteronomy 20:16)* This is a simple doctrine, with a clearly stated aim: to kill the enemy. The means, any means, of doing so are valid; they depend only on the extent of the technology at the disposal of the fighters.

By contrast, the doctrine of peace is entirely different. To attain it, one must actively pursue it. It demands infinite patience of those who practice it, and bestows upon them neither glory nor laurel wreaths. In general, those who make peace are not even thanked for their efforts. The labor of peace must be learned the hard way—usually following terrible wars that result in nothing more than new bloody conflicts. The greatness of the Bible is that its Prophets and teachers did not tire of teaching and preaching the doctrine of peace to a people saturated in battle and war throughout all of those thousand years.

After the end of the Biblical period, the Jews still had to face another three hundred years of nearly continuous war. This included the revolt against the Greeks and the establishment of the Hasmonean kingdom, the wars of the Jews and the Romans, the destruction of the Second Temple, and Bar-Kochba's revolt against the might of Rome.

The Jewish People, following the loss of its political independence, retained spiritual and religious autonomy in the Land of Israel. The School of Yavneh and its sages, which replaced the former center of political and military might—the kings, the generals, and the priests—gave rise to a wonderful structure of Oral Tradition, a doctrine of Jewish life—the Mishnah, and later the Talmud. The foundation of this structure was the Written Torah—that is, the Bible.

By this time, however, most of the Jewish People had already taken up the staff of the eternal Wandering Jew and had dispersed into countries near and far from their homeland. No wonder that the Jewish sages, in their efforts to create a philosophy that would save their people from the recurring human madness, found in the idea of peace the spiritual antidote necessary to keep up the fight against the devouring sword.

In their attempts to explain the savagery of nature and of humankind, the Sages of Israel and their spiritual heirs formed the doctrine of cosmic peace. According to that doctrine, peace exists in God's great universe: not in our small and insane world, but in the infinite worlds of Creation. For if peace cannot be found even there, there can be no explanation for all of God's order.

Accordingly, Jewish wisdom established a cosmology, not of eternal confusion within the universe but of harmony, order, and peace. That peace, though undoubtedly far from us, exists and is clearly visible in the pathways of the stars and the universal life cycle. To the sages, then, peace is the key to the understanding of both macro- and microcosm.

The Sages of Israel anchored this belief in a verse from the Book of Judges, which tells of the altar that Gideon built to God:

> So Gideon built there an altar to the Lord and called it "Adonai-shalom" (that is, the Lord is peace). (6:24)

It may thus be seen that the name of God, the Creator of heaven and earth, is "Peace"—that is, God not only makes peace; He *is* peace.

Rabbi Yudan, son of Rabbi Yossi, says:

> Great is peace, for the Holy One, blessed be He, is called Peace. (LEVITICUS RABBA 9:9)

The wonderful verse of Job—

> He imposes peace in His heights. (25:2)

—was transformed by the Sages of Israel into the cornerstone of the structure of divine order in the eternal universe. The concept of "peace in His heights" penetrated so deeply into the consciousness of Jews and their sages, and corresponded so well to their outlook on life, that it became part of the key passage which concludes the *Shemona Esreh* prayer recited three times each day. The passage—a jewel in the crown of prayer—begins with the words, "God, guard my tongue from evil," and ends with the verse:

> May He who makes peace in His high places make peace upon us and upon all Israel, and say: Amen.

Each morning, afternoon, and evening, devout Jews repeat this prayer for peace—for a peace that will resemble the wonderful peace of the heavenly high places. Jews recite this prayer summer and winter, fall and spring, in Israel and throughout the Diaspora. Even when the sword runs riot about them, shedding blood and ravening in war, they continue to pray and to believe, to pray and to hope, to pray and to cry out for peace. The cosmic importance of peace, and its place at the head of the scale of divine values, are described by the Sages of Israel:

> Great is peace, for the Holy One, blessed be He, has created no more beautiful attribute than peace. God created the world only so that there should be peace. (NUMBERS RABBA 1:17)

Furthermore, the sages give peace an importance equivalent to that of the creation of the entire world in all its glory, from the "unformed and void" to the creation of humankind:

> Great is peace, for it outweighs all the work of creation. (SIFREI NASO 42, pp. 46–47)

The creation of light and darkness out of the "unformed and void" also involved the making of peace; without peace, the universe must return to its primordial state. If there is no peace, there can be only infinite nothingness:

> If there is no peace, there is nothing. The Scriptures say: "And I will grant peace in the land." This shows that peace is equivalent to the whole land. (SIFRA BEHUKOTAI 26/LEVITICUS 26:6)

According to several sages of Jewish religion and philosophy, peace is also the connecting link between God's many worlds; without peace, there can be no order in the universe. Rabbi Isaac Amara, one of the great Jewish philosophers of fifteenth-century Spain and Italy, writes in his book *'Akedat Yitzhak*:

> For He, the Blessed One, binds together all the worlds and maintains them in their form and their position, their shape and size— it follows that peace is nature, which stabilizes the parts of reality—this was the purpose of the Torah in giving right order and complete guidance. (CHAP. 47)

The Maharal (Rabbi Yehuda Loew) of Prague also emphasizes the connecting role of peace:

He, the Blessed One, comprises all things, and binds and unites all things, and this is Peace itself, and because peace consists in the final form of the Blessed One, and this is not merely an attribute like the other attributes, but it is an independent thing, therefore his name is Peace. (NETIVOT HA-SHALOM, NETIV HA-SHALOM, 81)

The doctrine of Hasidism gives the value of peace a dimension not only cosmic, but nearly magical:

The completeness of the edifice exists only through the quality of peace. Thus the sages interpreted the verse "And great shall be the peace of thy children": Do not read *banayich* (thy children), but *bonayich* (thy builders), for the world is built by means of peace. (A TREASURY OF SAYINGS ABOUT THE TORAH, ED. RABBI L. A. LAVI)

The element of peace exists not only in the building of worlds, but in the creation of humankind. Even in the struggles between the mighty natural forces of the universe, the Sages of Israel found elements of compromise and peace, for whose sake the universe continues to exist and move along its preordained paths.

The sages knew very well the difficulty and complexity of peacemaking. By its very nature, the process takes place between two enemies who hate each other, and not between friends. This is a very difficult task: In order to get adversaries to approach each other, one must overcome enormous burdens of hostility, prejudice, and totally opposed opening positions. Yet precisely this effort was considered by the sages as a great challenge.

Rabbi Nachman of Bratslav formulates the peace process very decisively and successfully:

The main function of peace is to combine two opposites, and do not be upset if you see a man whose opinion is completely opposite to yours, and you imagine that it is absolutely impossible to stay at peace with him; or, when you see two men who are absolute opposites, do not say that it is impossible to make peace between them; on the contrary, it is the main element of the fullness of peace to try to make peace between two opposites. (ANTHOLOGY OF RABBI NACHMAN, PT. I)

After the first phase—that of accepting the challenge of making peace between opposites—one must begin effective action. The Sages of Israel took the Biblical concept of "pursuit of peace," and developed it into an entire doctrine in itself, expanding from the love of peace to its active pursuit, and then to its imposition, almost by force, on those who need it. As mentioned above, the sages transformed Aaron the High Priest into a symbol of "a man of peace and a pursuer of peace." The book *Avot* by Rabbi Natan includes a passage on the dynamic activism of the pursuit of peace:

> If a man sits still at home, how can he pursue peace between men? He should leave his home and go out into the world, and pursue peace in Israel, as it is said: "Seek peace, and pursue it." How is that to be done? Seek it from your home, and pursue it from another place. (AVOT DE-RABBI NATAN^A CH. 12)

Yet even after the peacemakers have pursued and caught up with peace, the work is not yet over. Peace must now be imposed, by whatever means necessary, upon the opposing sides. To this end, Rabbi Yonah of Gerondi, one of the great thirteenth-century sages of Spain, writes:

> And Jews must pick out select men who will impose peace, who will be able to run and enforce peace among men, and these select men should be capable of mollifying and conciliating men and imposing peace. (IGGERET TESHUVAH)

However, from their experience and that of their predecessors, the Sages of Israel knew that there can be no peace without compromise. The main principle of compromise is that none of the parties gets all of what it has been demanding or struggling for—that is, all of what seems just to that party.

The principle of Jewish compromise is found in the following Talmudic passage:

> If two laid hold of a cloak and one said, "I found it," and the other said, "I found it," or if one said, "The whole of it is mine," and the other said, "The whole of it is mine," each must take an oath that he claims not less than the half of it and they divide it between them. (MISHNAH BAVA METZIAH 1:1)

This principle is the opposite of that expressed in "the Judgment of Solomon" concerning the child and the two women, each of whom claimed to be its mother. This judgment was a special case: Solomon knew that a living child must not be cut in pieces, as such a "solution" would cause its death. He therefore sought to ascertain which of the two women would cry out: "Don't kill it!"

Cloaks, however, are not living children. A cloak can be divided—as can a room, or a house, or a territory, or any object; and in all cases when each of the two sides claims "The whole of it is mine," the object not only can, but must, be divided. Peace means a compromise, and when the conflict is over territory, as between Israelis and Palestinians, the only solution is to divide the cloak.

The Sages of Israel used the verse:

> Render true and perfect justice, leading to peace in your gates
> (ZECHARIAH 8:16)

to teach the judges of Israel that the principle of compromise, which leads to peace, must be maintained. As the sages rule:

> For where there is justice, there is no peace, and where there is peace, there is no justice. But what is the justice that brings peace? We must say: Arbitration. (MISHNAH SANHEDRIN 6:2)

The "division" discussed in the Mishnah is the dividing of the disputed object—in other words, compromise:

> A compromise has better force than a judgment. (SANHEDRIN 5b:2)

And:

> They that fear God are those who make a compromise in judgment. (MEKHILTA OF RABBI ISHMAEL, AMALEK, JETHRO 2)

In the long and bitter days of exile, the Jews pray and long for redemption, for the days of the Messiah. Legends of the coming of salvation, and the subsequent return to their homeland, fill their hearts with hope and expectancy. These legends also include considerable discussion of the dreadful "days of wrath" that would precede the coming of the Messiah, with wars of Gog and Magog, corruption and killing and mass murder. Yet even all of these apocalyptic descriptions recall the promise of future redemption. The Jews have always linked both the return to Zion and the coming of the Messiah with peace. Concerning Elijah the Prophet, who legend says will return before the Messiah, the Mishnah writes:

> Elijah will come ... neither to remove afar nor to bring nigh, but to make peace in the world. (MISHNAH 8:7)

Redemption itself will also come with peace—as the sages say, basing their words on those of the prophet:

> Great is peace, for when the Messianic King comes, he will begin with Peace, as it is said: "How beautiful upon the mountains are the feet of the messenger of good tidings, that bringeth peace." (LEVITICUS RABBA 9:9)

And:

> Great is peace, as the Holy One, blessed be He, foretells that the redeemed will dwell in Jerusalem in peace; and it is with peace that the Holy One, blessed be He, will console Jerusalem. (DEUTERONOMY RABBA 5:15)

The clear, concise conclusion is that there can be no redemption without peace, and there can be no peace without compromise. The longing for redemption through peace, in the doctrine of Hasidism, has extended not only to Jews but to all of humanity—a sort of reprise of the vision of Isaiah. An article attributed to Rabbi Israel Baal Shem Tov, founder of Hasidism, includes these lines:

> When a Jew looks forward to, and prays for, the redemption of Israel, he should take into consideration that the entire world looks forward to redemption, as all of creation is wrapped in the skins of Diaspora, so as not to break the vessels; thus, man must direct his efforts toward the salvation of worlds, as all worlds will be saved with Israel. (B. LANDAU, THE EXPECTATION OF PEACE IN HASIDIC DOCTRINE)

The doctrine of Hasidism, Landau explains, also stresses the great difficulty of obtaining peace, and thereby of bringing redemption closer:

The road to peace is not easy, as it is the way of peace to be veiled in bitterness. . . . But the bitterness will pass away in the end, and the remedy remains.

The Sages of Israel considered their Torah—which was their guiding light and oracle throughout their long and agonized exile—to be a doctrine of peace. With all their might, they clung to the doctrine of the Prophets, visionaries and heralds of peace; from those springs, they quenched the thirst of their people. The sages write of peace and its roots in the Torah of Israel:

> The Holy One, blessed be He, said: "The entire Torah is peace; to whom shall I give it? To the people that loves peace." (YALKUT SHIMONI, JETHRO, PAR. 273)

As they have moved to and fro, tossed by the winds of history and time, the Jews have carried in their hearts a double longing: a longing for the return to Zion, and for the kingdom of peace.

CHAPTER EIGHT

The Other Side

T HE BIBLE IS A BOOK OF DIVINE REVELATION; BUT IT IS ALSO a very human book. From its first chapters to its last page, the myriad variations and contradictions of humankind are revealed in every line. It describes some people who are utterly righteous, such as Noah, the "righteous and blameless man"; and a few who are utterly wicked, such as Haman the Agagite. However, most of its characters—including the founding fathers and great legislators, the greatly admired kings, and even the prophets of truth and justice—are flesh-and-blood human beings, with their good and evil instincts.

The Bible depicts no demigods. Unlike demigods and angels, the hearts of human beings combine evil instincts with the image of their Creator. This combination, and the struggle between these two basic elements, has followed humanity throughout its existence.

Not only does the Bible not conceal these two sides of the human personality—of every human personality; it strips them utterly bare before the reader's eyes. The biography of King David, the "sweet singer of Israel," is a classic example of the struggle between opposed instincts—cruelty and mercy, physical lust and spiritual exaltation, generosity and meanness—in the soul of a human being. In the case of King David, all of these contrasts plus more were housed within a single body and spirit.

No wonder that throughout the Bible, we find the entire span of qualities, values, and impulses that motivate human beings and society. In the preceding chapters, we have covered the values of the sanctity of life and peace, justice and freedom, equality, brotherhood, and mercy. Yet it is not at all difficult to discuss the opposites of these values as they appear in the Bible: war and death, violence and slavery, inequality, hatred, and cruelty. Moreover, these qualities, and even attempts at their justification, may be found in the words of

the same leaders, legislators, and prophets quoted above in our discussion of the values of good.

Anyone who attempts to discuss the most beautiful and exalted of Biblical values, while concealing the other side of the Great Book, "doeth his work with a slack hand"—indeed, with a dishonest hand—and cannot but fail to describe the fullness of the struggle between good and evil that the text portrays and understands. Consider, for example, a few instances of terrible hatred and jealousy, of merciless cruelty and revenge, from the pages of that same Bible that we have rightly viewed as the source of good and beauty.

We can begin with Moses, father of prophets and great legislator. It was Moses who led a people of wanderers and former slaves out of the "house of bondage" and to the Promised Land. The people, moreover, was an undisciplined, quarrelsome, rebellious lot. Many longed to return to the fleshpots of Egypt. Only by virtue of Moses' authoritarian personality and persistent leadership did they stay on course through the desert, en route to the Land of Canaan.

In its wanderings, the People of Israel encountered and fought against numerous enemy peoples. The worst of these, from Israel's standpoint, were the Amalekites, who trailed the weary Israelites and fell upon their hindmost ranks, nearly defeating Israel. Following that war, the Torah commands Israel to remember the foul deed of Amalek and to take revenge by annihilating that people altogether:

You shall blot out the memory of Amalek from under heaven. Do not forget! (DEUTERONOMY 25:19)

Other peoples, including the Midianites, also fought against the People of Israel with bitter rage. A rising desire for revenge swept over the people—and over Moses as well. The war of vengeance against Midian was very cruel: The Israelites killed every male of Midian, took their women and children prisoner, looted their cattle and beasts of burden, and burned their cities and palaces. The captive humans and animals were brought before Moses and Eleazar the priest. The Bible tells the rest of the story:

Moses became angry with the commanders of the army, the officers of thousands and the officers of hundreds, who had come back from the military campaign. Moses said to them, "You have spared every female! . . . Now, therefore, slay every male among the children, and slay also every woman who has known a man carnally; but spare every young woman who has not had carnal relations with a man. (NUMBERS 31:14–15, 17–18)

What, one might ask, is the difference between Pharaoh's terrible decree concerning the Hebrew children:

Every boy that is born you shall throw into the Nile but let every girl live (EXODUS 1:22)

—and Moses' dreadful decree that "every male among the children" of Midian is to be slain? The question must remain unanswered. Certainly, there can be no answer to it in the Torah—that Torah whose laws of life, justice, and mercy were handed down by Moses himself. Only a partial answer may be found in the fierce fires of revenge that burned in the bones of the great leader of Israel.

Joshua, Moses' successor, commands the People of Israel to fight and slay the Hittites, the Amorites, the Canaanites, the Perizzites, the Hivites, and the Jebusites:

In the towns of the latter peoples, however, which the Lord your God is giving you as a heritage, you shall not let a soul remain alive. No, you must proscribe them. . . . (DEUTERONOMY 20:16–17)

In fact, Joshua's wars of conquest and settlement are very cruel, and the verse "you shall not let a soul remain alive" is carried out in the most literal sense.

The following passage is a fearsome description of what took place in Jericho after that city's conquest by Joshua and his troops:

They exterminated everything in the city with the sword: man and woman, young and old, and ox and sheep and ass. (JOSHUA 6:21)

These words depict the consuming rage of the conquering soldiers who defeated an enemy city and slaughtered all its inhabitants without exception. This scene was to repeat itself many times, not just under Joshua and not only among the Hebrews. The sword of war devoured indiscriminately on all sides, before and since—and, to the despair of humanity, continues doing so to this very day: from Jericho to Hiroshima.

Yet, on reading the conquest of Jericho, we may once more ask the Biblical question:

> But these poor sheep, what have they done? (2 SAMUEL 24:17)

What was the sin of the lambs, oxen, and donkeys of Jericho—those poor unfortunate animals? Does not the Torah itself, in its mercy for animals, command that they rest on the Sabbath and not be slaughtered together with their young, nor muzzled while treading out the corn?

The terrible hatred of Amalek, and the will for revenge against that nation, continued long after Moses' and Joshua's day. The Prophet Samuel commands King Saul:

> Now go, attack Amalek, and proscribe all that belongs to him. Spare no one, but kill alike men and women, infants and sucklings, oxen and sheep, camels and asses. (1 SAMUEL 15:3)

When Saul and his army defeat the Amalekites, he slaughters them all by the sword—except for the Amalekite king, Agag, whom he captures alive. The Bible then relates how, in a surprising departure from Samuel's orders:

> Saul and the troops spared Agag and the best of the sheep, the oxen, the second born, the lambs, and all else that was of value. They would not proscribe them. . . . (15:9)

Saul imprisons Agag and takes him back to the Land of Israel, along with the best of the sheep and the oxen. Samuel, hearing of this, is furious at having been disobeyed. He comes to Saul's camp and addresses the king in anger:

> "Then what," demanded Samuel, "is this bleating of sheep in my ears, and the lowing of oxen that I hear?" (15:14)

Embarrassed, Saul tries to make excuses, explaining to Samuel that the sheep and cattle were spared in order to bring them as a victory sacrifice to God. Samuel, however, does not accept this explanation. Speaking in God's name, he chastises Saul and prophesies that the kingdom will be taken away from him. Samuel then kills Agag with his own hands:

> Samuel said: "Bring forward to me King Agag of Amalek." Agag approached him with faltering steps; and Agag said, "Ah, bitter death is at hand!" Samuel said: "As your sword has bereaved women, so shall your mother be bereaved among women." And Samuel cut Agag down before the Lord at Gilgal. (15:32–33)

Here we see, portrayed in all its strength, the eternal hatred of the People of Israel for Amalek, and the lust for revenge that permits neither mercy nor pity.

The essence of the insane cruelty of war is described by the writer of the Chronicles in a passage concerning the wars of Amaziah, king of Judah:

> Amaziah took courage and leading his army, he marched to the Valley of Salt. He slew 10,000 men of Seir; another 10,000 the men of Judah captured alive and brought to the top of Sela. They threw them down from the top of Sela and every one of them was burst open. (2 CHRONICLES 25:11–12)

The killing of prisoners in cold blood—is there any more dreadful deed? And does not the impulse for revenge at times drive even the loving and merciful Psalmist past the brink of sanity?

> Fair Babylon, you predator, a blessing on him who repays you in kind what you have inflicted on us; a blessing on him who seizes your babies and dashes them against the rocks. (137:8–9)

True, the Babylonians destroyed the Temple, laid waste to Judah, and drove its people into exile. True, the exiles' will to revenge, expressed in the Psalm, as they sat by the rivers of Babylon, weeping and swearing not to forget Jerusalem, is understandable. Nevertheless, the cruel "a blessing on him who . . . ," concluding their extraordinarily moving lament, is unusual in the context of the beautiful, peace-loving poetry of the Psalms.

Even the great Prophets of Israel sometimes burst out in unbridled rage and fury against the enemies of their people. Here, for example, is a prophecy of the "comforting" Isaiah, relating to God's vengeance on Edom:

> I trod them down in My anger, trampled them in My rage; their life-blood bespattered My garments, and all My clothing was stained. For I had planned a day of vengeance. . . . (63:3–4)

And Jeremiah, the prophet of peace, cries out against the nations that do not worship the One God of Israel:

> Pour out your wrath on the nations who have not heeded You, upon the clans that have not invoked Your name. For they have devoured Jacob, have devoured and consumed him, and have laid desolate his homesteads. (10:25)

And let us not forget the Prophet Joel, whose fearsome vision is the precise opposite of Isaiah's vision of "the end of days." Instead of "And they shall beat their swords into plowshares and their spears into pruning hooks: Nation shall not take up sword against nation; they shall never again know war," Joel foresees the day of God's judgment—a day of revenge against all the nations that persecuted Israel. Joel cries out to the people:

> Beat your plowshares into swords, and your pruning hooks into spears. (4:10)

This is no less than a vision of all-out world war.

Joel's vision of war, predicting a day when the nations will be judged by God in the Valley of Jehoshaphat in Jerusalem, is far removed from Isaiah's vision of world peace, with all nations flowing toward Zion, from where the Law will come. Yet, from far before Joel's time to this very day, it is chiefly his prophecy, rather than Isaiah's, that seems to be moving toward realization. In nearly every state and country—including, tragically, the Land of the Bible—plowshares are being beaten into swords and pruning hooks into spears. In fact, the largest and most sophisticated industry of today's world is that of modern weaponry—an industry that has gathered not only untold natural resources but also many of the world's best minds. To the question "Swords or plowshares?"—or, in its modern phrasing, "Guns or butter?"—the throats of humanity ring out time and again: "Swords!" "Guns!"

The other side of the Bible, then, cannot and must not be

denied. The Bible includes not only the exhortation that "You shall not take vengeance, nor bear any grudge," but also its exact opposite. Its immortal lines contain not only a sublime doctrine of world peace but also orders of cruel, primordial tribal war.

In short, the Bible is a relief map of humankind, as individuals and as a whole. Lurking in the depths and valleys of that relief map are death, war, hatred, violence, evil, slavery, and cruelty; yet shining forth upon its mountain tops, in all their beauty, are the imperatives of life and peace, love and justice, kindness, freedom, and mercy.

Whereas over the centuries fanatic fundamentalists—Jewish, Christian, and Moslem—have drawn their ammunition from Biblical fallout, great philosophers and moralists have made the Bible what it really is: a lighthouse for humanity. If humanity is to survive into the twenty-first century, in an age threatened by the combination of fanaticism and a technology of total annihilation, it will have to follow the light.

A Standard for Zion

T HE ETHICAL VALUES OF THE BIBLE AND JUDAISM WERE integral factors in the birth of Zionism some one hundred years ago. Zionism, the modern political movement to return the Jews to their ancestral homeland, was brought about by the integration of three forces. Two of these—the tribulations of the Jews and their hope for redemption in their ancient homeland—were age-old elements that marked the Jewish experience throughout the long exile. The third force, which tremendously accelerated the process, was the advent of modern nationalism. This force burst forth in Europe in the nineteenth century, spread throughout the world, and became dominant in the modern history of peoples and countries. The combination of these three forces created the national liberation movement of the Jewish People in its new form: the Zionist Movement.

The declared goals of Zionism included not only the return of the dispersed Jewish People to the Land of Israel but also the establishment of an independent entity in that homeland—that is, a Jewish State.

A small Jewish population had existed in the Land of Israel in nearly every generation of the centuries of exile. By the nineteenth century, this population had become somewhat larger; most of its members congregated in the four cities sacred to Judaism: Jerusalem, Hebron, Tiberias, and Safed. The major innovation of the 1870s and 1880s was the desire of Jews—at first, very few—to live as farmers and peasants, and to dwell as their ancestors had done in Biblical times.

In the mid-nineteenth century—even before modern Zionism, and certainly before the first Zionist Congress in 1897— a small group of Jews living in the Old City of Jerusalem had begun to move outside the city walls and to attempt to found agricultural settlements on the soil of the Land of Israel. As the Bible urged:

Every man shall sit under his grapevine or fig tree . . . (MICAH 4:4)

This form of life seemed to them the nearest approach to renewal of the old days of sovereignty that the Jews had formerly held in the Land of Israel. Accordingly, at the end of the nineteenth century, all kinds of Jews—students from pogrom-ridden Russia; simple Jews, "lovers of Zion," from Eastern Europe; and Jews from Yemen, longing for redemption—joined forces to form a small movement of settlers who established the first modern-day Jewish villages in the Land of Israel.

The very names given by these Jewish settlers to the first colonies are irrefutable proof of the close, direct relationship between the settlers and the Bible:

Mikvah Israel—"Hope of Israel" (JEREMIAH 14:8)
Petah Tikvah—"Door of Hope" (HOSEA 2:17)
Rosh Pina—"Chief Cornerstone" (PSALMS 118:22)
Rishon le-Zion—"Herald to Jerusalem" (ISAIAH 41:27)
Nes Ziona—"To Zion" (JEREMIAH 4:6)
Neve Shalom—"Peaceful Homes" (ISAIAH 32:18)
Ruhamma—"Lovingly Accepted" (HOSEA 1:3)

Who can fail to perceive the symbolism of these names, nor the settlers' desire to resemble their ancestors as lovers and workers of the soil? The young settlers from Eastern Europe called themselves by the name of BILU—an acronym for Hebrew words taken from the Bible, meaning:

O house of Jacob! Come, let us walk. (ISAIAH 2:5)

And, at the other end of the Jewish Diaspora, the Jews of Yemen who came to the Land of Israel in 1882 took the Hebrew letters whose numerical value denotes the year 1882 in the Jewish calendar and rearranged them into a word meaning "into the palm-tree"—recalling the poetic verse from the Song of Songs:

Let me climb the palm. (7:9)

The modern Hebrew literature written and read by these new settlers in the Promised Land abounds in romantic descriptions of the Biblical past. In "To the Bird"—the first, beautifully moving poem by Hayim Nachman Bialik, the great poet whose works constituted the jewel in the crown of nineteenth-century Hebrew poetry—the bird, which has just returned from the Land of Israel to the narrator's dwelling in exile, brings him greetings from his brothers, "happy in Zion"; tells him of a country "where springtime shall flourish forever"; speaks to him of "the Sharon Valley," of "the Fragrant Hill," of "the pearly dew of Mount Herman"; evokes his "brothers, the workers, who sow land in sorrow, yet bring in the sheaves with great joy." Hearing the bird, the narrator longs to take wing himself and fly to "the land where the palm and the almond are blooming."

These lines may appear to some as a sentimental collage of quasi-Biblical images. Yet they not only brought tears to their readers' eyes but moved thousands to decision and action. Thousands of young Diaspora Jews, impelled by Bialik's words and those of his literary contemporaries, arose and journeyed to that marvelous land where springtime would flourish forever, to sow in sorrow in the hope of reaping in joy.

The reality, however, was quite different: strange, bitter, and often cruel; gray and exhausting. The first settlers faced a period of struggle: with the land, which would not yield to them; with the hot, harsh climate and environment; with their dreadful inexperience; with unfamiliar diseases; and, most of all, with themselves. Many—indeed, some say most—of those who came to the Land of Israel in the first thirty years gave in, deserted the field, and returned to exile.

They also faced a struggle with another people. Many of the first pioneers considered themselves as "a people without a land," coming to redeem "a land without a people." Little did they know that the land was already inhabited by a people—the Arabs. Admittedly, large portions of that land were barren; quite a few of the Arabs were nomads, with no permanent base; and many of the Arab landworkers were poor serfs, indentured to rich effendis living far away. Nevertheless, the land was not empty. It contained towns and villages, and the majority of its population was Arab. Thus, the first Jewish settlers had to contend, from the very beginning, with the Arab presence.

At first this was not yet a struggle with "the Arab national problem," because the Jews did not yet constitute a "Jewish national problem." Still, the settler had to deal with problems of language and customs, lifestyles and relationships, while simultaneously trying to establish peaceful contacts and fighting off hostile Arab bands.

In a sense, the most hostile of all was the ruler of nineteenth- and early twentieth-century Palestine: the Ottoman Empire. The viziers of the "Sublime Porte" in Istanbul, headed by the Sultan—autocrat of an empire within which Palestine represented only a very small part—did not approve of the first steps of those strange Jews, who insisted on staking out land and setting up villages.

It may be assumed that the Jewish pioneers occasionally recalled the days of Ezra and Nehemiah, when their remote ancestors, returning from exile in Babylonia, encountered vast difficulties in the early days of the Return to Zion. As the Book of Ezra recounts:

> Thereupon the people of the land undermined the resolve of the people of Judah, and made them afraid to build. (4:4)

And Nehemiah describes the anger of the returning Jews' neighbors, who mocked them for wishing to rebuild the ruins of their country:

> What are the miserable Jews doing? . . . Will they revive those stones out of the dust heaps, burned as they are? (3:34)

Yet, despite the attitude of the Ottoman officials and the unfriendly Arab population, the Jewish settlers followed in the footsteps of Nehemiah, guarding at night and laboring during the day.

While the first practical measures were being taken in the Land of Israel, the Jewish People acquired a leader of stature: Theodor Herzl. It was Herzl who transformed his precursors' attempts to resettle the Land of the Bible into a real national movement—Zionism. His handsome physiognomy and splendid, commanding personality combined near-royal charisma with quasi-prophetic fervor. In the very short years of his life as leader of the Zionist Movement, he supplied Zionism with both an exciting vision and the modern tools for its implementation. Thus Herzl, the visionary, wrote in his diary at the conclusion of the First Zionist Congress in Basel in 1897:

> If I may sum up the Basel Congress in one phrase, which, for caution's sake, I will not utter in public, it is this: in Basel, I founded the Jewish State. Were I to say that in public today, the response would be laughter from all sides. Perhaps in another five years—at most, in another fifty years—everyone will recognize it.

This was the birth of Zionism: a unique national movement. In its daring dreams, its willingness to take on a "mission impossible," its readiness to swim against the tide of history and, as it were, to challenge the very laws of nature—in all of these, Zionism was truly unique. And no less unique was the spiritual, mental, material, and physical effort invested by Zionists in the realization of their ambitions, and in the face of many incomparably great difficulties in their path. This mighty effort, sustained over several decades, enabled Zionism—precisely fifty years after the above entry in Herzl's diary—to reach the threshold of establishing the Jewish State in the Land of Israel.

The Jews brought to Zionism not only its foundation—the doctrine of the Prophets of Israel—but all of the wisdom that they had accumulated throughout the generations of exile. This included the Oral Tradition and other Jewish learning, as well as the best of the world's great social doctrines and universal thought.

In the process of realization, Zionism split into numerous variant and ideologically opposed factions that incessantly argued over what each believed to be the best course of action. In general, however, it may be said that all of the Zionist groups and their leaders agreed in principle on several fundamental values, based on the principles propounded by the Prophets of Israel: the sanctity of life, peace, justice, freedom, equality, brotherhood, and mercy. These values, naturally, underwent a modern translation, in the spirit of the era in which Zionism was founded, so as to take the form of the following common goals: the establishment of a democratic, productive, tolerant, peace-loving Jewish State.

Let us now examine these goals one by one:

A JEWISH STATE

The terms *self-determination* and *nation-state* are the spiritual fruit of modern nationalism, first sown in Europe toward the mid-nineteenth century, following the French Revolution and the Napoleonic Era, and subsequently disseminated with great speed and strength throughout the world.

When the Zionists first issued their cry of "We are one people," punctuated by the troubles of the Jews in exile and their longing for Zion, it was only a matter of time until Herzl conceived his solution: the creation of a Jewish State in the Land of Israel. This state would once again provide the Jewish People with a territory of its own, a place where it could return to "self-determination" as a true people. This would be the one and only state in the world where the Jews would be in a majority. And, once that majority was attained, the Jewish people would be able—as every people does in its own country—to pass and keep its own laws and customs, speak its own language, set up its own institutions of government and defense, foster its own art and culture, maintain its own religious rituals for the believers among its population, and establish international relations according to its own interests.

In short, the Jewish State would enable the Jewish People to live as a nation in the family of nations, and no longer as a small minority in each of a large number of lands of exile— a minority at best considered strange, often mocked and scorned, and, in most instances, bitterly persecuted.

Herzl said all these things with wonderful clarity and simplicity, referring explicitly to "the Jewish State." However, he apparently had little or no knowledge of the Arabs living in the Land of Israel and did not understand the inherent problems their presence presented.

As the years went by and Zionism set out on its rocky, thorny course, its leaders tended to camouflage the goal of a Jewish State. In those first years, the Jewish settlers in the Land of Israel were a minority, and a weak one at that. Accordingly, the Zionist leaders, fearing to antagonize their gentile governors, contented themselves with achieving what they could. Yet, in their innermost hearts they never ceased to strive toward this goal, which they saw as essential to the realization of the prophecies of redemption, and, at the same time, as relevant to the reality in which they lived.

Only after the Holocaust—the greatest of disasters for the Jewish People and the most cruel outrage in the history of the world; an event whose unspeakable atrocity not even the Prophets could have foretold—only then did Zionism, backed by the majority of the Jewish People, unite and appeal for a national homeland for the tortured Jews.

This appeal was answered on November 29, 1947, by a resolution of the United Nations. In reality, however, the Jews only received their state after a cruel and bloody struggle—first against the British, and then in the War of Independence against the Arabs. In the midst of that war, on May 15, 1948, the Jews declared the establishment of their state. The "Declaration of the Independence of the State of Israel," signed on that day by the People's Council of the new state, included, *inter alia*, the following paragraphs:

> Eretz Israel was the birthplace of the Jewish people. Here their spiritual, religious and political identity was shaped. Here they first attained to statehood, created cultural values of national and universal significance, and gave to the world the eternal Book of Books. . . .
>
> This right is the natural right of the Jewish people to be masters of their own fate, like all other nations, in their own sovereign State.
>
> *Accordingly we, members of the People's Council, representatives of the Jewish Community of Eretz Israel and of the Zionist movement, are here assembled on the day of the termination of the British Mandate over Eretz Israel and, by virtue of our natural and historic right and on the strength of the resolution of the United Nations General Assembly, do hereby declare the establishment of a Jewish state in Eretz Israel, to be known as the state of Israel.*

A DEMOCRATIC STATE

Prior to the destruction of the Second Temple, the form of sovereign government under which the Jews lived in the Land of Israel was not much different from that of the neighboring peoples: a hereditary absolute monarchy. Earlier in this book, we observed how Samuel, the prophet-judge, attempted to dissuade his people from choosing kingly rule, and how he unsuccessfully tried to preserve the custom of government by judges selected according to their qualifications. Kingly rule, established in the days of King Saul, continued—though fitfully and intermittently—in Israel and Judah until the last days of the Hasmonean dynasty. Alongside the monarchy, throughout a considerable span of that long period, a hereditary hierarchy of priestdom existed.

The Prophets of Israel bore the torch of freedom through nearly the entire period of kingly rule, and their disciples dared to be a sort of opposition to the royal house and sometimes even to the priesthood. Whenever they witnessed corruption and oppression within the kingdom, their razor-sharp tongues struck out at kings and ministers, demanding true and righteous judgment.

With the loss of their political independence and the destruction of the Temple, the Jews began to develop institutions of partial government under foreign rule, at first in the Land of Israel and later throughout the various lands of exile. Deprived of any territory in which they could have established full sovereign rule, the Jews adopted ways of life that were much less formal and hierarchical than those under the royal house and the priesthood. Jewish community life focused on the synagogue and the house of study, or yeshiva. The zenith of the social pyramid was now occupied by the sages. It was they who passed laws, enacted customs, handed down rulings, interpreted the Torah, and adapted its precepts to the prevailing times and environment.

The accepted criteria for selection of the heads of Diaspora Jewish communities were knowledge of the Torah, scholarship, wisdom, and genius. In sociological language, it may be said that the ascribed characteristics of the royal house and the priesthood, which had been handed down from father to son, were replaced by achievement-oriented criteria, based on the leaders' personal accomplishments rather than their ascription to the kingly or priestly families.

At the same time, the Jewish community began to adopt

a democratic element *par excellence* in its lifestyle: the element of personal election. Rabbis, sages, heads of yeshivas, and so forth had to be instated by an electoral body, on the basis of personal achievement alone. It is important to note that this form of election continued throughout the entire period of exile, and that the achievements that constituted a basis for election concerned the spiritual, rather than the material. There were, of course, exceptions: Some rabbis and sages did attempt (in a few cases, even successfully) to establish dynasties and to derive material gains from their positions. These, however, only prove the great—and democratic—rule that characterized Jewish community life throughout the Diaspora. That rule expressed the free and personal election of leaders, in accordance with their spiritual qualifications, while maintaining an orderly rotation.

Naturally, as heads of small minority communities, these spiritual leaders had no power to assume actual rule. The true power was in the hands of the sovereign of whatever country the community happened to be part of. He controlled the army and the police, the law and its application; the Jewish communities and their leaders were dependent upon his mercies. At the same time, during considerable periods of their life in exile, various Jewish communities enjoyed a comparative degree of autonomy; their institutions were granted authority of taxation and judgment, enforcement and punition. And, of course, the functions of religious law continually remained in the hands of the Jews.

The form and structure of modern democratic government, which arose in England and spread through Europe and the entire world over the last few hundred years, affected the Jews as well. Such a structure, allowing the simultaneous operation of several political parties, coexistence of majority and minority, and orderly changes of government, was appropriate to Jewish needs. No wonder, then, that they, always the first to suffer from tyranny and oppression, adopted these ideas wholeheartedly.

The Jews of the Diaspora realized that only under democracy could they hope to attain and maintain equality and civil rights, safety from the merciless persecution of racism, and freedom to elect and be elected as equals to the legislative, executive, and judiciary institutions of the countries in which they lived. They also knew that this modern democracy was the form of government closest in spirit and principle to the prophetic doctrine of justice.

When the Jews established their own national movement, it was obvious to them that this would be a movement founded on democracy. The First Zionist Congress—a sort of National Assembly—was prepared by its founder, Dr. Herzl, in accordance with the best democratic tradition and practice. That congress elected the movement's executive institutions. Throughout the years, the Zionist Movement continued to hold free democratic elections. Various parties were founded, all of which maintained democratic procedure. The Zionist Congress became a sort of Jewish parliament in process: It had its coalitions and its oppositions, its debates, its majority rule, and its changes of leadership—all completely democratic.

Democracy was also practiced in the relatively small Jewish community within Palestine under Ottoman and British rule. From the beginning, the Zionist settlers established political bodies whose elected representatives participated in institutions common to the Jewish population. In time, the National Committee was established, to which the Jewish residents of Mandatory Palestine elected their delegates.

When the State of Israel was established, none of those involved in its establishment had the slightest doubt that this would be a democratic state. The state, they knew, would have its elected institutions and its legislature, and that legislature would elect a government responsible to it. The state would enact separation of the legislative, executive, and judicial authorities, and would define all of its citizens as equal in the eyes of the law. Affairs of state, large and small, would be determined by majority vote; and freedom of expression and organization would be anchored in law. In short, the Jewish State would be as democratic as the best and most enlightened of democratic states throughout the world.

The Declaration of the Independence of the State of Israel

expressed this fittingly, by drawing a parallel between the foundations of democracy and the doctrine of the Prophets:

> The State of Israel . . . will be based on freedom, justice and peace as envisaged by the Prophets of Israel; it will ensure complete equality of social and political rights to all its inhabitants irrespective of religion, race or sex.

A PRODUCTIVE STATE

The early Zionists were well aware that, if they wanted a Jewish State—that is, a state in which the overwhelming majority of the population would be Jewish—they would have to construct it so as to meet all the needs of a normal state. In other words, the residents of such a state would do all kinds of work and fulfill all of the requisite functions, and the Jewish society would be a complete society.

They knew that the Jewish People, scattered and dispersed throughout the Diaspora, was not "normal"; that, due to various historical and sociological factors, its members were included in only very specific strata of the foreign societies in whose midst they lived. They understood that the basic criterion for the realization of Zionism must be a revolutionary return to a structure in which the Jews would not only *sit* under their vines and fig trees but also *work* the fields, vineyards, and orchards. Accordingly, the return to the Land of Israel—even before the crystallization of Zionist ideology—involved a literal return to the land, with the pioneer Jewish settlers themselves becoming peasants and farmers.

The model for the first agricultural colonies in the Land of Israel came from the Bible. The first Jewish farmers, in the late nineteenth century, chose to emulate such beautiful examples as Boaz and his young men harvesting in the fields of Bethlehem, and Ruth gleaning behind them. With all their hearts, they longed to return to work the land their ancestors had loved.

Herzl and his colleagues understood that the Jewish State would have to be quite modern, incorporating the best of European technology. In his utopian work *Altneuland*, Herzl describes a Jewish State in the twentieth-century Land of

Israel—including a network of railroads and highways, deep-water ports, electrical power stations, canals, and state-of-the-art industry and agriculture.

Many years before the establishment of the State of Israel, the Socialist-Zionist Labor Movement conceived and constructed agriculture based on Jewish labor, exemplified by the kibbutz—a modern, egalitarian, productive commune. They invented the moshav—a productive cooperative village. They set up enterprises of construction and industry owned by the laborers themselves, organized strong professional unions, and established institutions of mutual aid in the fields of finance, health, culture, and sport.

Of course, they were not alone in these efforts. Alongside the Labor Movement and its enterprises, a private sector sprang up, with entrepreneurs active in crafts, agriculture, industry, and commerce. Private enterprise, too, helped greatly to advance the Zionist Movement and its development.

Under the British Mandate, the Jews in the Land of Israel set up a far-ranging network of educational and municipal institutions. In addition, from the earliest days of settlement in the Promised Land, the Jews secretly organized an underground infrastructure for armed defense. It may be said, with all certainty, that the State of Israel, at the time of its establishment, already enjoyed a firm productive base, built on decades of vision combined with labor and self-sacrifice. Standing side by side, supporting that base by their joint efforts, were Jewish farmers and industrial laborers, teachers and engineers, clerks and merchants, doctors and scientists, and, of course, scholars, writers, poets, and artists. The waves of Arab armies that surged against and threatened to destroy this structure, small in area and population, were shattered on colliding with its strong base and could not destroy it.

A TOLERANT STATE

If there was ever a people that paid the full price of intolerance, it was the Jewish People in exile. This strange, outlandish minority, vulnerable because of its religion and customs, was scorned and shunned, its members branded "heretics," "Christ-killers," and "spawn of Satan."

As they prepared to rebuild their own state, in which they could live and behave as they pleased, the creators and leaders of Zionism understood that such a state would have to be founded on the immutable principle of tolerance toward the strangers within their midst. They realized that on the road to recognition as one in the family of nations, Zionism would continuously encounter and have to deal with other peoples—primarily with the Arabs, and also with other minorities living within the future state in which the Jews hoped to establish their majority.

Zionism, however, realized that it would have to create norms of tolerance directed not only toward the strangers without, but toward itself within. Zionism, after all, was a very complex ideological and human construct. Most of its proponents were secular Jews who gave the movement itself a secular nature. However, from the beginning, Zionism also included a small but powerful religious faction, which served as a bridge between the modern Jewish national movement and the profundity of the Jewish religion. In addition, the Zionist ideology also incorporated strong elements drawn from all shades of socialism and all forms of liberalism. And, in its role as Ingatherer of the Exiles, assembling Jews from the four corners of the Diaspora, Zionism had to take into consideration encounters between Jews of different cultures, colors, aspects, and languages, who would find each other's mores foreign and odd at best.

Zionism realized that in order to survive and flourish, it would have to demand the greatest possible measure of tolerance from all its members and supporters. Tolerance, too, was amply documented in the Torah and the wisdom of the sages: "Love your neighbor as yourself," "And you shall love the stranger," "Do not do to others what you would not have them do to you"—all these dicta and many more are everlasting signposts, clearly pointing the way to tolerance.

Tolerance toward minorities within the Jewish society and within the Jewish State is expressly dictated by the Declaration of the Independence of the State of Israel:

The State of Israel ... as envisaged by the Prophets of Israel ... will guarantee freedom of religion, conscience, language, education and culture.

A PEACE-LOVING STATE

The Jews who wished for and worked toward a democratic, productive, tolerant Jewish State, naturally believed and hoped that that state would be established by peaceful means and without bloodshed. Indeed, some of the great figures of Zionism, including Herzl, actually thought—whether through naivete or ignorance—that the return of the Jews to their barren and desolate homeland would be welcomed by the Arabs and that the Jewish State would arise in peace.

Many of these early thinkers spoke of "a country without a people, waiting for a people without a country." Few of them knew about the people that already inhabited the Land of Israel—the Arabs. Even fewer knew anything about their lifestyle, their culture, or their hopes and aspirations for the future.

Herzl—who, in the course of his one and only visit to the Land of Israel, saw that there were Arabs dwelling within the confines of his future Jewish State—nevertheless describes in *Altneuland* a bloodless establishment of that state, without conflict or strife. According to his vision, the Arabs welcomed the arriving Jews with understanding and even with joy. After all, were not Jews and Arabs descended from a common father, Abraham? After all, were not Jews and Arabs both Semitic peoples? Why then, thought Herzl, should the Arabs not greet the returning Jews with open arms—especially since the Jews were the bringers of modern technology, progress, and development, for the general good? Thus, in Herzl's vision, the democratic Jewish State would arise by peaceful means, and the Arabs, who became a minority of their own free will, would be represented in the parliament, the government, the society, and the economy of that utopian land.

What neither Herzl and his colleagues, nor the settlers of the first Jewish colonies in the late nineteenth and early twen-

tieth centuries realized was that, alongside the development
of Zionism—the national Jewish liberation movement—there
was an ever-growing Arab national movement that aimed to
free the Arab peoples from the yoke of the Ottoman Empire
and other foreign rulers. This movement, in the course of
time, was to struggle for the right of Arab self-determination
and the establishment of more modern Arab states, which
would restore to the Arab peoples their former political, military, and cultural glory and greatness. While Jewish youth
dreamed, wrote, and began to organize for the realization of
Zionism in the Land of Israel, young Arab students and intellectuals, who had been exposed to the influence of modern
European nationalism, were beginning to work and organize
throughout the Ottoman Empire, especially in Syria and Lebanon, and also in awakening Egypt.

To the early builders of the Arab national movement, it
was clear that the Land of Israel—which, in their own language, they termed *Falastin*—would in the future become
part of Greater Syria; and that Greater Syria would itself be
part of an Arab state, or even superstate, stretching from the
Atlantic Ocean to the Persian Gulf (or, as the Arabs call it,
the Arabian Gulf).

Just as the early Zionists knew little, if anything, about the
beginnings of the Arab liberation movement, the early activ-
ists of that movement knew nothing about Zionism. They
had no idea that, somewhere in the darkness of the Diaspora,
a Jewish national movement was awakening to life. Nor could
they have known that, within a comparatively short time,
that movement and their own would clash head-on and become embroiled in a bloody conflict that was to last for
generations.

Yet, as early as the first years of the twentieth century, in
the decline of the Ottoman Empire, when dozens of modern
Jewish colonies had already been established in the Land of
Israel, both Jewish and Arab thinkers began to realize that
this problem of head-on collision between two young national
movements would become the main conflict in the area.

The Balfour Declaration of 1917, in which Britain, then a
great power, gave its authority for the establishment of "a

Jewish national home in Palestine" on one hand, and conflicting promises to the Arabs on the other hand, added tremendous impetus to the collision. Opposite Zionism—and, to no small extent, indirectly influenced by Zionism—an Arab-Palestinian national movement, which considered Zionism to be a deadly enemy, began to emerge.

During the thirty years of Mandatory rule, these two national movements crystallized and grew; and that growth was accompanied by increasingly severe and bloody clashes. The essence of the conflict became frighteningly clear: Both of the national movements demanded sole rights to the same territory. On one hand, Zionism demanded sole rights to all of "the Land of Israel"; on the other, the Palestinian-Arab national movement demanded sole rights to all of Falastin. And the Land of Israel and Falastin, from a geographical and territorial standpoint, were one and the same.

Proposals put forward by Britain's Peel Commission in 1937 for compromise and territorial partition between Arabs and Jews were summarily rejected by all the Arabs. Most of the Zionists also rejected them, following a stormy debate in which the main supporters of partition included such personalities as Chaim Weizmann and David Ben Gurion.

In the wake of the Holocaust and the subsequent struggle, the leaders of the United Nations decided that the disputed land should be partitioned into a Jewish state and an Arab state. This time, the great majority of Zionists accepted the decision; the Arabs, however, refused even to consider it.

In the ensuing 1948 War of Independence, which ended in a military victory for the Jews and a crushing defeat for the Arabs, the Land of Israel was bisected by the sword—and the State of Israel arose.

The Declaration of the Independence of the State of Israel includes an extension of "the hand of peace" and "good neighborliness" to the Arabs. In practice, however, the hands of both sides continued to clutch their weapons, and Israel's borders with its neighbors became a demarcation of war zones. Since then, war, the atmosphere of war, the threat of war, and the preparations for war have been dominant factors in the physical, economic, social, emotional, and spiritual life of the Jewish State.

The more than four decades that have elapsed since the establishment of the State of Israel may be divided into two approximately equal periods. The first consists of the nineteen years between the War of Independence in 1948 and the Six Day War in 1967; the second, of the years following that watershed event.

This division is an extremely significant one for Zionism and the State of Israel. The Zionist revolution may be compared to a great wave in the sea of Jewish life. Since its inception, and irrespective of temporary ups and downs, the tide of Zionism rose steadily until it reached its peak in the establishment of the state—a peak that continued until the end of the Six Day War. Following that war, Zionism entered a new period, which—again, irrespective of various ups and downs—has been generally characterized by a tendency to retreat from its original aims.

The first part of Israel's lifespan can be examined in accordance with the five Zionist goals discussed above. The first goal—*the establishment of a Jewish State*—was attained. For the first time since the Hasmonean Kingdom (or, perhaps, since the few short years of Bar-Kochba's revolt), the Jews established a state of their own and imposed their sovereignty over their own territory, the inheritance of their ancient ancestors. In order to stabilize and reinforce the goal thus gained, and to enable any Jew so desiring to settle in the Jewish State, the Law of Return was passed and the gates of Israel opened wide. Within a few short years, the new state absorbed some 1,500,000 Jewish immigrants, doubling and later tripling its Jewish population.

As a result of the War of Independence, following which hundreds of thousands of Palestinian Arabs fled Israel and became refugees, only a small Arab minority remained within the borders of the state. The large Jewish majority, which increased even farther with the waves of immigration, became the decisive force that stamped the State of Israel with its essential character as a Jewish State.

The second goal—*the establishment of a democratic state*—was implemented. The Jewish State of Israel, despite the pangs and sorrows of its birth, was, from the very beginning, a democratic state for its Jewish citizens. Later, following a difficult initial period of military government over the Arab minority, the government installed the basic elements of democracy—equality in the eyes of the law, and the right to elect and be elected—upon all of its citizens, Jews and Arabs alike, and gradually advanced upon the path of democratization.

The third goal—*the establishment of a productive state*—was considerably advanced during the first nineteen years of statehood. On the basis of labor and effort invested by four generations of pioneers, the State of Israel built and developed strong agricultural, industrial, military, administrative, educational, and scientific strata, as required by a modern state. Jews worked in all branches of the national economy, without exception.

The fourth goal—*the establishment of a tolerant state*—was fostered, with the State of Israel achieving a great degree of tolerance in its internal life. True, from the moment of its establishment, Israel encompassed numerous areas of friction: national—between Jews and Arabs; ethnic—between Jews of European and Oriental origin; and religious, economic, social, and class-oriented conflicts. Nevertheless, in general, it succeeded in approaching the goal of "live and let live."

The fifth goal—*the goal of peace*—was not achieved. The Palestinian Arabs considered Israel's War of Independence as an Arab disaster of epic proportions. They became overwhelmed with feelings of hatred and revenge, which spread throughout the entire Arab world. The refugee camps in the Arab states bordering on Israel became hotbeds for the Palestinian-Arab national movement, which inscribed upon its banners the slogans of "armed struggle," vengeance, return to the "stolen lands," and the ruin of Zionism. Israel, meanwhile, fortified itself, established a strong deterrent army, and devoted all its strength to advancing the basic goals of Zionism that it had been able to attain.

Through all those years, from 1949 to 1967, Israel de-

clared—and most of its population and leaders truly felt—
that it was content with the portion of the Land of Israel that
had become the State of Israel. Throughout those nineteen
years, Israel not only repeated this statement before the nations of the world, but taught the younger generation that
Zionism could achieve its full realization within the borders
of the State of Israel, and could honorably and successfully
absorb within those borders all Jews who wished to immigrate. Israel also explicitly declared that, if only the Arabs
would make peace, it would neither demand nor aspire to
any further territorial aims. The principle of partition between
the two peoples was widely accepted by the vast majority of
Zionists and of Israel's Jews.

These achievements—great though they are—should not
be interpreted as implying that the new Israeli society remained free of blemishes, nor that new and severe social
problems failed to arise within that society. The mass immigration in the 1950s, primarily of Jews from Islamic countries, created severe and complicated social and economic
problems. The absorption process gave rise to a heavy load
of negative feelings—deprivation, discrimination, bitterness—among several Jewish ethnic groups.

The Arab minority that remained within the State of Israel
initially was broken and leaderless, and subsequently was
subjected to many years of military administration. Even following the repeal of that administration, many Arabs continued to perceive themselves as second-class citizens, compared to the Jewish citizens of Israel.

At the same time, the "old guard" of Jewish settlers began
to exhibit some disturbing trends toward materialism, vanity,
and self-centeredness. These signs of corruption were soon
made manifest in the highest social and political circles.

The State of Israel did its best, under extremely trying
circumstances, to cope with these problems. Investing great
effort in attempts to correct errors and injustice, Israel continued to advance toward the establishment of a more just
society.

The Six Day War changed the entire situation. Victorious
Israel assumed control of the whole territory of the Land of

Israel, from the Mediterranean Sea in the west to the Jordan River in the east; it conquered all of the Sinai Peninsula and the Gaza Strip from the hands of Egypt, and the Golan Heights from the hands of Syria. This created a new situation, new borders, and powerful new dynamics, which exerted their influence on Zionism and its creation—the State of Israel. Without desiring or seeking it, Israel became a conqueror and an occupying power.

CHAPTER TEN

The Valley of Despair

S TEP BY STEP, ZIONISM IS RETREATING FROM THE REALIZATION
of its integral aims. The State of Israel, the creation of Zionism, is becoming less Jewish and less democratic; its society
is becoming less productive and less tolerant. If Israel continues on the "road to nowhere" along which it has been
traveling since the Six Day War, it will lose its one—admittedly great—achievement in the field of peace: the separate
peace agreement with Egypt.

The primary cause of this reactionary situation is Israel's
continuing military occupation of the West Bank and the
Gaza Strip, with their population of some 1,500,000 Palestinian Arabs. The results of the brilliant military victory achieved
in the 1967 war included a horrifying exposure of all the evil
impulses hidden within Israel as individual human beings and
as a people: arrogance, vanity, indifference to the fate of the
defeated, a strong desire to control the conquered territories
and to enslave their population to the economy of the victors,
and a mystic ritual of "sanctification" of the conquered lands.
And one more thing: the insouciance of those who led the
victory.

Drunk and dizzy with glory and fame, gorged on the fruits
of victory, the leaders imagined themselves all-powerful and
believed that time was bound to work on their behalf. They
began to think, speak, and act in terms of the supremacy of
force, of "might is right," to which they added a sort of "The
sword shall devour forever" fatalism on one hand, and a belief
in divine miracles, which would hasten the coming of the
Messiah, on the other.

These patterns of thought, speech, and action have led ever-
increasing sections of Israeli society, and primarily Israeli youth,
to hate the "strangers" in their midst, and to increase their
hostility toward the Arabs. This, in turn, has engendered the
settlements on the West Bank—some of them built upon the
tricks of land speculators. The "Greater Israel" movement,

whose main goal is to incorporate the West Bank and Gaza into the nation's borders, has led Zionism and Israel astray, diverting them from their proper path and deflecting them from the achievement of their fundamental goals.

We must now ask ourselves some painful questions: Is Israel still a Jewish state? Is Israel still a democratic state? Are Israel's economy and society still productive? Is Israel a state—or a society—of tolerance? And is Israel approaching peace?

A JEWISH STATE?

For an entire generation, ever since the Six Day War, Israel has controlled all of the land governed until 1948 by the British Mandate. This is the area then known to the British, and still known by the Arabs, as "Palestine," or, in Arabic, "Falastin." The regions it includes are the State of Israel in its pre-1967 borders, the West Bank, and the Gaza Strip.

The present population of the State of Israel is composed of 3,500,000 Jewish citizens and 750,000 Arab citizens. Residing in the occupied territories are 1,500,000 Arabs and several tens of thousands of Jews. Thus, the total number of residents living in or controlled by Israel is some 5,500,000: 3,500,000 Jews and more than 2,000,000 Arabs. The Arabs, then, currently comprise nearly 40 percent of the total population of what is known as "Greater Israel."

However, a closer study of the statistical data shows that, in the lowest age group—children up to four years old—there are already as many Arabs as Jews. The trends evidenced in the birth rates of Jews and Arabs are such that, not many years from now, the number of Arabs will equal the number of Jews. These trends will not be significantly affected by Jewish immigration to Israel, even if the latter should increase far in excess of its present proportions (about 20,000 per year). Moreover, Jewish emigration from Israel, a phenomenon that shows no sign of abating, will accelerate the process of numerical equalization even further. The demographic bombshell will not be defused.

It may thus be seen that the ideology of "Greater Israel" must inevitably lead to a state half Jewish and half Arab—in other words, to an explicitly binational state. Anyone who believes that the existing trends can be deflected by massive immigration of hundreds of thousands of Jews must either be totally unaware of the situation of Diaspora Jewry, including that of the Soviet Union, or believe in miracles. Very few young Jews, whether from the West or East, will want to immigrate to "Greater Israel"—a land that lives forever by the sword and tyrannizes half of its population; a land fragmented and polarized by religious extremism and social injustice.

There are, of course, those who count on an eventual "catastrophic Zionism": a situation whereby some future large-scale persecution of Jews, engendered by whatever apocalypse in Eastern and/or Western countries, will bring about mass Jewish emigration to Israel. It should, however, be remembered that the country and people of Israel do not constitute "a people that shall dwell alone." In any catastrophes liable to occur in the forseeable future—nuclear wars or world economic crises—little Israel will inevitably be among the first and most seriously affected victims.

Our conclusion, then, is that since 1967, the great Zionist dream of establishing a state characterized by a definite Jewish majority has been retreating farther and farther away.

A DEMOCRATIC STATE?

If we consider the State of Israel, the West Bank, and the Gaza Strip as a single administrative entity—which, in practice, has been the situation since 1967—then the manifestation of that administration has split the population of that entity into two drastically opposed life forms. The citizens of the State of Israel live in a democracy. They elect representatives from among themselves. They have freedom of speech and freedom of movement. They are permitted to form their own social and political organizations as they see fit. They enjoy all of the human rights and freedoms practiced in the State of Israel since its establishment.

The Palestinian Arabs, however, residents of the West Bank and the Gaza Strip, are ruled and dominated by a regime of military occupation. They do not enjoy even the most elementary democratic rights. They have no representative electoral institutions. They may not form political organizations. They are not even second- or third-class citizens; they are, so to speak, non-citizens. Their status is closer to that of "natives" deprived of rights, the Gibeonites of modern Israeli society.

Greater Israel, then, is a sort of monster with one body and two heads, one free and the other enslaved. Or, perhaps, a set of Siamese twins, inseparably joined by shared internal organs, but with separate heads and hearts filled with hatred for one another: Two societies, side by side and interwoven, yet each with its own set of laws and its own rules of acceptable behavior.

It has been said that the classic democracy—that of Athens—was, in fact, a false democracy, as the Athenian city-state had its socio-economic base in a vast layer of non-citizens and slaves who had no share in the creation and implementation of that "people's rule." How, then, are we to describe the democracy of Israel following the Six Day War? As long as the military occupation of the West Bank and the Gaza Strip persists, as long as Israel maintains sovereignty over 1,500,000 human beings by force of arms alone, there can be no true democracy in Israel. At best, there can be a semi-democracy, or a divided democracy, which will gradually wither away until it has ceased to exist.

In any state that occupies a conquered, hostile population, the elements of conquest—the supremacy of force, racism, and cruelty—must eventually penetrate and destroy the very cellular structure of democracy. Every Jewish citizen in Israel is liable to develop a split personality (and many of them have already begun to do so): one half a Dr. Jekyll, guided by a belief in democracy and Jewish ethics; the other a Mr. Hyde, impelled by a pseudo-Biblical drive to "utterly blot out the memory of Amalek from under heaven," and prepared to commit whatever atrocity toward this detestable goal.

Israeli democracy has taken a giant step backward since the Six Day War. If this retreat is not stopped, democracy in Israel will be irretrievably destroyed, and a rule of tyranny in "Greater Israel" will be established on its ruins.

A PRODUCTIVE STATE?

The "Normal Pyramid"—the goal upheld by early Zionist ideologists to describe the socio-economic structure of the future Jewish State—was based on the assumption that Jews would engage in all forms of work, and that the economy would be modern and extremely innovative. That pyramid, established in Israel by four generations of pioneer labor, has shown wider and wider cracks since the Six Day War. Some of the stones of its foundation have started to fall away, placing it in ever-greater danger of collapse into a random pile of rubble.

One of the greatest distortions is the transformation of Israel's economy—and, indeed, of Israel's entire society— into one primarily based on a gigantic military system. Admittedly, the State of Israel is obligated by circumstances to maintain a strong, brave, flexible, resourceful, and unconventional army in order to survive. This fact was realized and taken into account by Zionist and Israeli leaders from the very beginning. Yet from war to war—mainly following the Six Day War—Israel's army grew at a dizzyingly steep rate. Not even peace with Egypt could stop that growth, and the folly of the unfortunate military adventure in Lebanon accelerated it.

This uncalculated growth, and the resulting large-scale expansion of the country's military industries, have created a huge and constantly metastasizing military-industrial complex, whose tendrils permeate Israel's economy and society. This, in turn, has given rise to a serious disproportion in the allocation of resources to the defense establishment, compared with those allocated to the remaining elements of the economy, and to an increasing dependence on external factors, principally aid from the United States. The heads of this military-industrial complex have gained significant political leverage on the government of Israel, as they would on any government in similar circumstances. As Israel's largest single employer, they influence the activities of the entire economy and society. Only now, in the late 1980s, do some Israeli economists and statesmen appear to realize that the country can no longer bear unbridled expansion of the arms industry, without causing irreparable harm to education, health, and social welfare.

Ever since the Six Day War, those daring to criticize the military-industrial complex structure have been few and far between. The lack of peace, accompanied by the concept that there can be no solution but that of the sword, has naturally brought about the expansion of Israel's military establishment. Guided by a different political concept, that establishment could certainly have been reduced; and both the security and economy of Israel would certainly have stood to gain from such a gradual reduction.

The widest base of Israel's current normal pyramid, then, does not consist of agriculture and civilian industry, as envisioned by the country's ideological forebears, but of a vast military system, including tens of thousands of regular army enlisted persons and officers, tens of thousands of civil servants in the Ministry of Defense and related organizations, and many tens of thousands of military-industrial employees. It is both possible and necessary to maintain an equally efficient defense system on less than the enormous amounts of funding currently allotted to that system, and to improve stability by allocating more of the national budget to civilian production.

Any economy based on military and defense industries to an extent similar to that of Israel must, in order to preserve its viability, locate markets for the export of defense-related products and skilled personnel. Thus, Israel is fast becoming a hugely disproportionate exporter of the tools and doctrines of war. Moreover, the market for such tools and doctrines is dark, lawless, and subject to the uncontrolled competition of other countries. Therefore, if Israel is to succeed in playing by the non-rules of such a market, it must place its weapons and fighters at the disposal of causes foreign to its nature—indeed, at the disposal of some of the ugliest regimes in today's world. The events around "Irangate" speak for themselves.

As long as Israel continues on this path, it will not—cannot—achieve a normal economy or society. The burden of the military-industrial complex will distort the country's economy more and more grossly. Without help from outside sources, it is liable to fall apart altogether.

Another gaping crack in the post-1967 socio-economic pyramid concerns the ethic of "Jewish workers and Jewish work" in Israel—the mainstay of Zionism in its formative years. The opening of Israel's economy to residents of the West Bank and the Gaza Strip, following the Six Day War, brought about the influx of great numbers of Arab laborers from those areas. Instead of using aid money for building and developing an economic infrastructure capable of supporting the population of the occupied territories within the borders of those territories, Israel chose to mingle the two economies. Unorganized or semi-organized Arab labor began to penetrate one sector after another in the Israeli economy. These "cheap" laborers have now become an integral part of the distorted pyramid of the Jewish State.

The first sector to feel the effects of this penetration was that of the moshavim (cooperative agricultural villages), quickly followed by all other forms of agricultural settlement throughout the country. Jewish farmers rapidly became accustomed to a large and inexpensive labor force—including child labor. This external work force, in less than twenty years, has managed to undermine the internal social structure of many moshavim, which were originally based on doing their own work and mutual aid. Now, many Jewish crop growers have become "bosses," with Arab laborers squatting in "Uncle Ahmed's Cabin" at the edge of the farmer's field. In many areas, this blight has caused a return to more primitive agricultural methods, and a partial abandonment of mechanized agrotechnology and progress. As a result, many farms, and no small number of entire villages, have collapsed entirely.

But this phenomenon is not limited to agriculture. The Palestinian Arabs from the occupied territories have become Israel's "hewers of wood and drawers of water." Many of them plant, fertilize, prune, and chop down the Jews' trees. They pump fuel for the Jews' cars. They continue to build the Jews' houses—both in the new Jewish settlements in the occupied territories—which are diametrically opposed to the true pioneering spirit of Israel—and throughout the entire country. They cut the Jews' stone, spread the Jews' plaster, and do all kinds of hard labor and "dirty" work in the Jews' workshops and fields.

The excellent labor laws enacted by Israel's Knesset are not applied to these Arab laborers. Their status is by no means as good as that of the *Gastarbeiter* in the developed economies of Western Europe, as they have neither passport nor national identity. They do not belong to any state, not even to the State of Israel. They are "natives," brought by economic necessity to work on behalf of a society in which they have no share, and the social confusion resulting from the forced stratification of these laborers in the lowest level of Israel's social pyramid has grievously damaged attempts to bridge the class and social gaps within the country's Jewish population.

The transfer of manual labor—called "Black Work" in Hebrew—to the Arabs of the occupied territories has disgraced the value of this kind of work among Israel's Jews. In their haste to rid themselves of the taint now attached to such labor, many Jews have reverted to stereotypical Jewish occupations of the Diaspora: speculation, gambling on the Stock Exchange, and involvement in various black or gray markets. Many practice other doubtful occupations of the sort condemned by Zionist philosophers as a disease inherent within the Jewish Diaspora—a disease forced upon the Jews in their capacity as a persecuted minority, which could and should no longer exist within a Jewish state.

Another aspect of this phenomenon is that Arab laborers from the occupied territories who come to work in Israel are exposed to the vagaries of Israel's economy. Having no legal protection to speak of, they may all too easily be thrown to the claws of unemployment in time of economic crisis. By now, however, the Jewish economy may well have become so accustomed to the presence of these Arab laborers that many Jews have nearly forgotten how to do manual work. It will be tragic if these Arabs become indispensable to the continued functioning of Israel's economy. In summary, the phenomenon of Arab labor from the West Bank and the Gaza Strip has seriously endangered one of the most important of Zionist creations: the Jewish laborer, who honors his work and is honored by it, like the farmers and shepherds of the Bible. If nothing is done to remedy the situation, this creature will be doomed to vanish from the earth, to be replaced by the Jewish do-nothing, the Jewish *schnorrer*, and the Jewish *macher*. The dead weight of these negative occupations in the normal pyramid may well topple it completely, turning the utopian dream expressed by Theodor Herzl into a nightmare.

A TOLERANT STATE?

The schism between Israeli Jews and Palestinian Arabs has intensified immeasurably following the Six Day War. This is a polarization of two peoples at each other's throats—a polarization of Jewish victors versus vengeful Arab vanquished, of the conquerors' bayonets against the stones and molotov cocktails of the conquered. The protracted occupation of the West Bank and the Gaza Strip has led many of the Arab minority within Israel's pre-1967 borders (known as the Green Line) to join the seekers of revenge in the Arab camp, instead of working to bridge the gap with the Jews and to form a foundation for future peace.

This nationalist polarization has inevitably led to intolerance. It may be assumed that most Arab children learn their first lessons in Jew-hating at their mother's breast. In much the same way, too many Jewish children—especially since 1967—learn from their parents' lips such teachings as "The Arabs should be driven out of Israel," or even, "The only good Arab is a dead Arab." This small country is thus accumulating vast reserves of ill-suppressed hostility, which is bursting out through every crack in the wall of social behavior and leading to uncontrollable bloodshed and rebellion.

Moreover, Jewish society in Israel is becoming more and more internally polarized and divided. Orthodox religious movements attempt to force increasingly extremist viewpoints on the secular community, which must react in its own defense. Bitter rivalry and opposition still simmer between Jews of Ashkenazic (European) and Sephardic (Oriental) origin, between the miserable poor and the greedy *nouveaux riches*, between hawks and doves.

True, these and other polarizations existed, in some degree, before 1967. What society, anywhere in the world, is free of some internal disagreement? Yet Israel after the Six Day War and the two disastrous wars that followed it—an Israel characterized by a rickety economy, a daily life beset with tension, and a future uncertain at best—has become a hotbed of contrast and strife. What little tolerance and patience that still remain are fast running out. And the various extremes often tend to merge (for example: Orthodox Oriental Jews of limited means and hawkish ideology, versus secular, well-off, dovish Ashkenazim), forming divided, explosive clusters. The combination of Jewish-Arab intolerance with intra-Jewish intolerance is a strong factor fanning the flames of violence and lawlessness.

WHEN THERE IS NO PEACE

Since the beginning of Zionism, claims laid by both sides to the same territory—that called Falastin by Arabs and the Land of Israel by Jews—have been the major source of conflict and dispute between Israeli Jews and Palestinian Arabs. Following Israel's conquest of the territories bloodily disputed by the two national movements, leaders and people alike too often find themselves motivated by that primordial drive known as "the territorial imperative." This drive is well known throughout the history of humankind, and appears to affect most of the animal kingdom as well. At times, wars fought over territories may assume the guise of religious wars, holy wars, wars of "honor and dignity," or wars of blood feud and revenge. However, in reality, the great majority of wars are caused by that age-old territorial imperative.

The early wars waged by the People of Israel were not much different from territorial wars launched by other tribes and peoples. Such were the conquests of Joshua and the Judges after him; such were the wars of Saul and David, and many other Biblical wars. The maps of the Land of Israel verbally drawn in the Bible—some of them described as being protected by divine promise—are maps of territories contained within various borders. Those borders alternately grew and shrank, expanded and contracted, in the wake of wars, conquests, and counterconquests.

The factor that distinguishes the Bible as the Great Book of all humanity is the Prophets' ceaseless struggle against the evil instincts of humankind, and against society's instincts for violence, robbery, and warfare. This struggle may be termed unnatural, as it seems directly opposed to human nature. Territory as such was not among the Prophets' chief concerns. They were much more interested in what was being done *within* a given territory: the relationships of human beings with their God and with each other. Did their people believe in our merciful God, or worship bloodthirsty idols? Was their society one of righteousness and justice, or one of evil and injustice? Did the rich assist the poor, or did they oppress them?

Amos and Isaiah were not at all impressed by the extensive territorial gains made by the kings who ruled in their days. The military victories did nothing to still their outcry against oppression, deception, and injustice. The punishment and destruction foreseen by the Prophets had nothing to do with a greater or lesser extent of territory, but with the "evil in the sight of God" perpetrated within the Land of Israel—no matter how great or small that land was. Indeed, at a higher stage in their prophesying, the Prophets of Israel spoke of the total abolition of war. Their statement "Nation shall not take up sword against nation; they shall never again know war" really means that territories will no longer constitute an excuse for battle.

This vision of peace, as foretold by the Prophets, is linked with a vision in which the People of Israel will set a worldwide example of their laws of truth and righteousness, justice and mercy, freedom and lovingkindness. This People of Israel, which will live in peace in Zion, at peace with itself and its neighbors, is nowhere defined by the Prophets as being limited to any precise territorial boundaries. The Prophets' Zion, the central focus of this Chosen People, is indeed Jerusalem. The naming of this city, and of the land surrounding it, constitutes a territorial specification. However, the importance of the mission entrusted to the People of Israel as a "light to the nations" by far supersedes that of the physical dimensions of its land area.

The Prophets were aware of the territorial vastness that characterized the surrounding empires: Assyria, Babylonia, Egypt, and Greece. Yet the example that they demanded of their own people had nothing to do with territorial size. They considered Israel's contribution to the world to be the individual and collective conquest of its own evil impulses, especially those of murder and war.

Zionism sought to return the Jewish People to Zion, not only to reclaim a certain geographical territory but also to establish within that territory a model society of justice, and thereby to prove that the Jews could return to their homeland via the paths of truth and righteousness blazed by the Prophets of Israel.

When fate cast Zionism into the midst of a binational-territorial armed conflict, many Zionist leaders felt they would have to adopt a territorial compromise. Realizing that the territory known as the Land of Israel was being fought over by two peoples and two national movements, they concluded that the way to end the bloodshed was by partition, with each people receiving a separate part of the whole for its own national goals. Despite the Arabs' total refusal to compromise, many of the great Zionists, including Chaim Weizmann and David Ben Gurion, were prepared to agree to a solution of partition.

The 1948 War of Independence was, in fact, the partition of the disputed land by the sword. Zionism established the

State of Israel within Palestine, a part of the Land of Israel. The defeated Palestinian Arabs and the other Arab nations did not accept the partition. The various governments of Israel, up to the Six Day War, declared their acceptance of partition, adding that, if the Arabs would make peace, Israel would refrain from further territorial demands. The Arabs refused.

Following Israel's victory in the Six Day War and conquest of the entire expanse of disputed land area, the territorial imperative arose in Israel with all its might. Enlisted in the service of that imperative were each and every possible argument for not giving up a single inch of that land. Some of these arguments were religious, nationalist, and security-related; others rational, economic, and strategic; and still others irrational, mystical, and emotional.

During the years between the Six Day War and the Yom Kippur War, the territorial imperative was accompanied by a vainglorious sense of superiority on one hand, and a quasi-Messianic search for redemption on the other. Along with the increasing physical strength of the Israeli army came a belief that the 1967 war had been the first in a series of supposedly divine miracles. The territorial imperative soon led to the establishment of new Jewish settlements in the West Bank, the Gaza Strip, the Sinai, and the Golan Heights.

Only after the Yom Kippur War, the terrible shock brought about by that war, the change of government in Israel, from Labor to Likud, and Sadat's visit to Jerusalem, did some of Israel's leaders (first among them, ironically enough, Menachem Begin) start to regain some measure of sobriety. These leaders finally understood, albeit at a heavy toll of human lives, that peace could only be ensured by the return of territories. Thus, in return for peace with Egypt, Israel restored the entire Sinai Peninsula to Egyptian hands.

Yet many Israeli leaders still persisted in ignoring the problem of the two peoples and the two conflicting national movements simultaneously residing within the same land. Golda Meir's denial of the problem took the form of a simplistic statement that the Palestinian people did not exist, and that a nonexistent people could not possibly sponsor a national movement. Menachem Begin's denial was differently phrased: He believed the problem could be solved by the semantic trick of renaming the Palestinian Arabs "Arabs of the Land of Israel."

The leaders of Israel did not understand—and some still do not understand—that without a compromise between the two peoples and their national movements, there can be no peace in this part of the world. There can be no exit from the vicious cycle of terror, counter-terror, and endless war, unless there is territorial partition.

The present feeling of "no way out" is increasing the already fearsome depth of racism and extremism among both peoples. This feeling provides fertile ground for a multitude of social and political poisonous weeds. The protracted occupation of the West Bank and the Gaza Strip has transformed the outcome of the Six Day War into a Pyrrhic victory. Its insidious influences have exposed the evil instincts hidden in the hearts of all humanity—including Jews—and has spread their putrefaction throughout the tissues of Jewish society in Israel.

The lack of progress in untying the Gordian knot may result in its forced undoing by the sword. If no solution is found, the process of withdrawal from the original goals of Zionism will inevitably persist in the State of Israel. Israel will become less Jewish and less democratic; its economy will never achieve normal health; and the vicious growths of intolerance and xenophobia will run riot.

What, then, is the final balance of this process to date? Who has profited and who has lost in Israel after the Six Day War?

Those who have profited the most have been the members of the extremist-Orthodox-religious-nationalist stream of Zionism. Their greatest opportunity came with the conquest of the entire territory of what had been Mandatory Palestine by the Israeli army. They coined the term "Greater Israel" and formulated an ideology based on their own unilateral interpretation that that land, in its post-1967 borders, is sacrosanct.

They created what could well be termed "ritual Zionism"—

a process that transmuted the settling of the occupied territories into a ritual partly based on ancient tribal ways. Among those customs are sanctification of the land through conquest, and massive settlement by any possible means—including force, deception, and bribery.

This doctrine, founded on fragments of precepts, religious rulings, interpretations, and legends more or less vaguely descended from the Bible and the Oral Tradition of Judaism, teaches its disciples that some Arabs residing in the Land of Israel are the descendants of "Amalek," legendary enemy of the People of Israel.

This ritualistic doctrine has given rise to a generation of young religious fanatics, who do not hesitate to undermine and pervert the democratic and tolerant foundations of Israel as a nation and a state, for the sake of their self-established goals of mass settlement. In order to achieve those goals, they are prepared to deform beyond all recognition some of the most vital elements of Judaism. For the sake of the land ritual, they reject the fundamental Jewish belief in peace. In fact, they consider peace to be much less significant than the rite of mass settlement. Moreover, by their cruel and violent treatment of the conquered, they diminish the value of loving-kindness and mercy to all; they transform the Prophets' teachings of the sanctity of life, righteousness, and justice into an empty mockery.

These fanatic groups, not content with enslaving the Torah of Israel to their own grim ends, distort its wisdom by selective adoption of only those elements that they believe important to the fostering of those ends. From the impurities that have clung to Judaism (as to any great religion or civilization), they have forged the mask and idol of a primitive, jealous, and lightless religion.

Even worse, they are educating many of Israel's young people in their pseudo-religious and pseudo-nationalist ritual—which flourishes particularly well on the soil of ignorance. They refuse to take into consideration any sort of reality: neither that of the world, of the great powers, of the region, nor even the reality of their own people. The fact that the People of Israel within the State of Israel constitute a small nation in a small country (with or without the occupied territories), surrounded by a developing Arab world and a huge Moslem world, is utterly irrelevant to them. The fact that most of the world's nations, including the two super-powers, demand that Israel make peace via partition and compromise, is of no interest to them. They live in their own closed world of Messianic delusions and mirages, as "a people that shall dwell alone, and shall not be reckoned among the nations."

In their belief that they and they alone hold the key to the redemption of Israel, they are prepared to sweep their entire people along with them onto a course of no return. In their belief that the staking out of every hill and field in Judea, Samaria, and Gaza by Jews constitutes an act of sanctification and redemption, they not only deny the Prophets' vision of peace among Jews and throughout all humankind, but hasten the most terrible of fates—the end of the Zionist dream.

The vicious cycle of evil and bloodshed, in which the State of Israel has become enmeshed, now imperils its very existence. Both sides of the conflict are charged with vast energies of hostility. The extremism of madness and terror of the Arabs feeds the flames of the ritualistic, aggressive extremism now rising among Jews. If these energies are not neutralized and disarmed, they will one day result in a terrible chain of explosions liable to destroy both of the peoples inhabiting that land. Ritual Zionism, if left unchecked, may well turn Israel into a desperate, blind Samson, crying, "Let me die with the Philistines!"

And who are the great losers in Israel following the Six Day War?

Obviously, the first loser is Judaism: that pure, clear Judaism whose Prophets and sages, throughout an entire millennium in the Land of Israel and two millennia in exile, have invested vast efforts in purifying their people of the rites of violence, the impurities of cruelty, superstition, and tribal ritual.

The Judaism founded on the universal ethics of peace, goodness, blessing, life, grace, lovingkindness, and mercy has been sorely beaten by the proponents of ritual Zionism. Here and there, great figures of the Jewish religion have tried to warn against the nationalist fanaticism that has attached itself to Judaism, to suck the marrow of its bones and poison its very soul. Here and there, bold religious Jews have cried out against the dreadful perversion of Judaism before their very eyes. These, however, have comprised only a small minority, compared to the frenetic mobs inflamed by the false priests and prophets of the new ritualism. The pure stream of Judaism still runs—but it has been forced far down below the surface; and above it bubble the foul streams of the new zealotry called religious-ritual-Zionism.

The next great losers are Socialist Zionism and the Labor Movement. Socialist Zionism established as its watchword the values of equality, social justice, self-realization, and personal example. These values were embodied in the Labor Movement leaders, who harnessed themselves to the task of reclaiming the Land of Israel, and of educating generations of young pioneers in Israel and throughout the Diaspora.

The Labor Movement forged the most important organizations responsible for the defense of modern-day Judaism in its homeland, and imbued them with a set of values and codes to be maintained even in wartime. The Labor Movement headed the practical and political struggle for the founding of the State of Israel. With the realization of the age-old dream—a Jewish State in the Promised Land—it was only natural for the Labor Movement to be charmed by the glory of statehood in Israel.

Alas, it was that very glory—accompanied by the pomp and pleasures of stately rule—which eroded some of the Labor Movement's basic values. In the 1950s and 1960s, vanity and materialism spread through increasing sectors of Israel's Labor leadership. In its devotion to action and practical accomplishment, the Labor Movement did not give sufficient thought to the reinforcement of its ideological theory and education. Slowly, it began to divest itself of some of its former values, in favor of the splendor of statehood. Some of its leaders, who claimed to be "people of action," went so far as to consider Socialism an outmoded phenomenon of the past.

The Six Day War found the Labor Movement apparently at the peak of its strength and force; yet, in reality, some of its limbs had already fallen prey to rot. Following that fateful war, the Labor Movement became incapable of withstanding the challenges imposed by its role as a Jewish-Zionist-Socialist movement. Its leaders at the helm of government failed to exploit the brilliant military victory as the lever of a daring peace process. They climbed no peak from which they could have looked forward to the future. Rather, they "waited for a telephone call" from their defeated enemies, assuming that time would work in their favor. Dizzy from the fumes of victory, they rested on their laurels, and failed to develop the requisite ideological and educational antidote to the venom of conquest. On the contrary, the Labor leadership surrendered to the territorial imperative. Indeed, some of its leading personalities joined forces with the rite of Greater Israel, fabricating socialist justification for the conquest, annexation, and settlement of all the occupied territories.

During a crucial decade, from 1967 to the Likud electoral victory of 1977, the Labor Movement, headed by the Labor Party then in power, was swept further and further to the political right. Under the Labor government, Israel's economy became accustomed to the concept of cheap, unorganized labor from the occupied territories, and Arab children were put to work in Jewish fields. Under that government, from 1967 to 1973, the vainglorious "security concept" grew and flourished, culminating in the disaster of the Yom Kippur War. Under that government a class of *nouveaux riches* arose, fed on the fast, vast profits of war. Large sections of the country's Jewish population—especially its youth—began to consider *Socialism* a rude word. Throughout that period, anyone who opposed the party line was, at best, judged peculiar. At worst, they were vigorously condemned and excommunicated. By the time the Labor government finally fell in 1977, the Israel Labor Party, divested of most of its ideological assets, resembled an impoverished, distorted reflection of its former self.

The third loser after the Six Day War is Liberal Zionism. The ideology of Liberalism accompanied the formation of the

Zionist Movement from the very beginning—in fact, even before the rise of Socialist Zionism. The best and brightest of Liberalism was represented in Zionism by the teachings and writings of such famous thinkers as Pinsker and Ahad Ha'Am—and certainly by such illustrious names as Herzl, Nordau, and Weizmann. All of these were great Jews and great Liberals, who succeeded in combining the moral values of the prophetic doctrine with those of Liberalism.

No wonder, then, that the Liberal Zionists made common cause with the Labor Movement pioneers and the Religious Zionists. The wide-ranging covenant forged by those three ideological streams inspired Zionist thought and deed for many decades. Following the establishment of the State of Israel, the Liberal Zionists sought new allies, farther to the right of the political map. Their ideology was a difficult one for many of the new immigrants, who had never before encountered either Liberalism or Socialism. Accordingly, the Liberals allied themselves with the populist, rightist Herut (Liberty) Movement, which held greater appeal for the masses at the time.

After the Six Day War, the Liberal Zionists lost no time in peeling off one after another of the ideological elements of Liberalism. They became a miserable shadow of the Herut Movement, whose hour had arrived with the conquest and settlement of the occupied territories. Rejecting their own ideological and electoral foundations, the Liberals became tolerated parasites of Herut.

Of the basic Liberal values—"live and let live," protection of the weaker elements of society, rejection of the supremacy of force, universal justice, open-mindedness, "the art of the possible," the need for compromise, equality in the eyes of the law, and maximum protection of civil rights—only the merest vestiges remain. The term "Liberal Zionism" now wears the obligatory quotation marks of nationalism, narrow-mindedness, and dullness. Bowed down by these new encumbrances, Liberal Zionism has become a pale shadow on the political and ideological map of Israel.

To be sure, this is not the whole picture. There have indeed been prominent religious Jews who, following the Six Day

War, cried out against the dangers lying in wait for the religion and people of Israel, and pointed out the bottomless pit into which ritual Zionism threatens to lead the Jewish religion.

A number of Labor Movement leaders have warned against the rejection of Labor values, and cautioned that their movement's rightward drift was actually a deterioration. Several brave Liberals have demanded that their movement extricate itself from the talons of the political hawk and return to its own ways and its own values. Yet none of these were entirely able to withstand the rising waves of unchecked evil impulses, which now threaten to overcome Israeli society.

The various peace movements, the large-scale demonstrations of the Peace Now movement, the sensible articles by many of Israel's foremost intellectuals—all these, like "Stop" signs and "Danger" signals, stand in the hope of halting Israel's mad, nationalistic rush downhill.

CHAPTER ELEVEN

The Door of Hope

THOSE WHO HOLD ZIONISM DEAR, AND ALL JEWS WHO IDENTIFY
as Zionists all over the world—especially the great American
Jewish community—must now ask themselves a piercing
question: What was Zionism in the past, and what is Zionism
today? Was Zionism, as we have repeatedly stated in our
discussion, a national liberation movement of the Jewish People? Did that movement indeed aim to establish a Jewish state
in the Biblical homeland and to found that state on the principles of freedom, justice, and peace, as dictated by the visions
of the Prophets of Israel and as recorded in the Declaration
of Independence of the State of Israel?

Or was Zionism perhaps a sort of laboratory experiment,
in which some invisible "Minister of History" attempted to
test the group of humanity known as the Jewish People, in
order to see what would happen to a small people with a
great spiritual and moral heritage, that had been dispersed
across the globe as a religious and national minority among
the nations for two thousand years? What would happen to
that people when it returned to its own land, established its
own state, and became a majority for the first time in twenty
centuries?

How would such a people, under very difficult experi-
mental conditions, act toward the minorities within its midst?
Would it treat them as it was treated when it was itself a
minority? Or, perhaps, having become a majority, would it
manage not to do to the minorities what is distasteful to
itself—and thereby to withstand the test of the prophetic
heritage and vision?

If this is the test of Zionism—the test of Hillel the Sage,
and the test of Chaim Weizmann, first president of the State
of Israel, who said that the greatest test of the state would
be its attitude toward minorities—it is *a test that Israel and
Zionism have failed to withstand since 1967.* Does the realization of Zionism, then, prove the apparent rule of human

behavior that any oppressed minority that becomes a majority also eventually becomes an oppressor?

The penetrating question remains: Was it for this—to prove that the Jews, like any other nation, can become tyrannical rulers, once given the chance—that the Zionist undertaking exacted the labor and sacrifice of generations? Was the establishment of this Jewish State—a materialistic state that lives by the sword—a worthwhile effort? Does such a state solve the Jewish problem? Is the refuge that such a state offers the Jews one of real security? Does it radiate light upon the Jewish People and the world? Or is it no more than one more small, miserable, God-forsaken country, one of the many that crowd the edges of humanity?

A no less difficult question is this: Can Israel and its parent, Zionism, be redirected back toward their original goals, in the light of the vision of the Prophets of Israel? Is there a "door of hope" for Israel and Zionism; or are they doomed to languish in the "valley of despair"?

Before we attempt to answer these existential questions, we must first consider a question arising from the sum total of crucial subjects covered in the preceding chapters of this book. Our basic assumption was that Israel's deviation from its original path, following the Six Day War, resulted from its being overcome and deformed by the evil impulse of conquest and territorial domination. The question is: What about our Arab adversaries, both in general and the Palestinian Arabs in particular? Are they not controlled by these same impulses? Is the Palestinian Covenant—the PLO's "Constitution"—not merely an appeal for territorial domination over all of "Greater Palestine," to be established upon the ruins of Israel, in a campaign of bloodshed and revenge? Are they prepared for any sort of territorial compromise? Are any of the Arabs prepared to talk with the Israelis? And, if they are not, what point is there to all of the discussion on these pages? What point can there be to a one-sided chess game?

Yet none of these important questions are decisive regarding the future of Zionism. Zionism, from its very infancy, had to deal with a Palestinian-Arab national movement that was totally unwilling to compromise with it on any territorial issue: not half the territory, not one quarter of it, not even one inch of land. Nevertheless, despite protracted violence and strife, Zionism succeeded in remaining faithful to its Jewish and democratic goals, and even in implementing those goals in the spirit of the Prophetic vision.

The problem facing Israel and Zionism is not "Are they prepared to talk with us?" but "Are we prepared to talk among ourselves—and if so, what are we to say to ourselves?" This is a human and a Jewish problem; a problem that affects, first and foremost, our own existence.

Let us assume that, even today, the other side is not prepared to talk with us. Let us assume that each and every Arab longs to throw us out of the Middle East and to take over our territory for themselves. Even in this worst case scenario, we must answer for our own image as human beings and as Jews: What is the nature of the political and social regime in which we live; and what are the borders within which we are willing and able to survive?

If we state that we are prepared for territorial compromise and partition, we can, from a moral position of ethical and political power, hold the occupied territories as a surety for peace, until a willing partner in dialogue can be found. This answer—simple, yet based on principle—was not the one given by Israel following the Six Day War. Instead, Israel became inextricably tangled in the coils of annexation and settlement of the occupied territories.

Zionism could, and should, have observed the fate of the Palestinian-Arab nationalist movement. Zionism should have noted that the latter's intransigence and extremism led it to disaster after disaster. Zionism should have realized that it was the Arabs' original goal of Greater Palestine and standpoint declaring "Not one inch to the Zionists!" that eventually led the Palestinian Arabs to lose their own last inch of land.

We did not learn this lesson, nor did we face up to the major—primarily internal Jewish-Zionist—problem affecting our existence. Instead, we used the excuse of what was and was not happening on the other side; and, by so doing, made ourselves, our lives, and our future hostage to the extremist nationalists in the Arab camp. We laid ourselves open to a particularly vicious cycle in which the flames of vengeance and terror, fanned by fanatic Arab nationalists, serve those fanatics' ends by evoking kindred demons of extremism among Jews.

If we ever want to break this bloody chain, we must stop handing the keys to our fate and future to our most extremist enemies. We must first look within, examine our own essence as Jews and Zionists, and realize what a distortion of our humanity and Judaism we have brought upon ourselves, and what destructive ritualism we have adopted.

Only if, following that internal examination, we manage to comprehend that we must declare our readiness in principle for peace via compromise and partition, can we accurately examine the Arabs' response. This is the vantage point that Israel should have retained, while maintaining a strong, flexible, and unconventional army. Instead, we were smitten with a confusion of the senses and a gluttony for land.

Israel and Zionism, as they prepare to face the last decade of the twentieth century, have four options open to them. The first of these is to continue, more or less, on the course that Israel adopted following the Six Day War. Admittedly, that course is liable to bring about the atrophy of Zionism, transforming it into a claustrophobic, separatist movement; however, the State of Israel, as a state, will be able to survive on that course for a relatively long time. Other nations have dominated minorities in their midst for generations, have suffered many wars and rebellions, and yet have not collapsed. Even carrying the weight of the occupied territories and their population like some gigantic albatross around its neck, Israel will be able to keep dragging itself along from bog to bog, leaning on the crutches of the Jewish Diaspora and the United States for support. Yet, in the long run, such a state can have no future.

The second option is an almost certain recipe for rapid downfall and destruction. If, following an economic collapse, a social breakdown, or a serious failure in defense—and these three gruesome prospects haunt our doorstep like Gorgons— the deceived and disappointed masses cry out: "Give us a strong man who will bring us order!", they will most probably get what they ask for—and more. Such a leader will run Israel like a dictatorship, annex the occupied territories, drive out the Arabs, crumble any remaining democratic structure in Israel, and lead the country into a final, desperate, and hopeless war.

The third alternative involves exerting pressure and handing down solutions from outside. The assumption here is that the two superpowers, despite their mutually opposed interests, will reach the conclusion that peace must be forced on Israel and the Arabs by partitioning the country. Such a move may well take place, if both superpowers can succeed in reaching effective international arrangements to dispel the remaining tensions between them, so as to prevent nuclear world war.

If the United States and the Soviet Union choose this path, on which they have already begun—slowly and cautiously—to walk, they will also have to put out regional conflagrations and dismantle explosive charges in various parts of the world. Left unattended, these powder kegs could well blow up in their faces, setting off a chain reaction that would end all hope of peace between them. The Jewish-Arab conflict—or, more precisely, the quarrel between Jewish Israelis and Palestinian Arabs, around which the entire conflict is centered—is one of the most dangerous in today's world. An arrangement between the superpowers could bring about a coerced peace based on partition and guaranteed by the superpowers themselves.

Such a solution would save Israel as a state, but would not save Zionism as a movement. No ideological movement can survive without the oxygen of goal and path, vision and fulfillment. If Israel's path is forced on it by Washington and Moscow, its Jewish population will become embittered, humiliated, and degraded by the knowledge that it was incapable of finding its own way to a life of peace, dignity, and justice, but had to accept the dictates of others so as not to disturb the surrounding world. Many of the best young people born into such a society will not wish to continue living in it.

Israel's fourth option is to take its fate into its own hands,

with confidence and conviction, and to adopt a course leading
to peace via compromise and partition. This course is undoubtedly the hardest road of all, calling for an entire people,
raised on a ritual of land-worship, to give up a portion of its
ancestral heritage in exchange for peace. This course means
that for the sake of future life and peace, Israel—individually
and collectively—must overcome the evil impulse of the territorial imperative, which rules that any place that we have
conquered and occupied is ours.

It means that in order to survive, the People of Israel must
be given a new heart and a new spirit. This course will demand
true spiritual greatness, both of its leaders and its followers.
Yet it will unfailingly lead to a Jewish, democratic, productive, tolerant, and peaceful state in the spirit of the prophetic
vision of life, peace, justice, freedom, equality, brotherhood,
and mercy.

Admittedly, the chances of an entire people adopting this
new-old course are slim. It would be more probable to assume
that significant portions of the People of Israel will remain
on the confused course of ritual Zionism, or will bow to
solutions of coercion. Nonetheless, this course, and this alone,
leads to the true door of hope for the Jewish People, Zionism,
and Israel. Yet who will open this gate for us, before it is too
late? Who holds the key to this gate of hope, distant though
it may be?

The first to act in paving the road to the door of hope must
be the sages of the genuine Judaism of Israel, those undeceived
by the purveyors of a false Judaism. Such persons of faith
and purity exist in Israel and the Jewish world. It is up to
them to gather the spiritual and ethical strength to defuse the
mines now scattered in the fields of our life—mines charged
with the explosive of distorted Judaism and the shrapnel of
fragmented sources taken out of context, and triggered by
slogans of "sacred land" and "war by divine command."
Those who cherish the religion of Israel, and especially the
doctrine of the Prophets, must move through the minefields
like sappers, disarming the mines one by one.

They must eliminate the concept of "death before withdrawal" as it is applied to every inch of the Land of Israel,

and replace it with the Jewish value of sanctity of life. They must get rid of the idea of "war by divine command" for the sake of territory, and replace it with the value of peace, so characteristic of Israel's true religion and tradition. They must uproot the violence, whether against Jews or non-Jews, that has begun to flourish in our lives, and re-educate us in the values of righteousness and justice taught by the Prophets of Israel. They must remove oppression, discrimination, and hatred, and install in their stead doctrines of freedom, equality, and brotherhood. They must deflate the vanity of the conquerors and occupiers, and establish the Jewish values of humility, lovingkindness, and mercy.

Ritual Zionism has conquered and imprisoned Judaism and its doctrines. Judaism has become captive in the hands of those who raise the images of false ritual. The teachers of true religion and the leaders of pure faith must now redeem Judaism from its captivity and give it back its freedom. This is a difficult and thankless role, which only brave hearts and strong spirits can fulfill.

This is the historic role that they now must bear. It cannot, and will not, be fulfilled by anyone other than themselves. Only the teachers of true Judaism have the strength to contend with the misrepresenters of Judaism; only they have the spiritual authority to fight for the soul of Judaism within the camp of Orthodoxy. It is their role to purge the imperfections that have clung to Judaism. It is their role to make the true religion of Israel known to all, by preaching, writing, and explaining.

Such great spiritual figures do exist among the Jewish People. Many of them weep in their secret hearts over what the ritualists have done to the Torah of Israel. They must now understand that theirs is the role of rescue. They must cry out aloud and not cease until they have liberated Judaism and restored it to its purity and splendor, in the eyes of their own people and of the world.

If such a rescue process does take place, it will herald the coming of a new era—not only for Zionism, but for the State of Israel and all of Judaism. This new era will not arrive at once; it will not immediately bring the long-awaited peace, nor even the much-desired social reform. The way from the door of hope to the corridor, and from there to the main hall of the sanctuary, will be long and arduous. But the very entrance through that door will be the turning point, the first step in the renaissance of Zionism.

This process will bring Israel back to its original priorities: social justice, maximum equality, closing of the economic and social gaps within it, and granting of equal opportunities to all. This process will return the Galilee and the Negev to the top of Israel's priority list for development. By receiving Israel's best human and material resources, these areas will become a lodestone for innovative economic, social, and scientific creativity, as befits the new era of humanity on the threshold of the next century.

This internal purification, should it indeed come to pass, will become the new standard of Zionist Israel. Only when that standard has been raised on high will the Jews of Israel be able to prove—first and foremost, to themselves—that their society has overcome its misleading evil impulse, the territorial imperative, in a true expression of the ancient Jewish proverb:

> Who is mighty? He that subdues his (evil) nature. (MISHNAH AVOT 4:1)

This subduing will restore Zionism to its original role: the movement of a nation whose description, often translated as "the Chosen People," may more accurately be termed "the People of Choice." A people that has made the choice of peace, goodness, and blessing, rather than war, evil, and malediction; the choice of social justice and tolerance of strangers, rather than oppression and xenophobia; the choice of freedom for all, rather than enslavement of the weak. Such an Israel, and such a Zionism, will resume their rightful place as a source of pride to Jews throughout the world. Only then can we hope to provide them with positive reasons to build their lives in Israel.

Zionism has proved that Jews are capable of establishing and defending a state of their own. Only with a new heart and a new spirit can Zionism now prove that it is also capable of providing a focus of spiritual inspiration for world Jewry, by realizing the values of justice and peace, as reflected in the vision of the Prophets of Israel.

Once Israel has reoriented itself toward moral values, Jews throughout the Diaspora will be able to take pride in Israel as a state that practices the best of human and civil rights for all its citizens. Their pride in Israel will be based, not only on its physical and military strength, but mainly on its moral and ethical power. Such a purified Zionism can become a magnet for young Jews who long to live a better, more human, more Jewish, and more nearly perfect life.

At the outset of our discussion, we stated that the internal revolution of Zionism and Israel, accompanied by the process of creating "a new heart and a new spirit," is vital to the Jewish People and to Zionism itself; and, further, that it can never result from external occurrences or factors. It should be reiterated that these internal processes within Zionism will be no less essential and no less valid, even if they are not immediately followed by a parallel, positive reaction on the part of the Arabs; even if they do not immediately result in Arab acceptance of Israel and Arab willingness for peace.

Nevertheless, this internal process cannot fail to reap a vast external harvest. Only the heartless, blind, and deaf can fail to notice that the Arab world around us harbors not one, but many and varied political streams and processes; not only extremist fanatics, but moderate, realistic human beings. Arab states and leaders from the Atlantic Ocean to the Persian Gulf, have declared that following the solution of the Palestinian problem by compromise and partition they will be willing to accept and make peace with Israel.

If the internal change does occur within Israel, its image, form, and status in the eyes of the world will be immeasurably improved—in the most real-political sense. And this change in itself will provide impetus and acceleration for a new *rapprochement* between Jews and Arabs. If and when the two sides agree to compromise and partition, if and when (following a necessarily involved and complex process) peace prevails in the Middle East, the former enemies will find a new interrelationship—as neighbors who have accepted each other and joined forces in a common life and destiny.

Over the years, once the century-old minefields of fear, hatred, and jealousy have been slowly and patiently disarmed, Israel, the Palestinians, and the Jordanians may find themselves establishing a common market—and, perhaps, in the more distant future, even a confederation. Such a political entity could constitute a leading force in the Middle East, forging the path to a new and shining era of peace and progress, technological development, and religious and national tolerance.

This land, holy to the three great world religions and to most of humankind; this land, which bridges Europe, Asia, and Africa, and constitutes a geopolitical focus between the two superpowers of East and West; this land, poised on the demographic and sociological equator, between the rich, industrialized, northern third and the poor, deprived, southern two-thirds of humanity—this land can, and must, serve as the keystone in the arch of the One World.

The only alternative to the utter destruction of the human race in the fast-approaching twenty-first century is worldwide agreement, led by the superpowers, to a series of arrangements that will enable humankind to survive, in the simplest and most alarming sense of the word. This series of arrangements will grant decisive importance to the Middle East, and Israel will have a key role in achieving and maintaining peace in the region and throughout the world.

Isaiah, greatest of statesmen-prophets, foresaw such a development some 2,700 years ago. In his day, too, there were two great powers: the Assyrian Empire to the north and the Egyptian Empire to the south. Isaiah predicted that, following repeated clashes between Egypt and Assyria in their efforts to take over the world of his time, an era of peace would prevail in the world, and Israel would be the link between the two great powers:

> In that day, Israel shall be a third partner with Egypt and Assyria as a blessing on earth; for the Lord of Hosts will bless them,

saying, "Blessed be My people Egypt, My handiwork Assyria, and My very own Israel." (19:24–25)

All human beings, of all nations, are "God's handiwork"; and it is Israel, with its new heart and new spirit, that must be a blessing in the midst of the earth—the entire earth. Only by fulfilling this perfect and splendid goal can Israel become a whole land—a land of entire peace.

There will be those among you who may say: "These are but dreams." But who are those who cry "Dreams"? Jews, living by the age-old heritage of the visionary Prophets of Israel? Zionists, whose great enterprise was founded on Herzl's daydreams? Israelis, who have been fighting for their dreams for four generations?

"Dreams"? Is this terrible century in which we live not also characterized by great achievements on behalf of humankind?

Of all those who lived in Europe during and between the World Wars, who dared to dream that most of the European nations—including such traditional enemies as Germany and France—would become, in the last quarter of this century, an Economic Community with open borders?

Of all those who lived in Asia and America before, during, and following World War II, who dared to dream that the United States and Japan, after years at each other's throats, would dwell as allies, in a state of full-fledged peace?

Of all those who struggled under the yoke of colonialism in black Africa half a century ago, who dared to dream that, by the end of this century, that continent would include dozens of independent states, which—despite great difficulties and against all odds—had brought about their own liberation from imperialist conquest?

And who at the turn of the century dared to dream of a worldwide quantum leap in science and technology? A leap that could not only propel humanity into outer space but may yet see us into an era of unparalleled welfare and peace?

Besides Herzl, who of the participants in the First Zionist Congress in Basel in 1897 dared to dream that the Jewish State would arise within fifty years? And who, in Israel of

1967, dared to dream that the Israeli flag would fly, a few years later, over an Embassy in Cairo?

Let us keep moving, then, along the road from dream to action—the path of the Prophets and the Psalmist:

> When the Lord restores the fortunes of Zion—we see it as in a dream—our mouths shall be filled with laughter, our tongues with songs of joy. Then shall they say among the nations, "The Lord will do great things for them!" The Lord will do great things for us and we shall rejoice. Restore our fortunes, O Lord, like watercourses in the Negeb. They who sow in tears shall reap with songs of joy. Though he goes along weeping, carrying the seed-bag, he shall come back with songs of joy, carrying his sheaves. (PSALMS 126:1–6)

It is the path of Herzl, who wrote, in the last lines of his marvelous vision, *Altneuland*:

> Dream and action are not so different as people tend to think. For all human actions are founded upon dreams and will return to dreams.

And the path of a great Israeli poet, Saul Tschernichowsky:

> Laugh—yes, laugh—at all the dreams
> Which I, the dreamer, dare to weave;
> Laugh—yet I believe in humans,
> And in you I still believe.
>
> Let me still believe the future
> Holds a bright, though distant, day
> When one nation to another
> Peace and blessing will convey.
>
> ("I BELIEVE")

Out of faith in a future of hope, out of faith in a future of peace, let us draw the strength to keep moving along this difficult and obstacle-ridden path until we reach the light—the "light sown for the righteous," the "light of the seven days"—that selfsame light envisioned by the Prophets of Israel.